GOD'S
UNDERTAKER

GOD'S
UNDERTAKER

Has Science Buried God?

John C. Lennox

LION

A Lion Book
an imprint of
Lion Hudson plc
Wilkinson House, Jordan Hill Road,
Oxford OX2 8DR, England
www.lionhudson.com
ISBN 978 0 7459 5303 8
ISBN 978 0 8254 6188 0

First edition 2007
10 9 8 7 6 5 4 3 2 1

Acknowledgments

pp. 15, 29, 48, 50, 163, 167, 177, 178 Scripture quotations taken
from the Holy Bible, New International Version, copyright ©
1973, 1978, 1984 International Bible Society. Used by permission
of Zondervan and Hodder & Stoughton Limited. All rights reserved.
The 'NIV' and 'New International Version' trademarks are registered
in the United States Patent and Trademark Office by International Bible
Society. Use of either trademark requires the permission of International
Bible Society. UK trademark number 1448790.

This book originated in lectures given at a course entitled *Faith, Reason
and Science* at the University of Oxford, Department for Continuing Education
and at the Institute for the Philosophy of Science at Salzburg University, Austria.
It represents an attempt to evaluate the evidence of modern science in relation
to the debate between the atheistic and theistic interpretations of the universe
and to provide a basis for discussion.

The text paper used in this book has been made from wood
independently certified as having come from sustainable forests.

A catalogue record for this book is available
from the British Library

Distributed by:
UK: Marston Book Services Ltd, PO Box 269, Abingdon, Oxon OX14 4YN
USA: Trafalgar Square Publishing, 814 N Franklin Street, Chicago, IL 60610
USA Christian Market: Kregel Publications, PO Box 2607, Grand Rapids, Michigan 49501

Typeset in 10/12.5 GarammondITC
Printed and bound in the USA

Contents

To Sally
without whose love,
encouragement and support
this book – and much else –
would never have been completed.

Preface

'What is the meaning of it all?'

Richard Feynman

Why is there something rather than nothing? Why, in particular, does the universe exist? Where did it come from and where, if anywhere, is it heading? Is it itself the ultimate reality behind which there is nothing or is there something 'beyond' it? Can we ask with Richard Feynman: 'What is the meaning of it all?' Or was Bertrand Russell right when he said that 'The universe is just there, and that's all'?

These questions have lost nothing of their power to fire human imagination. Spurred on by the desire to climb Everest peaks of knowledge, scientists have already given us spectacular insights into the nature of the universe we inhabit. On the scale of the unimaginably large, the Hubble telescope transmits stunning images of the heavens from its orbit high above the atmosphere. On the scale of the unimaginably small, the scanning tunnelling microscope uncovers the incredibly complex molecular biology of the living world with its information-rich macromolecules and its micro-miniature protein factories whose complexity and precision make even advanced human technologies look crude by comparison.

Are we and the universe with its profusion of galactic beauty and subtle biological complexity nothing but the products of irrational forces acting on mindless matter and energy in an unguided way? Is human life ultimately only one, admittedly improbable, but nevertheless fortuitous, arrangement of atoms among many? In any case, how could we be in any sense special since we now know that we inhabit a tiny planet orbiting a fairly undistinguished star far out in an arm of a spiral galaxy containing billions of similar stars, a galaxy that is only one of billions distributed throughout the vastness of space?

What is more, say some, since certain basic properties of our universe, like the strength of the fundamental forces of nature and the number of observable space and time dimensions, are the result of random effects operating at the origin of the universe, then, surely, there could well be other universes with very different structures. May it not be that our universe is only one in a vast array of parallel universes forever separated from each other? Is it not therefore absurd to suggest that human beings have any ultimate significance? Their measure in a multiverse would seem effectively reduced to zero.

Thus it surely would be an intellectually stultifying exercise in nostalgia to hark back to the early days of modern science when scientists such as Bacon, Galileo, Kepler, Newton and Clerk Maxwell, for example, believed in an intelligent Creator God whose brain-child the cosmos was. Science has moved on from such primitive thinking, we are told, squeezed God into a corner, killed and then buried him by its all-embracing explanations. God has turned out to be no more substantial than the smile on a cosmic Cheshire cat. Unlike Schrödinger's cat, God is no ghostly superposition of dead and alive – he is certainly dead. Furthermore, the whole process of his demise shows that any attempt to reintroduce God is likely to impede the progress of science. We can now see more clearly than ever before that naturalism – the view that nature is all that there is, that there is no transcendence – reigns supreme.

Peter Atkins, Professor of Chemistry at Oxford University, while acknowledging the religious element in the history of the genesis of science, defends this view with characteristic vigour: 'Science, the system of belief founded securely on publicly shared reproducible knowledge, emerged from religion. As science discarded its chrysalis to become its present butterfly, it took over the heath. There is no reason to suppose that science cannot deal with every aspect of existence. Only the religious – among whom I include not only the prejudiced but the underinformed – hope there is a dark corner of the physical universe, or of the universe of experience, that science can never hope to illuminate. But science has never encountered a barrier, and the only grounds for supposing that reductionism will fail are pessimism on the part of scientists and fear in the minds of the religious.'[1]

A conference at the Salk Institute for Biological Sciences in La Jolla, California in 2006 discussed the theme: 'Beyond belief: science, religion, reason and survival.' Addressing the question whether science should do away with religion, Nobel Laureate Steven Weinberg said: 'The world needs to wake up from the long nightmare of religion... Anything we scientists can do to weaken the hold of religion should be done, and may in fact be our greatest contribution to civilization.' Unsurprisingly, Richard Dawkins went even further. 'I am utterly fed up with the respect we have been brainwashed into bestowing upon religion.'

And yet, and yet... Is this really true? Are all religious people to be written off as prejudiced and underinformed? After all, some of them are scientists who have won the Nobel Prize. Are they really pinning their hopes on finding a dark corner of the universe that science can never hope to illuminate? Certainly that is scarcely a fair or true description of most of the early pioneers in science who, like Kepler, claimed that it was precisely their conviction that there was a Creator that inspired their science to ever greater heights. For them it was the dark corners of the universe that science *did* illuminate that provided ample evidence of the ingenuity of God.

And what of the biosphere? Is its intricate complexity really only *apparently* designed, as Richard Dawkins, Peter Atkins' staunch ally in faith, believes? Can rationality really arise through unguided natural processes working under the constraints of nature's laws on the basic materials of the universe in some random way? Is the solution of the mind-body problem simply that rational mind 'emerged' from mindless body by undirected mindless processes?

Questions about the status of this naturalistic story do not readily go away, as the level of public interest shows. So, is naturalism actually demanded by science? Or is it just conceivable that naturalism is a philosophy that is brought to science, more than something that is entailed by science? Could it even be, dare one ask, more like an expression of faith, akin to religious faith? One might at least be forgiven for thinking that from the way in which those who dare ask such questions are sometimes treated. Like religious heretics of a former age they may suffer a form of martyrdom by the cutting off of their grants.

Aristotle is reputed to have said that in order to succeed we must ask the right questions. There are, however, certain questions that it is risky to ask – and even more risky to attempt to answer. Yet surely taking that kind of risk is in both the spirit and interests of science. From a historical perspective this is not a controversial point in itself. In the Middle Ages, for instance, science had to free itself from certain aspects of Aristotelian philosophy before it could get up a real head of steam. Aristotle had taught that from the moon and beyond all was perfection and, since perfect motion, in his view, had to be circular, the planets and stars moved in perfect circles. Beneath the moon motion was linear and there was imperfection. This view dominated thought for centuries. Then Galileo looked through his telescope and saw the ragged edges of lunar craters. The universe had spoken and part of Aristotle's deduction from his *a priori* concept of perfection lay in tatters.

But Galileo was still obsessed with Aristotle's circles: 'For the maintenance of perfect order among the parts of the Universe, it is necessary to say that movable bodies are movable only circularly.'[2] Yet the circles, too, were doomed. It fell to Kepler, on the basis of his analysis of the direct and meticulous observations of the orbit of Mars made by his predecessor as Imperial Mathematician in Prague, Tycho Brahe, to take the daring step of suggesting that astronomical observations were of more evidential value than calculations based on the *a priori* theory that planetary motion must be circular. The rest, as they say, is history. He made the ground-breaking suggestion that the planets moved in equally 'perfect' ellipses around the sun at one focus, a view later brilliantly illuminated by Newton's inverse-square law theory of gravitational attraction, which compressed all of these developments into one stunningly brief and elegant formula. Kepler had changed science forever by unleashing it from the inadequate philosophy that had constrained it for centuries. It would perhaps be a little presumptuous to assume that such a liberating step will never have to be taken again.

To this it will be countered by scientists like Atkins and Dawkins that, since the time of Galileo, Kepler and Newton, science has shown exponential growth and there is no evidence that the philosophy of naturalism, with which science is now so closely related (at least in the minds of many), is inadequate. Indeed, in their opinion, naturalism only serves to further science, which can now proceed unencumbered by the kind of mythological baggage that held it back so often in the past. The great merit of naturalism, it will be argued, is that it cannot possibly inhibit science for the very simply reason that it believes the scientific method to be supreme. It is the one philosophy that is absolutely compatible with science, essentially by definition.

But is that really the case? Galileo certainly found Aristotelian philosophy scientifically inhibiting in its *a priori* prescription of what the universe had to be like. But neither Galileo nor Newton, nor indeed most of the great scientific figures who contributed to the meteoric rise of science at that time, found belief in a Creator God inhibiting in this way. Far from it, they found it positively stimulating: indeed, for many of them it was their prime motivation for scientific investigation. That being the case, the vehemence of the atheism of some contemporary writers would spur one to ask: Why are they now so convinced that atheism is the only intellectually tenable position? Is it really true that everything in science points towards atheism? Are science and atheism such natural bedfellows?

Not so says the eminent British philosopher Anthony Flew, who was for many years a leading intellectual champion of atheism. In a BBC interview[3] he announced that a superintelligence is the only good explanation of the origin of life and of the complexity of nature.

The Intelligent Design debate

Such an announcement by a thinker of Flew's calibre gave a new twist of interest to the vigorous, if sometimes heated, debate on 'intelligent design'. At least some of the heat results from the fact that the term 'intelligent design' appears to convey to many people a relatively recent, crypto-creationist, anti-scientific attitude that is chiefly focussed on attacking evolutionary biology. This means that the term 'intelligent design' has subtly changed its meaning, bringing with it the danger that serious debate will be hijacked as a result.

Now 'intelligent design' strikes some as a curious expression, since usually we think of design as the result of intelligence – the adjective is therefore redundant. If we therefore simply replace the phrase with 'design' or 'intelligent causation' then we are speaking of a very respectable notion in the history of thought. For the notion that there is an intelligent cause behind the universe, far from being recent, is as ancient as philosophy and religion themselves. Secondly, before we address the question whether intelligent design is crypto-creationism we need to avoid another potential misunderstanding by considering the meaning of the term 'creationism' itself. For its meaning has changed as well. 'Creationism' used to denote simply the belief that there was a Creator. However, it has now come to mean not only belief in a Creator but also a commitment to a whole additional raft of ideas by far the most dominant of which is a particular interpretation of Genesis which holds that the earth is only a few thousand years old. This mutation in the meaning of 'creationism' or 'creationist' has had three very unfortunate effects. First of all it polarizes the discussion and gives an apparently soft target to those who reject out of hand any notion of intelligent causation in the universe. Secondly, it fails to do justice to the fact that there is a wide divergence of opinion on the interpretation of the Genesis account even among those Christian thinkers who ascribe final authority to the biblical record. Finally, it obscures the (original) purpose of using the term 'intelligent design', which is to make a very important distinction between the recognition of design and the identification of the designer.

These are different questions. The second of them is essentially theological and agreed by most to be outside the provenance of science. The point of making the distinction is to clear the way to asking whether there is any way in which science can help us with the answer to the first question. It is therefore unfortunate that this distinction between two radically different questions is constantly obscured by the accusation that 'intelligent design' is shorthand for 'crypto-creationism'.

The oft repeated question whether intelligent design is science can be rather misleading, certainly if we understand the term 'intelligent design' in its original sense. Suppose we were to ask the parallel questions: Is theism science? Is atheism science? Most people would give a negative answer. But if we were now to say that what we are really interested in is whether there is any scientific evidence for theism (or for atheism), then we are likely to be faced with the reply: Why, then, did you not say so?

One way to make sense of the question whether (intelligent) design is science or not is to reinterpret it as: Is there any scientific evidence for design? If this is how the question should be understood, then it should be expressed accordingly in order to avoid misunderstanding.

Now, as is well known, authors such as Peter Atkins, Richard Dawkins and Daniel Dennett argue that there is strong scientific evidence for atheism. They are therefore happy to make a scientific case for what is, after all, a metaphysical position. They, of all people, therefore, have no grounds for objecting to others using scientific evidence to support the opposing metaphysical position of theistic design. Of course, I am well aware that the immediate reaction on the part of some will be that there is no alternative case to be put. However, that judgement might just be a little premature.

Another way of interpreting the question of whether intelligent design is science is to ask whether the hypothesis of intelligent design can lead to scientifically testable hypotheses. We shall see later that there are two major areas in which such a hypothesis has already yielded results: the rational intelligibility of the universe and the beginning of the universe.

Our final comment on the term 'intelligent design' at this stage is that even the use of the word 'design' is inextricably associated in some peoples' minds with Newton's clockwork universe, beyond which science has been carried by Einstein. More than that, it conjures up memories of Paley and his nineteenth-century design arguments which many think have been demolished by David Hume. Without prejudging the latter issue, it might therefore be wiser, as suggested, to speak of intelligent causation or of intelligent origin, rather than intelligent design.

I have developed the arguments advanced in this book in lectures, seminars and discussions in many countries and, although I feel that there is still much work to be done, it is at the urging of many of those present on such occasions that I have made the attempt to put them into written form in a book that has been kept deliberately short by the suggestion that what was needed was a concise introduction to the main issues that could form a basis for further discussion and exploration of the more detailed literature. I am grateful for the many questions, comments and criticisms that have helped me in my task but, of course, I hold myself alone responsible for the remaining infelicities.

Some comments about procedure are in order. I shall attempt to set the discussion in the context of the contemporary debate as I understand it. Frequent use is made of quotations from leading scientists and thinkers with a view to getting a clear picture of what those in the forefront of the debate are actually saying. I am, however, aware that there is always a danger that, by quoting out of context, one not only ceases to be fair to the person being quoted but also, in that unfairness, may distort the truth. I hope that I have succeeded in avoiding that particular danger.

My mention of truth leads me to fear that some people of postmodernist persuasion may be tempted not to read any further, unless of course they are curious to read (and maybe even attempt to deconstruct) a text written by someone who actually believes in truth. For my part I confess to finding it curious that those who claim that there is no such thing as truth expect me to believe that what they are saying is true! Perhaps I misunderstand them, but they seem to exempt themselves from their general rubric that there is no such thing as truth when they are either speaking to me or writing their books. They turn out to believe in truth after all.

In any case, scientists have a clear stake in truth. Why, otherwise, would they bother to do science? And it is precisely because I believe in the category of truth that I have tried only to use quotations that seem fairly to represent an author's general position, rather than cite some statement which he or she made on some off day – any of us can be guilty of that kind of infelicity. In the end I must leave it to the reader to judge whether I have succeeded.

What about bias? No one can escape it – neither author nor reader. We are all biased in the sense that we all have a worldview that consists of our answers, or partial answers, to the questions that the universe and life throw at us. Our worldviews may not be sharply, or even consciously, formulated, but they are there nonetheless. Our worldviews are of course shaped by experience and reflection. They can and do change – on the basis of sound evidence, one would hope.

The question that is central to this book turns out to be in essence a worldview question: which worldview sits most comfortably with science – theism or atheism? Has science buried God or not? Let us see where the evidence leads.

War of the worldviews

'Science and religion cannot be reconciled.'

Peter Atkins

'All my studies in science... have confirmed my faith.'

Sir Ghillean Prance FRS

'Next time that somebody tells you that something is true, why not say to them: "What kind of evidence is there for that?" And if they can't give you a good answer, I hope you'll think very carefully before you believe a word they say.'

Richard Dawkins FRS

The last nail in God's coffin?

It is a widespread popular impression that each new scientific advance is another nail in God's coffin. It is an impression fuelled by influential scientific thinkers. Oxford Chemistry Professor Peter Atkins writes: 'Humanity should accept that science has eliminated the justification for believing in cosmic purpose, and that any survival of purpose is inspired only by sentiment.'[1] Now, how science, which is traditionally thought not even to deal with questions of (cosmic) purpose, could actually do any such thing is not very clear, as we shall later see. What is very clear is that Atkins reduces faith in God at a stroke, not simply to sentiment but to sentiment that is inimical to science. Atkins does not stand alone. Not to be outdone, Richard Dawkins goes a step further. He regards faith in God as an evil to be eliminated: 'It is fashionable to wax apocalyptic about the threat to humanity posed by the AIDS virus, "mad cow" disease and many others, but I think that a case can be made that *faith* is one of the world's great evils, comparable to the smallpox virus but harder to eradicate. Faith, being belief that isn't based on evidence, is the principal vice of any religion.'[2]

More recently, faith, in Dawkins' opinion, has graduated (if that is the right term) from being a vice to being a delusion. In his book *The God Delusion*[3] he quotes Robert Pirsig, author of *Zen and the Art of Motorcycle Maintenance*: 'When one person suffers from a delusion, it is called insanity. When many people suffer from a delusion, it is called Religion.' For Dawkins, God is not only a delusion, but a pernicious delusion.

Such views are at one extreme end of a wide spectrum of positions and it would be a mistake to think that they were typical. Many atheists are far from happy with the militancy, not to mention the repressive, even totalitarian overtones of such views. However, as always, it is the extreme views that receive public attention and media exposure with the result that many people are aware of those views and have been affected by them. It would, therefore, be folly to ignore them. We must take them seriously.

From what he says it is clear that one of the things that has generated Dawkins' hostility to faith in God is the impression he has (sadly) gained that, whereas 'scientific belief is based upon publicly checkable evidence, religious faith not only lacks evidence; its independence from evidence is its joy, shouted from the rooftops'.[4] In other words, he takes all religious faith to be blind faith. Well, if that is what it is, perhaps it does deserve to be classified with smallpox. However, taking Dawkins' own advice we ask: Where is the evidence that religious faith is not based on evidence? Now, admittedly, there unfortunately are people professing faith in God who take an overtly anti-scientific and obscurantist viewpoint. Their attitude brings faith in God into disrepute and is to be deplored. Perhaps Richard Dawkins has had the misfortune to meet disproportionately many of them.

But that does not alter the fact that mainstream Christianity will insist that faith and evidence are inseparable. Indeed, faith is a response to evidence, not a rejoicing in the absence of evidence. The Christian apostle John writes in his biography of Jesus: 'These things are written that you might believe...'[5] That is, he understands that what he is writing is to be regarded as part of the evidence on which faith is based. The apostle Paul says what many pioneers of modern science believed, namely, that nature itself is part of the evidence for the existence of God: 'For since the creation of the world God's invisible qualities – his eternal power and divine nature – have been clearly seen, being understood from what has been made, so that men are without excuse.'[6] It is no part of the biblical view that things should be believed where there is no evidence. Just as in science, faith, reason and evidence belong together. Dawkins' definition of faith as 'blind faith' turns out, therefore, to be the exact opposite of the biblical one. Curious that he does not seem to be aware of the discrepancy. Could it be as a consequence of his own blind faith?

Dawkins' idiosyncratic definition of faith thus provides a striking example of the very kind of thinking he claims to abhor – thinking that is not evidence based. For, in an exhibition of breathtaking inconsistency, evidence is the very thing he fails to supply for his claim that independence of evidence is faith's joy. And the reason why he fails to supply such evidence is not hard to find – there is none. It takes no great research effort to ascertain that no serious biblical scholar or thinker would support Dawkins' definition of faith. Francis Collins says of Dawkins' definition that it 'certainly does not describe the faith of most serious believers in history, nor of most of those in my personal acquaintance'.[7] Alister McGrath[8] points out in his recent highly accessible assessment of Dawkins' position that Dawkins has signally failed to engage with any serious Christian thinkers whatsoever. What then should we think of his excellent maxim: 'Next time that somebody tells you that something is true, why not say to them: "What kind of evidence is there for that?" And if they can't give you a good answer, I hope you'll think very carefully before you believe a word they say'?[9] One might well be forgiven for giving in to the powerful temptation to apply Dawkins' maxim to himself – and not believe a word that he says.

But Dawkins is not alone in holding the erroneous notion that faith in God is not based on any kind of evidence. Experience shows that it is relatively common among members of the scientific community, even though it may well be formulated in a somewhat different way. One is often told, for example, that faith in God 'belongs to the private domain, whereas scientific commitment belongs to the public domain', that 'faith in God is a different kind of faith from that which we exercise in science' – in short, it is 'blind faith'. We shall have occasion to look at this issue more closely in Chapter 4 in the section on the rational intelligibility of the universe.

First of all, though, let us get at least some idea of the state of belief/unbelief in God in the scientific community. One of the most interesting surveys in this regard is that conducted in 1996 by Edward Larsen and Larry Witham and reported in *Nature*.[10] For their survey was a repeat of a survey done in 1916 by Professor Leuba in which 1,000 scientists (chosen at random from the 1910 edition of American Men of Science) were asked whether they believed both in a God who answered prayer and in personal immortality – which is, be it noted, much more specific than believing in some kind of divine being. The response rate was 70 per cent of whom 41.8 per cent said yes, 41.5 per cent no and 16.7 per cent were agnostic. In 1996, the response was 60 per cent of whom

39.6 per cent said yes, 45.5 per cent no and 14.9 per cent[11] were agnostic. These statistics were given differing interpretations in the press on the half-full, half-empty principle. Some used them as evidence of the survival of belief, others of the constancy of unbelief. Perhaps the most surprising thing is that there has been relatively little change in the proportion of believers to unbelievers during those eighty years of enormous growth in scientific knowledge, a fact that contrasts sharply with prevailing public perception.

A similar survey showed that the percentage of atheists is higher at the top levels of science. Larsen and Witham showed in 1998[12] that, among the top scientists in the National Academy of Sciences in the USA who responded, 72.2 per cent were atheists, 7 per cent believed in God and 20.8 per cent were agnostics. Unfortunately we have no comparable statistics from 1916 to see if those proportions have changed since then or not, although we do know that over 90 per cent of the founders of the Royal Society in England were theists.

Now how one interprets such statistics is a complex matter. Larsen, for instance, also found that for income levels above $150,000 per year, belief in God falls off significantly, a trend not noticeably limited to those of the scientific fraternity.

Whatever the implications of such statistics may be, surely such surveys provide evidence enough that Dawkins may well be right about the difficulty of accomplishing his rather ominously totalitarian-sounding task of eradicating faith in God among scientists. For, in addition to the nearly 40 per cent of believing scientists in the general survey, there have been and are some very eminent scientists who do believe in God – notably Francis Collins, the current Director of the Human Genome Project, Professor Bill Phillips, winner of the Nobel Prize for Physics in 1997, Sir Brian Heap FRS, former Vice-President of the Royal Society, and Sir John Houghton FRS, former Director of the British Meteorological Office, co-Chair of the Intergovernmental Panel on Climate Change and currently Director of the John Ray Initiative on the Environment, to name but a few.

Of course our question is not going to be settled by statistics, however interesting they may be. Certainly the confessed faith in God even of eminent scientists does not seem to have any modulating effect on the strident tones used by Atkins, Dawkins and others as they orchestrate their war against God in the name of science. Perhaps it would be more accurate to say that they are convinced, not so much that science is at war with God, but that the war is over and science has gained the final victory. The world simply needs to be informed that, to echo Nietzsche, God is dead and science has buried him. In this vein Peter Atkins writes: 'Science and religion cannot be reconciled, and humanity should begin to appreciate the power of its child, and to beat off all attempts at compromise. Religion has failed, and its failures should stand exposed. Science, with its currently successful pursuit of universal competence through the identification of the minimal, the supreme delight of the intellect, should be acknowledged king.'[13] This is triumphalist language. But has the triumph really been secured? Which religion has failed, and at what level? Although science is certainly a delight, is it really the supreme delight of the intellect? Do music, art, literature, love and truth have nothing to do with the intellect? I can hear the rising chorus of protest from the humanities.

What is more, the fact that there are scientists who appear to be at war with God is not quite the same thing as science itself being at war with God. For example, some musicians are militant atheists. But does that mean music itself is at war with God? Hardly. The point here may be expressed as follows: *Statements by scientists are not necessarily statements of science.* Nor, we might add, are such statements necessarily true; although the prestige of science is such that they are often taken to be so. For example, the assertions by Atkins and Dawkins, with which we began, fall into that category. They are not statements of science but rather expressions of personal belief, indeed, of faith – fundamentally no different from (though noticeably less tolerant than) much expression of the kind of faith Dawkins expressly wishes to eradicate. Of course, the fact that Dawkins' and Atkins' cited pronouncements are statements of faith does not of itself mean that those statements are false; but it does mean that they must not be treated as if they were authoritative science. What needs to be investigated is the category into which they fit, and, most important of all, whether or not they are true.

Before going any further, we ought, however, to balance the account a little by citing some eminent scientists who do believe in God. Sir John Houghton FRS writes: 'Our science is God's science. He holds the responsibility for the whole scientific story... The remarkable order, consistency, reliability and fascinating complexity found in the scientific description of the universe are reflections of the order, consistency, reliability and complexity of God's activity.'[14] Former Director of Kew Gardens, Sir Ghillean Prance FRS, gives equally clear expression to his faith: 'For many years I have believed that God is the great designer behind all nature... All my studies in science since then have confirmed my faith. I regard the Bible as my principal source of authority.'[15]

Again, of course, the statements just listed are not statements of science either, but statements of personal belief. It should be noted, however, that they contain hints as to the evidence that might be adduced to support that belief. Sir Ghillean Prance explicitly says, for example, that it is *science itself* that confirms his faith. Thus we have the interesting situation in which, on the one hand, naturalist thinkers tell us that science has eliminated God, and, on the other hand, theists tell us that science confirms their faith in God. Both positions are held by highly competent scientists. What does this mean? Well, it certainly means that it is far too simplistic to assume that science and faith in God are inimical and it suggests that it could be worth exploring what exactly the relationships between science and atheism and between science and theism are. In particular, which, if any, of these two diametrically opposing worldviews of theism and atheism does science support?

We turn first to the history of science.

The forgotten roots of science

At the heart of all science lies the conviction that the universe is orderly. Without this deep conviction science would not be possible. So we are entitled to ask: Where does the conviction come from? Melvin Calvin, Nobel Prize-winner in biochemistry, seems in little doubt about its provenance: 'As I try to discern the origin of that conviction, I seem to find it in a basic notion discovered 2,000 or 3,000 years ago, and enunciated first in the Western world by the ancient Hebrews: namely that the universe is governed by a single God, and is not the product of the whims of many gods, each governing his own province according to his own laws. This monotheistic view seems to be the historical foundation for modern science.'[16]

This is very striking in view of the fact that it is common in the literature first to trace the roots of contemporary science back to the Greeks of the sixth century BC and then to point out that, for science to proceed, the Greek worldview had to be emptied of its polytheistic content. We shall return to the latter point below. We simply wish to point out here that, although the Greeks certainly were in many ways the first to do science in anything like the way we understand it today, the implication of what Melvin Calvin is saying is that the actual view of the universe that was of greatest help to science, namely the Hebrew view that the universe is created and upheld by God, was very much older than the worldview of the Greeks.

This is, perhaps, something that, to borrow Dawkins' language (which, we note, he himself borrowed from the New Testament!), ought to be 'shouted from the housetops' as an antidote to a summary rejection of God. For it means that the foundation on which science stands, the base from which its trajectory has swept up to the edge of the universe, has a strong theistic dimension.

One person who drew attention to this circumstance much earlier than Melvin Calvin was the eminent historian of science and mathematician Sir Alfred North Whitehead. Observing that medieval Europe in 1500 knew less than Archimedes in the third century BC and yet by 1700 Newton had written his masterpiece, *Principia Mathematica*, Whitehead asked the obvious question: How could such an explosion of knowledge have happened in such a relatively short time? His answer: 'modern science must come from the medieval insistence on the rationality of God... My explanation is that the faith in the possibility of science, generated antecedently to the development of modern scientific theory, is an unconscious derivative from medieval theology.'[17] C.S. Lewis' succinct formulation of Whitehead's view is worth recording: 'Men became scientific because they expected law in nature and they expected law in nature because they believed in a lawgiver.' It was this conviction that led Francis Bacon (1561–1626), regarded by many as the father of modern science, to teach that God has provided us with two books – the book of Nature and the Bible – and that to be really properly educated, one should give one's mind to studying both.

Many of the towering figures of science agreed. Men such as Galileo (1564–1642), Kepler (1571–1630), Pascal (1623–62), Boyle (1627–91), Newton (1642–1727), Faraday (1791–1867), Babbage (1791–1871), Mendel (1822–84), Pasteur (1822–95), Kelvin (1824–1907) and Clerk Maxwell (1831–79) were theists; most of them, in fact, were Christians. Their belief in God, far from being a hindrance to their science, was often the main inspiration for it and they were not shy of saying so. The driving force behind Galileo's questing mind, for example, was his deep inner conviction that the Creator who had 'endowed us with senses, reason and intellect' intended us not to 'forgo their use and by some other means to give us knowledge which we can attain by them'. Johannes Kepler described his motivation thus: 'The chief aim of all investigations of the external world should be to discover the rational order which has been imposed on it by God, and which he revealed to us in the language of mathematics.'[18] Such discovery, for Kepler, amounted, in his famous phrase, to 'thinking God's thoughts after him'.

How different, as British biochemist Joseph Needham records, was the reaction of the Chinese in the eighteenth century when the news about the great developments in science that had taken place in the West was brought to them by Jesuit missionaries. For them the idea that the universe could be governed by simple laws which human beings could and had discovered was foolish in the extreme. Their culture simply was not receptive to such notions.[19]

Lack of appreciation of the precise point we are making here can lead to confusion. We are not claiming that *all* aspects of religion in general and Christianity in particular have contributed to the rise of science. What we are suggesting is that the doctrine of a unique Creator God who is responsible for the existence and order of the universe has played an important role. We are not suggesting that there never has been religious antagonism to science. Indeed, T.F. Torrance,[20] commenting on Whitehead's analysis, points out that the development of science was often 'seriously hindered by the Christian church even when within it the beginnings of modern ideas were taking their rise'. As an example he states that the Augustinian theology that dominated Europe for 1,000 years had a power and beauty that led to great contributions to the arts in the Middle Ages, but its 'eschatology which perpetuated the idea of decay and collapse of the world and of salvation as redemption out of it, directed attention away from the world to the superterrestrial, while its conception of the sacramental universe allowed only a symbolic understanding of nature and a religious, illustrative use of it' thus 'taking up and sanctifying a cosmological outlook that had to be replaced if scientific progress was to be made'. Torrance also says that what often seriously discouraged the scientific mind was a 'hardened notion of authority and its relation to understanding that went back to Augustine… which first gave rise to bitter complaints against the church'.[21] Galileo is a case in point, as we shall see below.

Torrance nevertheless gives strong support to the general tenor of Whitehead's thesis: 'In spite of the unfortunate tension that has so often cropped up between the advance of scientific theories and traditional habits of thought in the church, theology can still claim to have mothered throughout long centuries the basic beliefs and impulses which have given rise especially to modern empirical science, if only through its unflagging faith in the reliability of God the Creator and in the ultimate intelligibility of his creation.'

John Brooke, Oxford's first Professor of Science and Religion, is more cautious than Torrance: 'In the past religious beliefs have served as a presupposition of the scientific enterprise insofar as they have underwritten that uniformity… a doctrine of creation could give coherence to scientific endeavour insofar as it implied a dependable order behind the flux of nature. … this need not entail the strong claim that without a prior theology, science would never have taken off, but it does mean that the particular conceptions of science held by its pioneers were often informed by theological and metaphysical beliefs.'[22]

More recently, John Brooke's successor at Oxford, Peter Harrison, has made an impressive case that a dominant feature in the rise of modern science was the Protestant attitude to the interpretation of biblical texts, which spelt an end to the symbolic approach of the Middle Ages.[23]

It is, of course, notoriously difficult to know 'what would have happened if...', but it is surely not too much to say that the rise of science would have been seriously retarded if one particular doctrine of theology, the doctrine of creation, had not been present – a doctrine that is common to Judaism, Christianity and Islam. Brooke issues a healthy warning against overstating the case: Just because a religion has supported science does not prove that the religion is true. Quite so – and the same can, of course, be said of atheism.

The doctrine of creation was not only important in the rise of science because of its entailment of order in the universe. It was important for another reason which we hinted at in the introduction. In order for science to develop, thinking had to be freed from the hitherto ubiquitous Aristotelian method of deducing from fixed principles how the universe ought to be, to a methodology that allowed the universe to speak directly. That fundamental shift in perspective was made much easier by the notion of a *contingent* creation – that is, that God the Creator could have created the universe any way he liked. Hence, in order to find out what the universe is really like or how it actually works, there is no alternative to going and looking. You cannot deduce how the universe works simply by reasoning from *a priori* philosophical principles. That is precisely what Galileo and, later, Kepler and others did: they went and looked – and revolutionized science. But, as everyone knows, Galileo got into trouble with the Roman Catholic Church. We need, therefore, to turn to his story to see what is to be gleaned from it.

Myths of conflict: Galileo and the Roman Catholic Church, Huxley and Wilberforce

One of the main reasons for distinguishing clearly between the influence of the doctrine of creation and the influence of other aspects of religious life (and, be it said, religious politics) on the rise of science is so that we can better understand two of the paradigmatic accounts from history that are often used to maintain the widespread public impression that science has been constantly at war with religion – a notion often referred to as the 'conflict thesis'. These accounts concern two of the most famous confrontations in history: the first, just mentioned above, between Galileo and the Roman Catholic Church; and the second, the debate between Huxley and Wilberforce on the subject of Charles Darwin's famous book *The Origin of Species*. Upon closer investigation, however, these stories fail to support the conflict thesis, a conclusion that comes as a surprise to many, but a conclusion, nonetheless, that has history on its side.

First of all we note the obvious: Galileo appears in our list of scientists who believed in God. He was no agnostic or atheist, at loggerheads with the theism of his day. Dava Sobel, in her brilliant biography, *Galileo's Daughter*[24], effectively debunks this mythical impression of Galileo as 'a renegade who scoffed at the Bible'. It turns out in fact that Galileo was a firm believer in God and the Bible, and remained so all of his life. He held that 'the laws of nature are written by the hand of God in the language of mathematics' and that the 'human mind is a work of God and one of the most excellent'.

Furthermore, Galileo enjoyed a great deal of support from religious intellectuals – at least at the start. The astronomers of the powerful Jesuit educational institution, the Collegio Romano, initially endorsed his astronomical work and fêted him for it. However, he was vigorously opposed by secular philosophers, who were enraged at his criticism of Aristotle.

This was bound to cause trouble. But, be it emphasized, not at first with the church. At least that is the way that Galileo perceived it. For in his famous *Letter to the Grand Duchess Christina* (1615) he claims that it was the academic professors who were so opposed to him that they were trying to influence the church authorities to speak out against him. The issue at stake for the professors was clear: Galileo's scientific arguments were threatening the all-pervading Aristotelianism of the academy.

In the spirit of developing modern science Galileo wanted to decide theories of the universe on the basis of evidence, not of argument based on an appeal to *a priori* postulates in general and the authority of Aristotle in particular. And so he looked at the universe through his telescope and what he saw left some of Aristotle's major astronomical speculations in tatters. Galileo observed sunspots, which blemished the face of Aristotle's 'perfect sun'. In 1604 he saw a supernova, which called into question Aristotle's 'immutable heavens'.

Aristotelianism was the reigning worldview, not simply the paradigm in which science had to be done, but it was a worldview in which cracks were already beginning to appear. Furthermore, the Protestant Reformation was challenging the authority of Rome and thus, from Rome's perspective, religious security was under increasing threat. It was therefore a very sensitive time. The embattled Roman Catholic Church, which had, in common with almost everyone else at the time, embraced Aristotelianism, felt itself unable to allow any serious challenge to Aristotle although there were the beginnings of rumblings (particularly among the Jesuits) that the Bible itself did not always support Aristotle. But those rumblings were not yet strong enough to prevent the powerful opposition to Galileo that would arise from both the Academy and the Roman Catholic Church. But, even then, the reasons for that opposition were not merely intellectual and political. Jealousy, and also, it must be said, Galileo's own lack of a sense of diplomacy, were contributing factors. He irritated the elite of his day by publishing in Italian and not in Latin, in order to give some intellectual empowerment to ordinary people. He was committed to what later would be called the public understanding of science.

Galileo also developed an unhelpfully short-sighted habit of denouncing in vitriolic terms those who disagreed with him. Neither did he promote his cause by the way in which he handled an official direction to include in his *Dialogue Concerning the Two Principal Systems of the World* the argument of his erstwhile friend and supporter Pope Urban VIII (Maffeo Berberini) to the effect that, since God was omnipotent, he could produce any given natural phenomenon in many different ways and so it would be presumption on the part of the natural philosophers to claim that they had found the unique solution. Galileo dutifully obliged but he did so by putting this argument into the mouth of a dull-witted character in his book whom he called Simplicio ('buffoon'). One might see this as a classic case of shooting oneself in the foot.

There is, of course, no excuse whatsoever for the Roman Catholic Church's use of the power of the Inquisition to muzzle Galileo, nor for subsequently taking several centuries 'rehabilitating' him. It should, however, be noted that, again contrary to popular belief, Galileo was never tortured; and his subsequent 'house arrest' was spent, for the most part, in luxurious private residences belonging to friends.[25]

There are important lessons to be gleaned from the Galileo story. First a lesson for those who are disposed to take the biblical account seriously. It is hard to imagine that there are any today who believe that the earth is the centre of the universe with the planets and sun revolving around it. That is, they accept the heliocentric Copernican view for which Galileo fought and they do not think that it conflicts with the Bible, although almost everyone at and before the time of Copernicus thought with Aristotle that the earth was at the physical centre of the universe and they used their literalistic reading of parts of the Bible to support that idea. What has happened to make the difference? Simply that they now take a more sophisticated, nuanced view of the Bible,[26] and can see that when, for example, the Bible talks of the sun 'rising', it is speaking phenomenologically – that is, giving a description as it appears to an observer, rather than implying commitment to a particular solar and planetary theory. Scientists today do just the same: they also speak in normal conversation of the sun rising, and their statements are not usually taken to imply that they are obscurantist Aristotelians.

The important lesson is that we should be humble enough to distinguish between what the Bible says and our interpretations of it. The biblical text just might be more sophisticated than we first imagined and we might therefore be in danger of using it to support ideas that it never intended to teach. So, at least, thought Galileo in his day and history has subsequently proved him right.

Finally, another lesson in a different direction, but one not often drawn, is that it was Galileo, who believed in the Bible, who was advancing a better *scientific* understanding of the universe, not only, as we have seen, against the obscurantism of some churchmen,[27] but (and first of all) against the resistance (and obscurantism) of the secular philosophers of his time who, like the churchmen, were also convinced disciples of Aristotle. Philosophers and scientists today also have need of humility in light of facts, even if those facts are being pointed out to them by a believer in God. Lack of belief in God is no more of a guarantee of scientific orthodoxy than is belief in God. What is clear, in Galileo's time and ours, is that criticism of a reigning scientific paradigm is fraught with risk, no matter who is engaged in it. We conclude that the 'Galileo affair' really does nothing to confirm a simplistic conflict view of the relationship of science to religion.

The Huxley–Wilberforce Debate, Oxford 1860

Nor in fact does that other frequently-cited incident, the debate on 30 June 1860 at the British Association for the Advancement of Science held in Oxford's Natural History Museum, which took place between T.H. Huxley (Darwin's bulldog) and Bishop Samuel Wilberforce (Soapy Sam). The debate was occasioned by a lecture delivered by John Draper on Darwin's theory of evolution – *The Origin of Species* having been published seven months earlier. This encounter is often portrayed as a simple clash between science and religion, where the competent scientist convincingly triumphed over the ignorant churchman. Yet historians of science have shown that this account is also very far from the truth.[28]

In the first place, Wilberforce was no ignoramus. A month after the historic meeting in question, he published a 50-page review of Darwin's work (in the *Quarterly Review*), which Darwin regarded as 'uncommonly clever; it picks out with skill all the most conjectural parts, and brings forward well all the difficulties. It quizzes me most splendidly.' Secondly, Wilberforce was no obscurantist. He was determined that the debate should not be between science and religion, but a scientific debate – scientist versus scientist on scientific grounds – an intention which figures significantly in his summary of the review: 'We have objected to the views with which we are dealing, solely on scientific grounds. We have done so from the fixed conviction that it is thus that the truth or falsehood of such arguments should be tried. We have no sympathy with those who object to any facts or alleged facts in nature, or to any inference logically deduced from them, because they believe them to contradict what it appears to them is taught by revelation. We think that all such objections savour of a timidity which is really inconsistent with a firm and well-intrusted faith.'[29] The robustness of this statement might come as a surprise to many people who have simply swallowed the legendary view of the encounter. One might even be excused for detecting in Wilberforce a kindred spirit to that of Galileo.

Nor was it the case that the only objections to Darwin's theory came from the side of the church. Sir Richard Owen, the leading anatomist of the day (who, incidentally, had been consulted by Wilberforce), was opposed to Darwin's theory; as was the eminent scientist Lord Kelvin.

As to contemporary accounts of the debate, John Brooke[30] points out that initially the event seemed to cause little or no stir: 'It is a significant fact that the famous clash between Huxley and the Bishop was not reported by a single London newspaper at the time. Indeed, there are no official records of the meeting; and most of the reports came from Huxley's friends. Huxley himself wrote that there was "inextinguishable laughter among the people" at his wit and "I believe that I was the most popular man in Oxford for full four and twenty hours afterwards." ' However, the evidence is that the debate was far from one-sided. One newspaper later recorded that one previous convert to Darwin's theory was de-converted as he witnessed the debate. The botanist Joseph Hooker grumbled that Huxley didn't 'put the matter in a form or way that carried the audience' so he had had to do it himself. Wilberforce wrote three days later to archaeologist Charles Taylor: 'I think I thoroughly beat him.' *The Athenaeum*'s report gives the impression that honours were about even, saying that Huxley and Wilberforce 'have each found foemen worthy of their steel'.

Frank James, historian at the Royal Institution in London, makes the suggestion that the widespread impression that Huxley was victorious may well have arisen because Wilberforce was not well-liked, a fact that is missing from most of the accounts: 'Had Wilberforce not been so unpopular in Oxford, he would have carried the day and not Huxley.'[31] Shades of Galileo!

On careful analysis, then, two of the main props commonly used to support the conflict thesis crumble. Indeed research has undermined that thesis to such an extent that historian of science Colin Russell can come to the following general conclusion: 'The common belief that... the actual relations between religion and science over the last few centuries have been marked by deep and enduring hostility... is not only historically inaccurate, but actually a caricature so grotesque that what needs to be explained is how it could possibly have achieved any degree of respectability.'[32]

It is clear, therefore, that powerful forces must have been at play, in order to account for the depth to which the conflict myth has become embedded in the popular mind. And indeed there were. As in the case of Galileo, the real issue at stake was not simply a question of the intellectual merits of a scientific theory. Once more, institutional power played a key role. Huxley was on a crusade to ensure the supremacy of the emerging new class of professional scientists against the privileged position of clerics, however intellectually gifted. He wanted to make sure that it was the scientists who wielded the levers of power. The legend of a conquered bishop slain by a professional scientist suited that crusade, and it was exploited to the full.

However, it is apparent that even more was involved. A central element in Huxley's crusade is highlighted by Michael Poole.[33] He writes, 'In this struggle, the concept of "Nature" was spelt with a capital N and reified. Huxley vested "Dame Nature", as he called her, with attributes hitherto ascribed to God, a tactic eagerly copied by others since. The logical oddity of crediting *nature* (every physical thing there is) with planning and creating every physical thing there is, passed unnoticed. "Dame Nature", like some ancient fertility goddess, had taken up residence, her maternal arms encompassing *Victorian scientific naturalism*.' Thus a mythical conflict was (and still often is) hyped up and shamelessly used as a weapon in another battle, the real one this time, that is, that between naturalism and theism.

The real conflict – naturalism versus theism

With this we come to one of the major points we wish to make in this book which is that there is a conflict, a very real one, but it is not really a conflict between science and religion at all. For if that were so, elementary logic would dictate that one would find that scientists were all atheists and only non-scientists believed in God, and this, as we have seen, is simply not the case. No, the real conflict is between two diametrically opposed worldviews: naturalism and theism. They inevitably collide.

For the sake of clarity, we note that naturalism is related to, but not identical with, materialism; although they are sometimes very hard to tell apart. *The Oxford Companion to Philosophy* says that the complexity of the concept of matter has meant that 'the various materialist philosophies have tended to substitute for "matter" some notion like "whatever it is that can be studied by the methods of natural science", thus turning materialism into naturalism; though it would be an exaggeration to say the two outlooks have simply coincided'.[34] Materialists are naturalists. But there are naturalists who hold that mind and consciousness are to be distinguished from matter. They regard the former as 'emergent' phenomena; that is, dependent on matter, but occurring on a higher level which is not reducible to the lower-level properties of matter. There are also other naturalists who hold that the universe consists purely of 'mind stuff'. Naturalism, however, in common with materialism, stands opposed to supernaturalism, insisting that 'the world of nature should form a single sphere without incursions from outside by souls or spirits, divine or human'.[35] Whatever their differences, materialism and naturalism are therefore intrinsically atheistic.

We should also note that materialism/naturalism comes in different versions. For example, E.O. Wilson distinguishes two. The first is what he calls political behaviourism: 'Still beloved by the now rapidly fading Marxist–Leninist states, it says that the brain is largely a blank slate devoid of any inborn inscription beyond reflexes and primitive bodily urges. As a consequence the mind originates almost wholly as a result of learning, and it is the product of a culture that itself evolves by historical contingency. Because there is no biologically based "human nature", people can be moulded to the best possible political and economic system, namely, as urged upon the world through most of the twentieth century, communism. In practical politics, this belief has been repeatedly tested and, after economic collapses and tens of millions of deaths in a dozen dysfunctional states, is generally deemed a failure.' The second, Wilson's own view, he calls scientific humanism, a worldview that he thinks 'drains the fever swamps of religion and blank-slate dogma'. He defines it as follows: 'Still held by only a tiny minority of the world's population, it considers humanity to be a biological species that evolved over millions of years in a biological world, acquiring unprecedented intelligence yet still guided by complex inherited emotions and biased channels of learning. Human nature exists and it was self-assembled. It is the commonality of the hereditary responses and propensities that define our species.' Wilson asserts that it is this Darwinian view that 'imposes the heavy burden of individual choice that goes with intellectual freedom'.[36]

It goes beyond the scope of this book to consider the various nuances of these and other views. We wish here to concentrate on what is essentially common to all of them, something that astronomer Carl Sagan expressed with elegant economy in the opening words of his acclaimed television series *Cosmos*: 'The cosmos is all there is, or was, or ever shall be.' This is the essence of naturalism. Sterling Lamprecht's definition of naturalism is longer but nevertheless worth recording. He defines it to be: 'a philosophical position, empirical method that regards everything that exists or occurs to be conditioned in its existence or occurrence by causal factors within one all-encompassing system of nature'.[37] Thus there is nothing but nature. It is a closed system of cause and effect. There is no realm of the transcendent or supernatural. There is no 'outside'.

Diametrically opposed to naturalism and materialism is the theistic view of the universe that finds clear expression in the opening words of Genesis: 'In the beginning God created the heavens and the earth.'[38] Here is an assertion that the universe is not a closed system but a creation, an artefact of the mind of God, maintained and upheld by him. It is an answer to the question: Why does the universe exist? It exists because God causes it to be.

The Genesis statement is a statement of belief, not a statement of science, in exactly the same way as Sagan's assertion is not a statement of science, but of his personal belief. Thus the key issue is, we repeat, not so much the relationship of the discipline of science to that of theology, but the relationship of science to the various worldviews held by scientists, in particular to naturalism and theism. Thus, when we ask if science has buried God, we are talking at the level of the interpretation of science. What we are really asking is: Which worldview does science support, naturalism or theism?

E.O. Wilson is in no doubt of the answer: Scientific humanism is 'the only worldview compatible with science's growing knowledge of the real world and the laws of nature'. Quantum chemist Henry F. Schaeffer III is in no doubt of his answer either: 'A Creator must exist. The Big Bang ripples (1992) and subsequent scientific findings are clearly pointing to an *ex nihilo* creation consistent with the first few verses of the book of Genesis.'[39]

In order to tease out the relationship between worldviews and science we must now ask a surprisingly difficult question: What exactly is science?

2

The scope and limits of science

'Whatever knowledge is attainable, must be attained by scientific methods; and what science cannot discover, mankind cannot know.'

Bertrand Russell

'The existence of a limit to science is, however, made clear by its inability to answer childlike elementary questions having to do with first and last things – questions such as "How did everything begin?"; "What are we all here for?"; "What is the point of living?" '

Sir Peter Medawar

The international character of science

Whatever else science is, it is certainly international. For many of us, including the author, one of the highlights of being a scientist is that of belonging to a truly international community transcending all kinds of frontiers: race, ideology, religion, political conviction and the myriad other things that can divide people from one another. All of these things are forgotten as we together try to get to grips with the mysteries of mathematics, make sense of quantum mechanics, fight against debilitating disease, investigate the properties of strange materials, formulate theories about the interiors of stars, develop new ways of producing energy, or study the complexity of proteomics.

It is precisely because of this ideal of an international community, free to get on with its scientific work untrammelled by extraneous and potentially divisive intrusions, that scientists understandably begin to get nervous when metaphysics threatens to rear its head, or worse still when the God question appears. Surely, if there is one area that can (and should) be kept religiously and theologically neutral, it is science? And, for the most part, it is so. Vast tracts of the natural sciences, in fact, probably far and away the major part, are just like that. After all, the nature of the elements, the periodic table, the values of the fundamental constants of nature, the structure of DNA, the Krebs cycle, Newton's Laws, Einsteins's Equation and so on have essentially nothing to do with metaphysical commitment. Isn't it all like that?

Defining science

And that brings us back to our question: What is science? Contrary to popular impression, there is no one agreed scientific method, though certain elements crop up regularly in attempts to describe what 'scientific' activity involves: hypothesis, experiment, data, evidence, modified hypothesis, theory, prediction, explanation, and so on. But precise definition is very elusive. By way of illustration, consider the following attempt by Michael Ruse. He holds that science 'by definition deals only with the natural, the repeatable, that which is governed by law'.[1]

On the positive side this definition would certainly allow us to distinguish between astronomy and astrology. However, the most obvious weakness in this definition is that, if allowed to stand, it would rule out most of contemporary cosmology as science. It is hard to see how the standard model for the origin of the universe can be describing anything other than unique events – the origin of the universe is not (easily) repeatable. Cosmologists might understandably be peeved to be told that their activities did not qualify as science.

For, there is another way of looking at things that is an essential part of the methodology of contemporary science, and that is the method of inference to the best explanation (or abduction, as it is sometimes called). Now with repeatable events to be sure we trust that our explanations of them are the best explanation in that they have predictive power, but with unrepeatable events it is still possible to ask: What is the best explanation of this event or phenomenon? The logic is: If A, then B is likely. We observe B, so A becomes a candidate to be a possible explanation for B. Ruse's definition seems to miss this.

Nevertheless, his inadequate definition does serve a useful purpose in that it reminds us that not all science carries with it the same kind of authority. Scientific theory that is based on repeated observation and experimentation is likely to, and should, carry more authority than that which is not. There is always the danger of failing to appreciate this point and thus endowing the latter with the authority of the former – a consideration to which we shall return.

To complicate matters even further, the Enlightenment ideal of the coolly rational scientific observer, completely independent, free of all preconceived theories, prior philosophical, ethical and religious commitments, doing investigations and coming to dispassionate, unbiased conclusions that constitute absolute truth, is nowadays regarded by serious philosophers of science (and, indeed, most scientists) as a simplistic myth. In common with the rest of humanity, scientists have preconceived ideas, indeed, worldviews that they bring to bear on every situation. This can be seen from some of the statements we have already examined. And observations themselves tend to be unavoidably 'theory laden' – we cannot even take a temperature, without having an underlying theory of heat.

At the much deeper level of elementary particle behaviour physicists have discovered that the very process of observation gives rise to disturbances that cannot be ignored. Nobel Prize-winner Werner Heisenberg deduces that 'the natural laws formulated mathematically in quantum theory no longer deal with the elementary particles themselves but with our knowledge of them'.[2]

There are also vigorous contemporary discussions as to whether science is observation-and-prediction-based, or problem-and-explanation-based. And when we in the end set up our theories, they tend to be underdetermined by the data: for instance, infinitely many curves can be drawn through a given finite set of points. By its very nature, therefore, science inevitably possesses a certain degree of tentativeness and provisionality.

We hasten to add that this is far from granting that science is some kind of totally subjective and arbitrary social construct, as is held by some thinkers of postmodern persuasion.[3] It is probably fair to say that many, if not most, scientists are 'critical realists', believing in an objective world which can be studied and who hold that their theories, though not amounting to 'truth' in any final or absolute sense, give them an increasingly firm handle on reality, as exemplified, say, in the development of the understanding of the universe, from Galileo via Newton to Einstein.[4]

But back to Ruse and his definition of science, for there is more to be said. What does he mean by saying that science deals only with the 'natural'? It surely means at least that the things studied by science are the things found in nature. But it may also imply that the explanations to be given of such things can count as scientific only if they are couched solely in terms of physics, chemistry and natural processes. Certainly this is a very common view. For example, Professor of Ecology and Evolution Massimo Pigliucci states that 'The basic assumption of science is that the world can be explained entirely in physical terms, without recourse to godlike entities.'[5] In a similar vein Nobel Laureate Christian de Duve writes: 'Scientific enquiry rests on the notion that all manifestations in the universe are explainable in natural terms, without supernatural intervention. Strictly speaking, this notion is not an *a priori* philosophical stand or profession of belief. It is a *postulate*, a working hypothesis that we should be prepared to abandon if faced with facts that defy every attempt at rational explanation. Many scientists, however, do not bother to make this distinction, tacitly extrapolating from hypothesis to affirmation. They are perfectly happy with the explanations provided by science. Like Laplace, they have no need for the 'God hypothesis' and equate the scientific attitude with agnosticism, if not with outright atheism.'[6]

Here is a clear admission that, for many, science is practically inseparable from a metaphysical commitment to an agnostic or atheistic viewpoint. We notice in passing the subtle implication that 'supernatural intervention' is to be equated with 'defying every attempt at rational explanation'. In other words 'supernatural' implies 'non-rational'. To those of us who have engaged in serious theological reflection, this will seem quite wrong-headed: the notion that there is a Creator God is a rational notion, not a non-rational one. To equate 'rational explanation' with 'natural explanation' is at best an indicator of a strong prejudice, at worst a category mistake.

De Duve's view is shared by many scientists. It is, for example, the view expressed by the judge in Kitzmiller et al. vs Dover Area School District (2005) in deciding that 'Intelligent Design' is a religious and not a scientific view. Judge Jones states forthrightly: 'Expert testimony reveals that since the scientific revolution of the sixteenth and seventeenth centuries, science has been limited to the search for natural causes to explain natural phenomena.... While supernatural explanations may be important and have merit, they are not part of science... This self-imposed convention of science which limits inquiry to testable, natural explanations about the natural world, is referred to by philosophers as "methodological naturalism" and is sometimes known as the scientific method... Methodological naturalism is a "ground rule" of science today which requires scientists to seek explanations in the world around us based upon what we can observe, test, replicate, and verify.'

Philosopher Paul Kurtz holds similarly that 'What is common to naturalistic philosophy is its commitment to science. Indeed, naturalism might be defined in its more general sense as the philosophical generalizations of the methods and conclusions of the sciences.'[7]

Now, one can understand why such an approach is attractive. In the first place it makes for a clear distinction between good science and superstition, between astronomy and astrology or between chemistry and alchemy, for instance. It also helps avoid lazy 'God of the gaps' thinking that says of some phenomenon, 'I cannot understand it therefore God or the gods did it.'

However, there is at least one serious down-side. Such a close tie between science and naturalism could lead to the situation in which any data, phenomena, or interpretations of such, that did not comfortably fit the naturalistic way of thinking might not be taken seriously, and might even be fiercely resisted. Now, of course, this is only a down-side if naturalism is false as a philosophy. If naturalism is true, then there will simply never (ultimately) be any such problem even if the naturalistic explanation of a given phenomenon takes many years to discover.

Which comes first – science or philosophy?

Such a view would appear to be held by Kurtz. He defines naturalism as a philosophy that arises out of the natural sciences. That is, the scientist first studies the universe, formulates his theories, and then sees that a naturalistic or materialistic philosophy is demanded by them.

However, as we have already pointed out, the picture of a scientific 'tabula rasa', of a completely open mind free of philosophical pre-commitment brought to the study of the natural world, is seriously misleading. For, it is even possible that what happens is precisely the reverse of what Kurtz suggests. For instance, the immunologist, George Klein, states categorically that his atheism is not based on science, but is an *a priori* faith commitment. Commenting on a letter in which one of his friends described him as an agnostic, he writes: 'I am not an agnostic. I am an atheist. My attitude is not based on science, but rather on faith... The absence of a Creator, the non-existence of God is my childhood faith, my adult belief, unshakable and holy.'[8]

We notice in passing the idea that Klein, in common with Dawkins, holds that faith and science are in opposition, a notion to which we shall take exception.

Similarly, in his review of Carl Sagan's last book, the Harvard geneticist Richard Lewontin makes it abundantly clear that his materialistic convictions are *a priori*. He not only confesses that his materialism does not derive from his science, but he also admits, on the contrary, that it is his materialism that actually consciously determines the nature of what he conceives science to be: 'Our willingness to accept scientific claims that are against common sense is the key to an understanding of the real struggle between science and the supernatural. We take the side of science in spite of the patent absurdity of some of its constructs... in spite of the tolerance of the scientific community for unsubstantiated just-so stories, because we have a prior commitment... to materialism. It is not that the methods and institutions of science somehow compel us to accept a material explanation of the phenomenal world but, on the contrary, that we are forced by our *a priori* adherence to material causes to create an apparatus of investigation and a set of concepts that produce material explanations, no matter how counter-intuitive, no matter how mystifying to the uninitiated.'[9,10]

This statement is as astonishing as it is honest. And it is the reverse of Kurtz's position.

Lewontin claims that there is a struggle between 'science and the supernatural', and yet at once contradicts himself by admitting that science carries no compulsion within itself to force materialism upon us. This supports our contention that the real battle is not so much between science and faith in God, but rather between a materialistic, or more broadly, a naturalistic worldview and a supernaturalistic, or theistic, worldview. After all Lewontin's faith commitment to materialism is self-confessedly *not* rooted in his science but on something completely different, as becomes clear from what he says next: 'Moreover that materialism is absolute, for we cannot allow a Divine foot in the door.'

I am not so sure that Dawkins would be as enthusiastic about eradicating this kind of 'blind faith' in materialism as he is about eradicating faith in God, though consistency would argue that he should. And what, in any case, is the precise force of the word 'cannot' in connection with allowing a Divine foot in the door? If, as Lewontin says, science does not force us to be materialists, then the 'cannot' clearly does not refer to science as being incapable of pointing in the direction of the existence of a Divine foot. It must simply mean that 'we materialists cannot allow a Divine foot in the door'. Well, of course, it is a tautology to say that 'materialists cannot allow a Divine foot in the door'. Materialism rejects both the Divine foot and, come to think of it, the door as well. There is after all, no 'outside' for a materialist – the 'cosmos is all that is, was, or ever shall be'. But that rejection carries no implications whatsoever about the existence of such a foot or door beyond the mere unsubstantiated assertion that Lewontin personally does not believe in either of them. After all, if a physicist deliberately designs a machine that is capable of detecting radiation only within the visible spectrum, then, however useful her machine is, it would be absurd for her to try to use it to deny the existence of, for example, X-rays, that it cannot by construction see.

It would, of course, be as false to deny that good science can be done by scientists committed to materialistic or naturalistic assumptions as it would be to deny that good science can be done by theists. What is more, lest we lose our sense of proportion, we should bear in mind that, by and large, science done on atheistic presuppositions will lead to the same results as science done on theistic presuppositions.[11] For example, when trying to find out in practice *how* an organism functions, it matters little whether one assumes that it is *actually* designed, or only *apparently* designed. Here the assumption of either 'methodological naturalism' (sometimes called 'methodological atheism') or what we might term 'methodological theism' will lead to essentially the same results. This is so for the very simple reason that the organism in question is being treated methodologically as if it had been designed in both cases.

The danger of terms such as 'methodological atheism' or 'methodological naturalism' is that they might appear to lend support to an atheistic worldview, and to give the impression that the atheism had something to do with the success of the science – which might not necessarily be the case at all. To see this point even more clearly, just imagine what would happen if the term 'methodological theism' were to be employed in the literature instead of the term 'methodological atheism'. It would be howled down at once on the basis that it could give the impression that it was the theism that contributed to the success of the science.

And yet we find, rather incongruously, that there are scientists with *theistic* convictions who insist on defining science in such explicitly naturalistic terms. For example, Ernan McMullin writes: '… methodological naturalism does not restrict our study of nature, it just lays down which sort of study qualifies as science. If someone wants to pursue another approach to nature – and there are many others – the methodological naturalist has no reason to object. Scientists have to proceed in this way; the methodology of science gives no purchase on the claim that a particular event or type of event is to be explained by invoking God's creative action directly.'[12]

There is an important difference between Lewontin and McMullin. Lewontin will not allow a Divine foot – period. For McMullin there may well be a Divine foot but science has nothing to say about it. For him there are other approaches to nature, but they do not qualify as scientific and so they may inevitably be regarded as less authoritative. We would like to suggest that neither the expression 'methodological naturalism' nor the expression 'methodological theism' is particularly helpful: better to avoid both.

However, it is one thing to eschew the use of certain unhelpful terminology. What no scientist can avoid is having his or her own philosophical commitments. Those commitments, as we have just said, are not likely to figure very largely, if at all, when we are studying *how things work*, but they may well play a much more dominant role when we are studying *how things came to exist in the first place*, or when we are studying things that bear on our understanding of ourselves as human beings.

Following where the evidence leads – always?

Instead of begging the question and defining science to be essentially applied naturalism and, therefore, metaphysically *a priori*, suppose we understand it to be investigation of and theorizing about the natural order so that we give weight to what is surely of the essence of true science – that is, a willingness to follow empirical evidence, wherever it leads. The key question now arises as to what happens if our investigations in such areas begin to turn up evidence that conflicts with our worldview commitment – if such a circumstance is even thinkable.

As famously studied by Kuhn,[13] tensions can arise when empirical evidence conflicts with the accepted scientific framework, or 'paradigm' as Kuhn called it, within which most scientists in a given field are working.[14] The notorious refusal of some churchmen to look through Galileo's telescope is a classic expression of that kind of tension. For them, the implications of the physical evidence were too much to face, since there was no way in which their favoured Aristotelian paradigm could be false. But it is not only churchmen who can be guilty of such obscurantism. In the early twentieth century, for example, Mendelian geneticists were persecuted by Marxists because Mendel's ideas on heredity were regarded as inconsistent with Marxist philosophy, and so the Marxists refused to allow the Mendelians to follow where the evidence led.

As in the case of the overthrow of Aristotelianism, entrenched attitudes may mean that it can take a long time before an accumulation of evidence favouring a new paradigm leads to the replacement of the existing one. For a scientific paradigm does not necessarily immediately crumble the moment some inconsistent evidence is found, although it must be said that the history of science throws up noteworthy exceptions. For example, when Rutherford discovered the nucleus of the atom he at once overthrew a dogma of classical physics and an immediate paradigm shift resulted. And DNA replaced protein as the basic genetic material virtually overnight. In these cases, of course, no deep-lying, uncomfortable, worldview issues were involved. A comment from Thomas Nagel is apposite: 'Of course belief is often controlled by the will; it can even be coerced. The obvious examples are political and religious. But the captive mind is found in subtler form in purely intellectual contexts. One of its strongest motives is the simple hunger for belief itself. Sufferers from this condition find it difficult to tolerate having no opinion for any length of time on a subject that interests them. They may change their opinions easily when there is an alternative that can be adopted without discomfort, but they do not like to be in a condition of suspended judgement.'[15]

However, alternatives cannot always be adopted without discomfort and particularly in cases where worldviews may be, or appear to be, threatened by evidence there can be enormous resistance and even antagonism shown to anyone who wishes to follow where the evidence appears to lead. It takes a strong person to swim against the tide and risk the opprobrium of his peers. And yet, some of impressive intellectual stature do precisely that. 'My whole life has been guided by the principle of Plato's Socrates,' writes Anthony Flew, in connection with his recent turning from atheism to theism. 'Follow the evidence wherever it leads.' And what if people don't like it? 'That's too bad,' he says.[16]

Summing up so far

There would seem then to be two extremes to be avoided. The first is to see the relationship between science and religion solely in terms of conflict. The second is to see all science as philosophically or theologically neutral.[17] The word 'all' is important here since it is all too easy to get things out of proportion and see the whole of science as hostage to philosophical fortune. We cannot emphasize too much that vast tracts of science remain unaffected by such philosophical commitments. But not quite all – and that is where the problem lies.

The limits of scientific explanation

Science explains. For many people this encapsulates the power and the fascination of science. Science enables us to understand what we did not understand before; and by giving us understanding of nature, it gives us power over nature. But how much does science explain? Are there any limits?

Some think not and, at the materialistic end of the spectrum, there are those who hold that science is the only way to truth and it can, at least in principle, explain everything. This view is called 'scientism'. Peter Atkins gives a classic expression of this view: 'There is no reason to suppose that science cannot deal with every aspect of existence.'[18] That, in a nutshell, is the essence of scientism.

Those like Atkins who hold this view regard all talk of God, religion and religious experience as outside of science, and therefore not objectively true. They admit of course that many people think about God; and they can see that thinking about God can have emotional and even physical effects, some of which may be beneficial. But, for them, thinking about God is like thinking about Father Christmas, dragons, hobgoblins, or fairies and leprechauns at the bottom of the garden.

Richard Dawkins makes this point in dedicating his book *The God Delusion* to the memory of Douglas Adams with a quote: 'Isn't it enough to see that a garden is beautiful without having to believe that there are fairies at the bottom of it?'

The fact that you can think about fairies and be enchanted or terrified by them does not mean that they exist. The scientists of whom we are speaking, therefore, are (often, but not always, as we have seen) happy to let people go on thinking about God and religion if they want to, as long as they do not claim that God has any objective existence, or that religious belief constitutes knowledge. In other words, science and religion can peacefully co-exist as long as religion does not invade the realm of science. For only science can tell us what is objectively true; only science can deliver knowledge. The bottom line is: science deals with reality, religion does not.

Certain elements of these assumptions and claims are so outlandish that they call for immediate comment. Take the Douglas Adams quote cited by Dawkins above. It gives the game away. For it shows that Dawkins is guilty of committing the error of proposing false alternatives by suggesting that it is either fairies or nothing. Fairies at the bottom of the garden may well be a delusion, but what about a gardener, to say nothing about an owner? The possibility of their existence cannot be so summarily dismissed – in fact, most gardens have both.

Furthermore, take the claim that only science can deliver truth. If it were true it would at once spell the end of many disciplines in schools and universities. For the evaluation of philosophy, literature, art, music lies outside the scope of science strictly so-called. How could science tell us whether a poem is a bad poem or a work of genius? Scarcely by measuring the lengths of the words or the frequencies of the letters occurring in them. How could science possibly tell us whether a painting is a masterpiece or a confused smudge of colours? Certainly not by making a chemical analysis of the paint and the canvas. The teaching of morality likewise lies outside science. Science can tell you that, if you add strychnine to someone's drink, it will kill them. But science cannot tell you whether it is morally right or

wrong to put strychnine into your grandmother's tea so that you can get
your hands on her property.

In any case, the statement that only science can deliver knowledge is
one of those self-refuting statements that logicians like Bertrand Russell
love to point out. All the more surprising that Russell himself appears to
have subscribed to this particular view when he wrote: 'Whatever
knowledge is attainable, must be attained by scientific methods; and what
science cannot discover, mankind cannot know.'[19] In order to see the self-
contradictory nature of this statement we simply have to ask: How does
Russell know this? For his statement is not itself a statement of science and
so if it is true then (according to the statement itself) it is unknowable – and
yet Russell believes it to be true.

Aunt Matilda's cake

Perhaps a simple illustration will help convince us that science is limited.
Let us imagine that my Aunt Matilda has baked a beautiful cake and we take
it along to be analyzed by a group of the world's top scientists. I, as master
of ceremonies, ask them for an explanation of the cake and they go to
work. The nutrition scientists will tell us about the number of calories in
the cake and its nutritional effect; the biochemists will inform us about the
structure of the proteins, fats etc. in the cake; the chemists, about the
elements involved and their bonding; the physicists will be able to analyze
the cake in terms of fundamental particles; and the mathematicians will no
doubt offer us a set of elegant equations to describe the behaviour of those
particles.

Now that these experts, each in terms of his or her scientific discipline,
have given us an exhaustive description of the cake, can we say that the
cake is completely explained? We have certainly been given a description
of *how* the cake was made and *how* its various constituent elements relate
to each other, but suppose I now ask the assembled group of experts a
final question: *Why* was the cake made? The grin on Aunt Matilda's face
shows she knows the answer, for she made the cake, and she made it for
a purpose. But all the nutrition scientists, biochemists, chemists,
physicists and mathematicians in the world will not be able to answer the
question – and it is no insult to their disciplines to state their incapacity
to answer it. Their disciplines, which can cope with questions about the
nature and structure of the cake, that is, answering the 'how' questions,
cannot answer the 'why' questions connected with the purpose for which
the cake was made.[20] In fact, the only way we shall ever get an answer is
if Aunt Matilda reveals it to us. But if she does not disclose the answer to

us, the plain fact is that no amount of scientific analysis will enlighten us.

To say with Bertrand Russell that, because science cannot tell us why Aunt Matilda made the cake, we cannot know why she made it, is patently false. All we have to do is ask her. The claim that science is the only way to truth is a claim ultimately unworthy of science itself. Nobel Laureate Sir Peter Medawar points this out in his excellent book *Advice to a Young Scientist*: 'There is no quicker way for a scientist to bring discredit upon himself and upon his profession than roundly to declare – particularly when no declaration of any kind is called for – that science knows, or soon will know, the answers to all questions worth asking, and that questions which do not admit a scientific answer are in some way non-questions or "pseudo-questions" that only simpletons ask and only the gullible profess to be able to answer.' Medawar goes on to say, 'The existence of a limit to science is, however, made clear by its inability to answer childlike elementary questions having to do with first and last things – questions such as: "How did everything begin?"; "What are we all here for?"; "What is the point of living?".' He adds that it is to imaginative literature and religion that we must turn for answers to such questions.[21] Francis Collins, Director of the Human Genome Project, also emphasizes this: 'Science is powerless to answer questions such as "Why did the universe come into being?" "What is the meaning of human existence?" "What happens after we die?".'[22] There is clearly no inconsistency involved in being a passionately committed scientist at the highest level while simultaneously recognizing that science cannot answer every kind of question, including some of the deepest questions that human beings can ask.

It is only fair to say also that Russell, in spite of the fact that he wrote the very scientistic sounding statement we cited above, indicated elsewhere that he did not subscribe to full-blown scientism. He did, however, think that all definite knowledge belongs to science, which certainly sounds like incipient scientism, but then he immediately goes on to say that most of the interesting questions lie outside the competence of science: 'Is the world divided into mind and matter, and, if so, what is mind, what is matter? Is mind subject to matter, or is it possessed of independent powers? Has the universe any unity or purpose? Is it evolving towards some goal? Are there really laws of nature, or do we believe in them only because of our innate love of order? Is man what he seems to the astronomer, a tiny lump of impure carbon and water impotently crawling on a small and unimportant planet? Or is he what he appears to Hamlet? Is there a way of living that is noble and another that is base, or are all ways of living merely futile? ... To such questions no answers can be found in the laboratory.' [23]

Now what we are saying here has been familiar since the time of Aristotle, who famously distinguished what he called four causes: the material cause (the material of which the cake is made); the formal cause (the form into which the materials are shaped); the efficient cause (the work of Aunt Matilda the cook); and the final cause (the purpose for which the cake was made – someone's birthday). It is the fourth of Aristotle's causes, the final cause, which is outside the scope of science.

Austin Farrar writes: 'Every science picks out an aspect of things in the world and shows how it goes. Everything that lies outside such a field lies outside the scope of that science. And since God is not a part of the world, still less an aspect of it, nothing that is said about God, however truly, can be a statement belonging to any science.'[24]

In light of this, Peter Atkins' statements 'There is no reason to suppose that science cannot deal with every aspect of existence' (cited above) and 'There is nothing that cannot be understood'[25] seem to be completely off the wall.

Not surprisingly, there is a high price to pay for his attribution of such omni-competence to science: 'Science has no need of purpose... all the extraordinary, wonderful richness of the world can be expressed as growth from the dunghill of purposeless interconnected corruption.'[26] One wonders what Aunt Matilda would make of that as an ultimate explanation for the fact that she made the cake for her nephew Jimmy's birthday, indeed as an ultimate explanation of why she, Jimmy and the birthday cake existed in the first place. She might even prefer a 'primeval soup' to a 'dunghill of corruption', if she were offered the choice.

It is one thing to suggest that science cannot answer questions of ultimate purpose. It is quite another to dismiss purpose itself as an illusion because science cannot deal with it. And yet, Atkins is simply taking his materialism to its logical conclusion – or perhaps not quite. After all, the existence of a dunghill presupposes the existence of creatures capable of making dung! Rather odd then to think of the dung as creating the creatures. And if it is a 'dunghill of corruption' (in line with, one might suppose, the Second Law of Thermodynamics) one might wonder how the corruption gets reversed. The mind boggles.

But what destroys scientism completely is the fatal flaw of self-contradiction that runs through it. Scientism does not need to be refuted by external argument: it self-destructs. It suffers the same fate as in earlier times did the verification principle that was at the heart of the philosophy of logical-positivism. For, the statement that only science can lead to truth is not itself deduced from science. It is not a scientific statement but rather a statement about science, that is, it is a metascientific statement. Therefore, if scientism's basic principle is true, the statement expressing scientism must be false. Scientism refutes itself. Hence it is incoherent.

Medawar's view that science is limited is, therefore, no insult to science.

The very reverse is the case. It is those scientists who make exaggerated claims for science who make science look ridiculous. They have unintentionally and perhaps unconsciously wandered from doing science into myth-making – incoherent myths at that.

Before we leave Aunt Matilda we should note that her simple story helps to sort out another common confusion. We have seen how unaided scientific reasoning cannot find out why she made the cake; she must reveal it to us. But that does not mean reason is from that point on either irrelevant or inactive. The contrary is the case. For, understanding what she says when she tells us for whom the cake was made requires the use of our reason. We further need our reason to assess the credibility of her explanation. If she says she made the cake for her nephew Jimmy and we know that she has no nephew of that name, we will doubt her explanation; if we know she has a nephew of that name then her explanation will make sense. In other words, reason is not opposed to revelation – it is simply that her revelation of the purpose for which she made the cake supplies to reason information that *unaided* reason cannot access. But reason is absolutely essential to process that information. The point is that in cases where *science* is not our source of information, we cannot automatically assume that *reason* has ceased to function and *evidence* has ceased to be relevant.

Thus, when theists claim that there is Someone who stands in the same relationship to the universe that Aunt Matilda stands to her cake and that that Someone has revealed why the universe was created, they are not abandoning reason, rationality and evidence at all. They are simply claiming that there are certain questions which unaided reason cannot answer and to answer them we need another source of information – in this instance, revelation from God, to understand and evaluate which, reason is essential. It was in this spirit that Francis Bacon talked of God's Two Books – the Book of Nature and the Bible. Reason, rationality and evidence apply to both.

God – an unnecessary hypothesis?

Science has been spectacularly successful in probing the nature of the physical universe and elucidating the mechanisms by which the universe works. Scientific research has also led to the eradication of many horrific diseases, and raised hopes of eliminating many more. And scientific investigation has had another effect in a completely different direction: it has served to relieve a lot of people from superstitious fears. For instance, people need no longer think that an eclipse of the moon is caused by some frightful demon, which they have to placate. For all of these and myriad other things we should be very grateful.

But in some quarters the very success of science has also led to the idea that, because we can understand the mechanisms of the universe without bringing in God, we can safely conclude that there was no God who designed and created the universe in the first place. However, such reasoning involves a common logical fallacy, which we can illustrate as follows.

Take a Ford motor car. It is conceivable that someone from a remote part of the world, who was seeing one for the first time and who knew nothing about modern engineering, might imagine that there is a god (Mr Ford) inside the engine, making it go. He might further imagine that when the engine ran sweetly it was because Mr Ford inside the engine liked him, and when it refused to go it was because Mr Ford did not like him. Of course, if he were subsequently to study engineering and take the engine to pieces, he would discover that there is no Mr Ford inside it. Neither would it take much intelligence for him to see that he did not need to introduce Mr Ford as an explanation for its working. His grasp of the impersonal principles of internal combustion would be altogether enough to explain how the engine works. So far, so good. But if he then decided that his understanding of the principles of how the engine works made it impossible to believe in the existence of a Mr Ford who designed the engine in the first place, this would be patently false – in philosophical terminology he would be committing a category mistake. Had there never been a Mr Ford to design the mechanisms, none would exist for him to understand.

It is likewise a category mistake to suppose that our understanding of the impersonal principles according to which the universe works makes it either unnecessary or impossible to believe in the existence of a personal Creator who designed, made, and upholds the universe. In other words, we should not confuse the mechanisms by which the universe works either with its cause or its upholder.

Michael Poole, in his published debate with Richard Dawkins,[27] puts it this way: '… there is no logical conflict between reason-giving explanations which concern mechanisms, and reason-giving explanations which concern the plans and purposes of an agent, human or divine. This is a logical point, not a matter of whether one does or does not happen to believe in God oneself.'

In total disregard of this logical point, a famous statement made by the French mathematician Laplace is constantly misused to buttress atheism. On being asked by Napoleon where God fitted into his mathematical work, Laplace, quite correctly, replied: 'Sir, I have no need of that hypothesis.' Of course God did not appear in Laplace's mathematical description of how things work, just as Mr Ford would not appear in a scientific description of the laws of internal combustion. But what does that prove? That Henry Ford did not exist? Clearly not. Neither does such an argument prove that God does not exist. Austin Farrer comments on the Laplace incident as follows: 'Since God is not a rule built into the action of forces, nor is he a block of force, no sentence about God can play a part in physics or astronomy... We may forgive Laplace – he was answering an amateur according to his ignorance, not to say a fool according to his folly. Considered as a serious observation, his remark could scarcely have been more misleading. Laplace and his colleagues had not learned to do without theology; they had merely learned to mind their own business.' [28]

Quite so. But suppose Napoleon had posed a somewhat different question to Laplace: 'Why is there a universe at all in which there is matter and gravity and in which projectiles composed of matter moving under gravity describe the orbits encapsulated in your mathematical equations?' It would be harder to argue that the existence of God was irrelevant to that question. But then, that was not the question that Laplace was asked. So he did not answer it.

3

Reduction, reduction, reduction...

'If cows and horses or lions had hands and could draw, then horses would draw the forms of gods like horses, cows like cows, making their bodies similar in shape to their own.'

Xenophanes, 500 BC

'I am not postulating a "God of the gaps", a god merely to explain the things that science has not yet explained. I am postulating a God to explain why science explains; I do not deny that science explains, but I postulate God to explain why science explains.'

Richard Swinburne

The God of the gaps

There is another important issue that arises from this story about Laplace. In any debate about science and religion, sooner or later the question of the 'God of the gaps' will be raised. This is the idea that the introduction of a god or God is an evidence of intellectual laziness: we cannot explain something scientifically and so we introduce 'God' to cover our ignorance. We shall have more to say about this later, but at this juncture it is important to point out that Mr Ford is not to be found in the gaps in our knowledge about the workings of internal combustion engines. More precisely, he is not to be found in any reason-giving explanations that concern mechanisms. For Henry Ford is not a mechanism: he is no less than the agent who is responsible for the existence of the mechanism in the first place so that it *all* bears the marks of his handiwork – and that means the bits we do understand and the bits we don't.

So it is with God. At the more abstract level of the explanatory power of science itself, philosopher Richard Swinburne in his book *Is there a God?*[1] says: 'Note that I am not postulating a 'God of the gaps', a god merely to explain the things that science has not yet explained. I am postulating a God to explain why science explains; I do not deny that science explains, but I postulate God to explain why science explains. The very success of science in showing us how deeply ordered the natural world is provides strong grounds for believing that there is an even deeper cause for that order.' Swinburne is using inference to the best explanation and saying that God is the best explanation for the explanatory power of science.

The point to grasp here is that, because *God is not an alternative to science as an explanation*, he is not to be understood merely as a God of the gaps. On the contrary, he is the ground of all explanation: it is his existence which gives rise to the very possibility of explanation, scientific or otherwise. It is important to stress this because influential authors such as Richard Dawkins will insist on conceiving of God as an explanatory alternative to science – an idea that is nowhere to be found in theological reflection of any depth. Dawkins is therefore tilting at a windmill – dismissing a concept of God that no serious thinker believes in anyway. Such activity is not necessarily to be regarded as a mark of intellectual sophistication.

De-deifying the universe – the very first scientists

We need, however, to probe a little more thoroughly the claim made by many scientists that atheism is a necessary presupposition for true science to be carried out. They think that any move to bring in God as an explanation of the universe at any level will prove to be the end of science. If, for example, when it thunders, we suppose, like some of the ancients, that it is a god who is actually making the noise, then we would not, and could not, investigate the mechanism behind the noise. Only by assuming that there are no gods can we be free to investigate the mechanisms of nature in a truly scientific manner: introduce gods at any stage, and science stops. God, for them, is a science-stopper.

Well, we certainly need to remove deifications of the forces of nature in order to be able to be free to study nature – a revolutionary step in thinking which was taken by the early Greek natural philosophers Thales, Anaximander and Anaximenes of Milesia over 2,500 years ago. They were not content with mythological explanations, such as those that had been written down by Homer and Hesiod around 700 BC. They sought explanations in terms of natural processes and chalked up some notable scientific successes. Thales is accredited with determining the length of the year to be 365 days, accurately predicting a solar eclipse in 585 BC and using geometric methods to calculate the heights of pyramids from their shadows and even to estimate the size of the earth and the moon. Anaximander invented a sundial and a weatherproof clock and made the first world and star-maps. The Milesians were therefore among the earliest scientists.

Of great interest in the present context is Xenophanes (c. 570–478 BC) of Colophon (near Izmir in present day Turkey), who, though known for his attempts to understand the significance of the fossils of sea-creatures found in Malta, is even more famous for his trenchant denunciation of the mythological worldview. He pointed out that behaviour was attributed to the gods that among humans would be regarded as utterly shameful: the gods were rogues, thieves and adulterers. Indeed, he held that these gods had clearly been made in the images of the peoples that believed in them: Ethiopians have gods that are dark and flat-nosed, Thracians made them blue-eyed and red-haired. He added deridingly: 'If cows and horses or lions had hands and could draw, then horses would draw the forms of gods like horses, cows like cows, making their bodies similar in shape to their own.' Thus for Xenophanes these gods were but obvious childish fictions of the fertile imaginations of those who believed in them.

The influential Greek atomist philosopher Epicurus (born in 341 BC just after the death of Plato), who gave his name to Epicurean philosophy, wished to remove the myths from explanation in order to improve understanding: 'Thunderbolts can be produced in several different ways – just be sure the myths are kept out of it! And they will be kept out of it if one follows rightly the appearances and takes them as signs of what is unobservable.'[2]

Such denunciation of the gods, together with a determination to investigate the natural processes hitherto almost exclusively understood to be the activity of those gods, inevitably led to the decline of mythological interpretations of the universe and to the advance of science.[3]

Xenophanes was, however, not the only ancient thinker to criticize the polytheistic worldview. More importantly, nor was he the first. Unknown to him (presumably – there does not, alas, seem to be much information on the matter) and centuries beforehand, Moses had warned against worshipping 'other gods, bowing down to them, or to the sun or the moon or the stars of the sky'.[4] The Hebrew prophet Jeremiah, for example, writing in around 600 BC, similarly denounced the absurdity of deifying nature and worshipping the sun, moon and stars.[5]

At this point we could easily make the mistake of jumping to the conclusion that getting rid of gods either necessitates or is the same as getting rid of God. Far from it. For Moses and the Prophets it was absurd to bow down to various bits of the universe such as the sun, moon and stars as gods. But they regarded it as equally absurd not to believe in and bow down to the Creator God who made both the universe and them. And here, it is to be noted, they were not introducing a radically novel idea. They did not have to have their universe de-deified as did the Greeks, for the simple reason that they had never believed in the gods in the first place. What had saved them from that superstition was their belief in One True God, Creator of heaven and earth. That is, the idolatrous and polytheistic universe described by Homer and Hesiod was not the original world-picture of humankind – an impression that is often gained from the fact that most books on science and philosophy start with the ancient Greeks and emphasize the importance of the de-deification of the universe, singularly failing to point out that the Hebrews had protested against idolatrous interpretations of the universe long before the time of the Greeks. This serves to obscure the fact that polytheism arguably constitutes a perversion of an original belief in One Creator God.[6] It was this perversion that needed to be corrected, by recovering, not by jettisoning, belief in the Creator. Precisely the point made by Melvin Calvin, as cited earlier.

There is, therefore, a deep gulf between the Greek and Hebrew view of the universe that ought to be highlighted even further. Commenting on Hesiod's poem 'Theogony' (The Genesis of the gods), Werner Jaeger writes: 'If we compare this Greek hypostasis of the world-creative Eros with that of the *Logos* in the Hebrew account of creation, we may observe a deep-lying difference in the outlook of the two peoples. The *Logos* is a substantialization of an intellectual property or power of God the Creator, who is stationed *outside* the world and brings that world into existence by his own personal fiat. The Greek gods are stationed *inside* the world; they are descended from Heaven and Earth... they are generated by the mighty power of Eros who likewise belongs within the world as an all-engendering primitive force. Thus they are already subject to what we should call natural law.... When Hesiod's thought at last gives way to truly philosophical thinking, the Divine is sought inside the world – not outside it, as in the Jewish Christian theology that develops out of the book of Genesis.'[7]

It is therefore a very striking fact that Xenophanes, in spite of his being steeped in a polytheistic culture, did not make the mistake of confusing God with the gods and thus reject the former with the latter. He believed in one God who ruled the universe. He wrote: 'There is one God... similar to mortals neither in shape nor in thought... remote and effortless he governs all there is.'[8]

The work of Thomas Aquinas in the thirteenth century is also relevant to this discussion. He regarded God as the First Cause – the ultimate cause of all things. God directly caused the universe to exist and it was thus dependent on him. This is what we might call direct causation. But then Aquinas held that there was a second level of causation (sometimes called secondary causation) that operated within the universe. This consisted in the cause-effect web that is spun out of the vast interlocking and interdependent system that is the universe. Thus, the fact that explanations of secondary causation can be given in terms of laws and mechanisms does not imply the non-existence of the Creator on which the very existence of the cause-effect web depends.

The notion that belief in a Creator God who created and who upholds the universe would bring science to an end is frankly fallacious. Indeed it could be said to be a somewhat strange idea in light of the role that this belief has played in the rise of science – for if it were true, science might never have started. Believing that the engine of the car had been designed by Mr Ford would not stop anybody from investigating scientifically how the engine worked – in fact it might well spur them on to do so. However, and this is crucial, if they came to superstitiously believe that Mr Ford *was* the engine, that would stop their science dead. This is the key issue: there is a great difference between God and the gods, and between a God who is the Creator and a god who is the universe, as James Clerk Maxwell well knew when he had inscribed over the door of the famous Cavendish Physics laboratory in Cambridge the words: 'Great are the works of the Lord; they are pondered by all who delight in them.'[9]

As we look back over the history of science we have every reason to be grateful to the brilliant thinkers who took the brave step of questioning the mythological view of nature that endowed various bits of the universe with divine powers they did not possess. We have seen that some of them did so, not only without rejecting the concept of a Creator, but in the very name of that Creator. Perhaps there is a subtle danger today that, in their desire to eliminate the concept of a Creator completely, some scientists and philosophers have been led, albeit unwittingly, to re-deify the universe by endowing matter and energy with creative powers that they cannot be convincingly shown to possess. Banishing the One Creator God they would then end up with what has been described as the ultimate in polytheism – a universe in which every particle has god-like capacities.

When we discussed the limits of science above, we pointed out that there were certain questions that science was not geared to answer, particularly 'why' questions that have to do with purpose as distinct from function. We must now turn to the way in which science tries to answer those questions that do fall within its competence.

Reductionism

The object of 'explaining' something is to give an accessible and intelligible description of its nature and function. One obvious thing to try to do is to split the problem up into separate parts or aspects, and thus 'reduce' it to simpler components that are individually easier to investigate. This kind of procedure, often called *methodological reductionism*, is a major part of the normal process of science (and, indeed of many other activities), and has proved spectacularly effective.

Then there is the way in which the language of mathematics is used to reduce or compress the description of often very complex phenomena into short and elegant equations. Think of the phenomenal achievement of Kepler in taking Tycho Brahe's many observations of the motion of the planets and compressing them into the single statement that the planets moved in elliptical orbits with the sun at one focus. Or take Newton's further compression or reduction of Kepler's work in his law of gravitation. Similarly, the equations of Maxwell, Einstein, Schrödinger and Dirac are among the most famous iconic examples of the triumph of mathematical reductionism, and the ongoing quest for a TOE (Theory of Everything) is driven by the desire to achieve the ultimate mathematical compression by uniting the four fundamental forces of nature.

The great mathematician David Hilbert, spurred on by the singular achievements of mathematical compression, thought that the reductionist programme of mathematics could be carried out to such an extent that in the end all of mathematics could be compressed into a collection of formal statements in a finite set of symbols together with a finite set of axioms and rules of inference. It was a seductive thought with the ultimate in 'bottom-up' explanation as the glittering prize. Mathematics, if Hilbert's Programme were to succeed, would henceforth be reduced to a set of written marks that could be manipulated according to prescribed rules without any attention being paid to the applications that would give 'significance' to those marks. In particular, the truth or falsity of any given string of symbols would be decided by some general algorithmic process. The hunt was on to solve the so-called Entscheidungsproblem by finding that general decision procedure.

Experience suggested to Hilbert and others that the Entscheidungsproblem would be solved positively. But their intuition proved wrong. In 1931 the Austrian mathematician Kurt Gödel published a paper entitled 'On Formally Undecidable Propositions of Principia Mathematica and Related Systems'. His paper, though only twenty-five pages long, caused the mathematical equivalent of an earthquake whose reverberations are still palpable. For Gödel had actually *proved* that Hilbert's Programme was doomed in that it was unrealizable. In a piece of mathematics that stands as an intellectual tour-de-force of the first magnitude, Gödel demonstrated that the arithmetic with which we are all familiar is incomplete: that is, in any system that has a finite set of axioms and rules of inference and which is large enough to contain ordinary arithmetic, there are always true statements of the system that cannot be proved on the basis of that set of axioms and those rules of inference. This result is known as Gödel's First Incompleteness Theorem.

Now Hilbert's Programme also aimed to prove the essential consistency of his formulation of mathematics as a formal system. Gödel, in his Second Incompleteness Theorem, shattered that hope as well. He proved that one of the statements that cannot be proved in a sufficiently strong formal system is the consistency of the system itself. In other words, if arithmetic is consistent then that fact is one of the things that cannot be proved in the system. It is something that we can only believe on the basis of the evidence, or by appeal to higher axioms. This has been succinctly summarized by saying that if a religion is something whose foundations are based on faith, then mathematics is the only religion that can prove it is a religion!

In informal terms, as the British-born American physicist and mathematician Freeman Dyson puts it, 'Gödel proved that in mathematics the whole is always greater than the sum of the parts'.[10] Thus there is a limit to reductionism. Therefore, Peter Atkins' statement, cited earlier, that 'the only grounds for supposing that reductionism will fail are pessimism in the minds of the scientists and fear in the minds of the religious' is simply incorrect.

That there are limits for reductionism in science itself is borne out by the history of science, which teaches us that it is important to balance our justifiable enthusiasm for reductionism by bearing in mind that there may well be (and usually is) more to a given whole than simply what we obtain by adding up all that we have learned from the parts. Studying all the parts of a watch separately will not necessarily enable you to grasp how the complete watch works as an integrated whole. There is more to water than we can readily see by investigating separately the hydrogen and oxygen of which it is composed. There are many composite systems in which understanding the individual parts of the system may well be simply impossible without an understanding of the system as a whole – the living cell, for instance.

Besides methodological reductionism, there are two further important types of reductionism: *epistemological* and *ontological*. Epistemological reductionism is the view that higher level phenomena can be explained by processes at a lower level. The strong epistemological reductionist thesis is that such 'bottom-up' explanations can always be achieved *without remainder*. That is, chemistry can ultimately be explained by physics; biochemistry by chemistry; biology by biochemistry; psychology by biology; sociology by brain science; and theology by sociology. As the Nobel Prize-winning molecular biologist Francis Crick puts it: The ultimate aim of the modern development in biology is, in fact, to explain all biology in terms of physics and chemistry.'[11]

This view is shared by Richard Dawkins. 'My task is to explain elephants, and the world of complex things, in terms of the simple things that physicists either understand, or are working on.'[12] Leaving aside for the moment the very questionable assertion to which we must return below that the subject matter of physics is simple (think of quantum mechanics, quantum electrodynamics or string theory), the ultimate goal of such reductionism is evidently to reduce all human behaviour – our likes and dislikes, the entire mental landscape of our lives – to physics. This view is often called 'physicalism', a particularly strong form of materialism. It is not, however, a view which commends universal support, and that for very good reasons. As Karl Popper points out: 'There is almost always an unresolved residue left by even the most successful attempts at reduction.'[13]

Scientist and philosopher Michael Polanyi[14] helps us see why it is intrinsically implausible to expect epistemological reductionism to work in every circumstance. He asks us to think of the various levels of process involved in constructing an office building with bricks. First of all there is the process of extracting the raw materials out of which the bricks have to be made. Then there are the successively higher levels of making the bricks – they do not make themselves; brick-laying – the bricks do not 'self-assemble'; designing the building – it does not design itself; and planning the town in which the building is to be built – it does not organize itself. Each level has its own rules. The laws of physics and chemistry govern the raw material of the bricks; technology prescribes the art of brick-making; brick-layers lay the bricks as directed by the builders; architecture teaches the builders; and the architects are controlled by the town planners. Each level is controlled by the level above. But the reverse is not true. The laws of a higher level cannot be derived from the laws of a lower level – although what can be done at a higher level will, of course, depend on the lower levels. For example, if the bricks are not strong there will be a limit on the height of the building that can safely be built with them.

Or take another example, quite literally to your hand at this moment. Consider the page you are reading just now. It consists of paper imprinted with ink (or perhaps it is a series of dots on the computer screen in front of you). It is surely obvious that the physics and chemistry of ink and paper (or pixels on a computer monitor) can never, even in principle, tell you anything about the significance of the shapes of the letters on the page; and this has nothing to do with the fact that physics and chemistry are not yet sufficiently advanced to deal with this question. Even if we allow these sciences another 1,000 years of development it will make no difference, because the shapes of those letters demand a totally new and higher level of explanation than physics and chemistry are capable of giving. In fact, complete explanation can only be given in terms of the higher level concepts of language and authorship, the communication of a message by a person. The ink and paper are carriers of the message, but the message certainly does not arise automatically from them. Furthermore, when it comes to language itself, there is again a sequence of levels. You cannot derive a vocabulary from phonetics, or the grammar of a language from its vocabulary, etc.[15]

As is well known, the genetic material DNA carries information. We shall describe this later on in some detail; but the basic idea is that DNA can be thought of as a long tape on which there is a string of letters written in a four-letter chemical language. The sequence of letters contains coded instructions (information) that the cell uses to make proteins. But the order of the sequence is not generated by the chemistry of the base letters.

In each of the situations described above, we have a series of levels, each higher than the previous one. What happens on a higher level is not completely derivable from what happens on the level beneath it. In this situation it is sometimes said that the higher level phenomena 'emerge' from the lower level. Unfortunately, however, the word 'emerge' is easily misunderstood, and even misleadingly misused, to mean that the higher level properties arise *automatically* from the lower level properties without any further input of information or organization – just as the higher level properties of water emerge from combining oxygen and hydrogen. However, this is clearly false in general, as we showed earlier by considering building and writing on paper. The building does not emerge from the bricks nor the writing from the paper and ink without the injection of both energy and intelligent activity.

The same argument applies to the illustration of emergence offered by Dawkins in a public lecture in Oxford (20 January 1999) when he claimed that the capacity to do word-processing is an 'emergent' property of computers. It is; but only at the expense of the input of the considerable quantities of information contained in an intelligently designed software package like Microsoft Word.

The British theologian and scientist Arthur Peacocke wrote, 'In no way can the concept of "information", the concept of conveying a message, be articulated in terms of the concepts of physics and chemistry, even though the latter can be shown to explain how the molecular machinery (DNA, RNA and protein) operates to carry information...'[16]

Yet, notwithstanding the fact that writing on paper, computer software and DNA have in common the fact that they encode a 'message', those scientists committed to materialistic philosophy insist that the information-carrying properties of DNA must ultimately have emerged automatically out of matter *by a mindless, unguided, process*. The driving force behind their insistence is obvious. For if, as materialism holds, matter and energy are all that exists, then it follows logically that matter and energy must possess the inherent potential to organize themselves in such a way that eventually all the complex molecules necessary for life, including DNA, will emerge. On the basis of their materialistic hypotheses no other possibility is conceivable or allowable. Whether there is any evidence that matter and energy actually possess this 'emergent' capacity is another thing altogether, which will be discussed in detail later.

Next we must consider the third type of reductionism, *ontological reductionism*, which is closely related to epistemological reductionism. A classic example of it is given by Richard Dawkins: 'The universe is nothing but a collection of atoms in motion, human beings are simply machines for propagating DNA, and the propagation of DNA is a self-sustaining process. It is every living object's sole reason for living.'[17]

The words 'nothing but', 'sole', or 'simply', are the tell-tale signature of ontological reductionist thinking. If we remove these words we are usually left with something unobjectionable. The universe certainly is a collection of atoms, and human beings do propagate DNA. Both of these statements are statements of science. But immediately we add the words 'nothing but', the statements go beyond science and become expressions of materialistic or naturalistic belief. The question is, do the statements remain true when we add those tell-tale words? Is there really nothing more to the universe and life than that? Are we going to say with Francis Crick: 'You, your joys and your sorrows, your memories and ambitions, your sense of personal identity and free will, are in fact no more than the behaviour of a vast assembly of nerve cells and their associated molecules'?[18]

What shall we think, then, of human love and fear? Are they meaningless neural behaviour patterns? Or what shall we make of the concepts of beauty or truth? Is a Rembrandt painting nothing but molecules of paint scattered on canvas? Crick seems to think they are. One then wonders by what means we would recognize it. After all, if the concept of truth itself results from 'nothing more than the behaviour of a vast assembly of nerve cells' how in the name of logic would we know that our brain was composed of nerve cells? As Fraser Watts has pointed out,[19] Crick himself seems to realize that there must be more to it than this, for he radically modifies his 'astonishing' hypothesis by weakening it to the almost innocuous statement 'You are *largely* the behaviour of a vast population of neurones'[20] (italics added). But such a modified hypothesis ceases to astonish. Come to think of it, even if the astonishing hypothesis were true how would it astonish? For how could we begin to know or understand it? And what meaning would 'astonishment' have? The idea is intrinsically incoherent.

These arguments are extensions of what has come to be known as Darwin's Doubt: 'With me, the horrid doubt always arises whether the convictions of man's mind, which has been developed from the mind of the lower animals, are of any value or at all trustworthy.'[21]

By far and away the most devastating criticism of ontological reductionism is that it, like scientism, is self-destructive. John Polkinghorne describes its programme as 'ultimately suicidal. If Crick's thesis is true we could never know it. For, not only does it relegate our experiences of beauty, moral obligation, and religious encounter to the epiphenomenal scrap-heap. It also destroys rationality. Thought is replaced by electro-chemical neural events. Two such events cannot confront each other in rational discourse. They are neither right nor wrong. They simply happen... The very assertions of the reductionist himself are nothing but blips in the neural network of his brain. The world of rational discourse dissolves into the absurd chatter of firing synapses. Quite frankly, that cannot be right and none of us believes it to be so.'[22]

Precisely. There is a patent self-contradiction running through all attempts, however sophisticated they may appear, to derive rationality from irrationality. When stripped down to their bare bones, they all seem uncannily like futile attempts to lift oneself by one's bootstraps, or to construct a perpetual motion machine.[23] After all, it is the use of the human mind that has led people to adopt ontological reductionism, which carries with it the corollary that there is no reason to trust our minds when they tell us anything at all; let alone, in particular, that such reductionism is true.

4

Designer universe?

'To the majority of those who have reflected deeply and written about the origin and nature of the universe, it has seemed that it points beyond itself to a source which is non-physical and of great intelligence and power. Almost all of the great classical philosophers – certainly Plato, Aristotle, Descartes, Leibniz, Spinoza, Kant, Hegel, Locke, Berkeley – saw the origin of the universe as lying in a transcendent reality. They had different specific ideas of this reality, and different ways of approaching it; but that the universe is not self-explanatory, and that it requires some explanation beyond itself, was something they accepted as fairly obvious.'

Keith Ward

'Astronomy leads us to a unique event, a universe which was created out of nothing, one with the very delicate balance needed to provide exactly the right conditions required to permit life, and one which has an underlying (one might say 'supernatural') plan.'

Arno Penzias, Physics Nobel Prize-winner

Evidence for design?

In recent years science has been taking us on a journey full not only of surprises but also of mystery. Cosmology on an unimaginably large scale, and elementary particle physics on the incredibly small scale, have gradually laid bare to us the spectacularly beautiful structure of the universe in which we live. Its sheer size makes us aware of and simultaneously amazed at our own tinyness. On the linear scale of size, we are insignificant – specks of dust in a vast galaxy, which is itself scarcely more than a speck in the universe – although it ought to be said that on a logarithmic scale we are about half-way between the incredibly small and the incredibly large dimensions revealed to us by nuclear physics and astronomy, respectively. Just what are we human beings? And what is this universe? Is it really our home, or are we just tiny transient beings that it has happened to throw up as matter and energy, mindlessly to exploit the inherent potential in the laws of nature?

None of us faces these questions dispassionately. The universe is far too awe-inspiring for that. Nor do we face them disinterestedly. We cannot remain untouched by such questions – after all, we are here. And so our minds insist on asking about the nature of our relationship to the universe.

As ever, the answers we get to these questions are of very different kinds. Some scientists think that we are aliens in the cosmos, 'an eczema on the face of the universe', thrown up by the vast maelstrom of chance and necessity that governs our universe's physical behaviour. We are 'the product of a mindless and purposeless natural process which did not have us in mind', to quote biologist George Gaylord Simpson.[1]

But there are others who do not feel like aliens in the universe. Physicist Freeman Dyson is one such. He writes: 'As we look out into the universe and identify the many accidents of physics and astronomy that have worked together to our benefit, it almost seems as if the universe must in some sense have known we were coming.'[2] Nor is another physicist, Paul Davies, convinced that we are mere insignificant specks of animated dust. He writes: 'I cannot believe that our existence in this universe is a mere quirk of fate, an accident of history, an incidental blip in the great cosmic drama. Our involvement is too intimate... We are truly meant to be here.'[3] Davies is clearly suggesting that there is a Mind behind the universe, which had humans in view when the universe was made. Why do Dyson and Davies think the way they do? Does the universe itself give us any clues that would be grounds for thinking that we human beings have significance? It does. The first ground is:

The rational intelligibility of the universe

However much we may debate the essence of the scientific method, there is no question as to the foundation on which that method rests: the rational intelligibility of the universe. It was Albert Einstein's astonishment at this that prompted him to make the famous comment, 'The most incomprehensible thing about the universe is that it is comprehensible.'[4]

The very concept of the intelligibility of the universe presupposes the existence of a rationality capable of recognizing that intelligibility. Indeed, confidence that our human mental processes possess some degree of reliability and are capable of giving us some information about the world is fundamental to any kind of study, not only the study of science. This conviction is so central to all thinking that we cannot even question its validity without assuming it in the first place, since we have to rely on our minds in order to do the questioning. It is the bedrock belief upon which all intellectual inquiry is built. I shall argue that theism gives it a consistent and reasonable justification whereas naturalism seems powerless to do so.

Rational intelligibility is one of the main considerations that have led thinkers of all generations to conclude that the universe must itself be a product of intelligence. Philosopher Keith Ward sums up: 'To the majority of those who have reflected deeply and written about the origin and nature of the universe, it has seemed that it points beyond itself to a source which is non-physical and of great intelligence and power. Almost all of the great classical philosophers – certainly Plato, Aristotle, Descartes, Leibniz, Spinoza, Kant, Hegel, Locke, Berkeley – saw the origin of the universe as lying in a transcendent reality. They had different specific ideas of this reality, and different ways of approaching it; but that the universe is not self-explanatory, and that it requires some explanation beyond itself, was something they accepted as fairly obvious.'[5] Thus the inference to the best explanation from the origin and nature of the universe to an underlying non-physical intelligence has a long and impressive pedigree.

The nature and role of faith in science

For Albert Einstein the comprehensibility of the universe was something to be wondered at: 'You find it strange that I consider the comprehensibility of the world (to the extent that we are authorized to speak of such a comprehensibility) as a miracle or as an eternal mystery. Well, *a priori*, one should expect a chaotic world, which cannot be grasped by the mind in any way... the kind of order created by Newton's theory of gravitation, for example, is wholly different. Even if man proposes the axioms of the theory, the success of such a project presupposes a high degree of ordering of the objective world, and this could not be expected *a priori*. That is the 'miracle' which is being constantly reinforced as our knowledge expands.'[6]

For, as the example of Newton's theory shows, it is not only the fact that the universe is intelligible which is amazing; it is the mathematical nature of that intelligibility which is remarkable. We tend to take the usefulness of mathematics as obvious because we are so used to it. But why? Paul Davies is among those not satisfied with the glib response of people who say that the fundamental laws of nature are mathematical simply because we define as fundamental those laws that are mathematical. One of the main reasons for his dissatisfaction is that much of the mathematics found to be successfully applicable 'was worked out as an abstract exercise by pure mathematicians, long before it was applied to the real world. The original investigations were entirely unconnected with their eventual application.'[7] It is very striking that the most abstract mathematical concepts that seem to be pure inventions of the human mind can turn out to be of vital importance for branches of science, with a vast range of practical applications.[8]

Davies here echoes a famous essay by Eugene Wigner, a Nobel Laureate in Physics, in which he wrote: 'The enormous usefulness of mathematics in the natural sciences is something bordering on the mysterious, and there is no rational explanation for it... it is an article of faith.'[9] The relationship between mathematics and physics goes very deep and it is very hard to think of it as some random accident. Professor of Mathematics Sir Roger Penrose FRS, whose understanding of that relationship is unquestioned, has this to say about it: 'It is hard for me to believe... that such SUPERB theories could have arisen merely by some random natural selection of ideas leaving only the good ones as survivors. The good ones are simply much too good to be the survivors of ideas that have arisen in a random way. There must be, instead, some deep underlying reason for the accord between mathematics and physics.'[10] Certainly science itself cannot account for this phenomenon. Why? Because, in the words of John Polkinghorne: 'Science does not explain the mathematical intelligibility of the physical world, for it is part of science's founding faith that this is so.'[11]

We cannot fail to note that here we have two leading scientists, Wigner and Polkinghorne, explicitly drawing our attention to the foundational role that faith plays in science. Yes, faith. This may come as a surprise, even as a shock, to many, especially if they have been exposed to the very common fallacy mentioned at the beginning of this book and spread with memetic speed by Richard Dawkins and others, that 'faith' means 'blind faith' and belongs exclusively to the domain of religion, whereas science does not involve faith at all. Dawkins is simply wrong: faith is inseparable from the scientific endeavour. Gödel's Second Theorem gives further evidence for this: you cannot even do mathematics without faith in its consistency – and it has to be faith because the consistency of mathematics cannot be proved.

But there is more. Think of Newton's inverse square law of gravitational attraction. Because we are so familiar with it as an explanation of how the planets orbit the sun in ellipses and use it (or rather, the experts do) to predict all kinds of astronomical events, eclipses and such like, we often fail to realize that there is a hidden faith dimension even here. It is betrayed by our belief that what happened today will happen again tomorrow. This is the well-known problem of induction in philosophy that was memorably illustrated by Bertrand Russell in his story of the 'inductivist turkey'. The hero of the story is a turkey that, because it had been regularly fed in the days preceding Christmas, reasoned that it would be fed every day. However it hit a serious crisis on Christmas Day that, for a split-second at least, might just have revealed to it the perils of induction! Paul Davies comments: 'Just because the sun has risen every day of your life, there is no guarantee that it will rise tomorrow. The belief that it will – that there are indeed dependable regularities of nature – is an act of faith, but one which is indispensable to the progress of science.'[12] This aspect of the rational intelligibility of the universe is often referred to as the principle of uniformity of nature. It is an article of the scientist's faith.

Our answer to the question of why the universe is rationally intelligible will in fact depend, not on whether we are scientists or not, but on whether we are theists or naturalists. Theists will argue that Wigner is wrong when he says there is no rational explanation for that intelligibility. On the contrary, they will say that the intelligibility of the universe is grounded in the nature of the ultimate rationality of God: both the real world and mathematics are traceable to the Mind of God who created both the universe and the human mind. It is, therefore, not surprising when the mathematical theories spun by human minds created in the image of God's Mind, find ready application in a universe whose architect was that same creative Mind.

Keith Ward strongly supports this view: 'The continuing conformity of physical particles to precise mathematical relationships is something that is much more likely to exist if there is an ordering cosmic mathematician who sets up the correlation in the requisite way. The existence of laws of physics... strongly implies that there is a God who formulates such laws and ensures that the physical realm conforms to them.'[13]

Theism, therefore, upholds and makes sense of the rational intelligibility of the universe; whereas, as we saw earlier, the reductionist thesis undermines it and dissolves it into meaninglessness. Far from science abolishing God, it would seem that there is a substantial case for asserting that it is the existence of a Creator that gives to science its fundamental intellectual justification. Even Stephen Hawking, who occupies the professorial chair once held by Sir Isaac Newton at Cambridge, and who is not known to be particularly sympathetic to theism, admitted in a television interview: 'It is difficult to discuss the beginning of the universe without mentioning the concept of God. My work on the origin of the universe is on the borderline between science and religion, but I try to stay on the scientific side of the border. It is quite possible that God acts in ways that cannot be described by scientific laws.'[14]

It is for this kind of reason that it is possible to see even a certain consonance between scientific and religious ways of thinking about the universe. In his debate on atheism and theism with J. J. C. Smart, J. J. Haldane makes precisely this point, arguing that scientific and religious approaches are similar: 'Thus science is faith-like in resting upon "creedal" presuppositions, and inasmuch as these relate to the order and intelligibility of the universe they also resemble the content of a theistic conception of the universe as an ordered creation. Furthermore it seems that the theist carries the scientific impulse further by pressing on with the question of how perceived order is possible, seeking the most fundamental descriptions-cum-explanations of the existence and nature of the universe.'[15]

The existence of the universe

Another vital element in the scientist's credo is the conviction that the universe is there to study – so self-evident a fact, indeed, that we can easily take it for granted. And that is a pity. For one of the fundamental problems of philosophy is: Why is there a universe at all, why is there something rather than nothing?

Now there are some scientists and philosophers who think that we should not even ask this question. For them there is no point in looking for a reason for the existence of the universe since, according to them, there simply isn't one. Their view is that, since any chain of reasoning must start somewhere, we might as well start with the existence of the universe. Echoing Bertrand Russell, E. Tryton writes: 'Our universe is simply one of those things which happen from time to time.'[16] However, the kind of answer that says that the universe just sprang into existence sounds about as scientific as answering the question why apples fall to the ground, by saying that they just do. In addition, it would be distinctly odd, as Keith Ward points out, 'to think that there is a reason for everything, except for that most important item of all – that is, the existence of everything, the universe itself'.[17] The insatiable human desire for explanation will not let that question rest.

Others maintain that the universe is self-explanatory. For instance, Peter Atkins believes that 'Space-time generates its own dust in the process of its own self-assembly.'[18] He calls this the 'Cosmic bootstrap', referring to the self-contradictory idea of a person lifting himself by pulling on his own bootlace. Keith Ward is surely right to say that Atkins' view of the universe is as blatantly self-contradictory as the name he gives to it, pointing out that it is 'logically impossible for a cause to bring about some effect without already being in existence'. Ward concludes: 'Between the hypothesis of God and the hypothesis of a cosmic bootstrap, there is no competition. We were always right to think that persons, or universes, who seek to pull themselves up by their own bootstraps are forever doomed to failure.'[19] Neither universes nor Aunt Matilda's cake are self-generating or self-explanatory. Atkins' 'self-generation' explanation is demanded from him by his materialism, not his science.

Stephen Hawking, on the other hand, seems to agree with the point made in our Aunt Matilda story, namely that science cannot answer the question of why there is a universe. He writes: 'The usual approach of science of constructing a mathematical model cannot answer the questions of why there should be a universe for the model to describe. Why does the universe go to all the bother of existing? Is the unified theory so compelling that it brings about its own existence? Or does it need a Creator, and, if so, does he have any other effect on the universe?'[20]

Hawking's first suggestion here is, not that the universe is self-generating, but that it is brought into existence by a theory. Paul Davies says something similar in an interview: 'There's no need to invoke anything supernatural in the origins of the universe or of life. I have never liked the idea of divine tinkering: for me it is much more inspiring to believe that a set of mathematical laws can be so clever as to bring all these things into being.'[21]

It is strange that a scientist of Davies' standing is prepared to decide how things started on the basis of like or dislike. That is no better than someone who says, 'I like to think that there are fairies at the bottom of my garden.' Furthermore, he is here ascribing intelligence (if not personality) to a set of mathematical laws – and believing that they could be intelligent on the basis that he finds it inspiring! Is this wishful thinking or what?

Leaving aside the dubious-sounding motivation we might well ask what could possibly be meant by a *theory* or *laws* bringing the universe into existence. We certainly expect to be able to formulate theories involving mathematical laws that describe natural phenomena, and we can often do this to astonishing degrees of precision. However, the laws that we find cannot themselves cause anything. Newton's laws can describe the motion of a billiard ball, but it is the cue wielded by the billiard player that sets the ball moving, not the laws. The laws help us map the trajectory of the ball's movement in the future (provided nothing external interferes), but they are powerless to move the ball, let alone bring it into existence.

And, if one dare say so, the much maligned William Paley[22] said as much long ago. Speaking of the person who had just stumbled on a watch on the heath and picked it up he says that such a person would not be 'less surprised to be informed, that the watch in his hand was nothing more than the result of the laws of *metallic* nature. It is a perversion of language to assign any law, as the efficient, operative cause of any thing. A law presupposes an agent; for it is only the mode, according to which an agent proceeds: it implies a power; for it is the order, according to which that power acts. Without this agent, without this power, which are both distinct from itself, the *law* does nothing; is nothing.'[23]

In the world in which most of us live the simple law of arithmetic, $1+1 = 2$, never brought anything into being by itself. It certainly has never put any money into my bank account. If I first put £1,000 into the bank and then later another £1,000, the laws of arithmetic will rationally explain how it is that I now have £2,000 in the bank. But if I never put any money into the bank myself and simply leave it to the laws of arithmetic to bring money into being in my bank account, I shall remain permanently bankrupt. The world of strict naturalism in which clever mathematical laws all by themselves bring the universe and life into existence, is pure (and, one might add, poor) fiction. To call it science-fiction would besmirch the name of science. Theories and laws simply do not bring anything into existence. The view that they nevertheless somehow have that capacity seems a rather desperate refuge (and it is hard to see what else it could be but a refuge) from the alternative possibility contained in Hawkings's final question cited above: 'Or does it need a Creator?'

Allan Sandage, widely regarded as one of the fathers of modern astronomy, discoverer of quasars and winner of the Crafoord Prize, astronomy's equivalent of the Nobel Prize, is in no doubt that the answer to that question is positive: 'I find it quite improbable that such order came out of chaos. There has to be some organizing principle. God to me is a mystery but is the explanation for the miracle of existence – why there is something rather than nothing.'[24]

The beginning of the universe

The question of the existence of the universe is regarded as logically distinct from the question of whether or not the universe had a beginning. Whether the universe had a beginning or not is a question of central importance to the history of thought. It is connected with questions about the nature of ultimate reality. For, if the universe had no beginning, it is eternal and one might argue that it is simply a brute fact of existence. On the other hand, if it had a beginning, it is not eternal and, therefore, not ultimate.

Throughout history many views have been put forward. Plato held that the universe was made out of pre-existent matter.[25] Aristotle believed that the earth was the centre of an eternal universe. In a variation on the theme of an eternal universe, other ancient cosmologies, like the Hindu cosmology, for example, thought in terms of the universe going through endlessly repeating cycles, much like the rhythm of nature but of immense duration – sometimes measured in trillions of years.

However, long before the ancient Greeks, the Hebrews believed that time was linear and that the universe had a beginning. It had been created, and the Creator was God. This biblical view was held by leading thinkers such as Augustine, Irenaeus and Aquinas. It dominated the intellectual landscape for many centuries.

Now it is of particular interest that Aquinas in the thirteenth century attempted to reconcile the biblical position with Aristotelian philosophy by stressing that, in his view, the concept of creation had much more to do with existence than with process. Following Augustine he held that God had created 'with time' rather than in time. According to him, therefore, creation meant simply that the universe depends on God for its existence. Aquinas thought that it was impossible to tell from philosophical considerations whether the universe was eternal or not: yet he conceded that divine revelation showed that it did indeed have a beginning.

For much of the modern scientific era following Copernicus, Galileo and Newton, belief in general reverted to the idea of a universe infinite in both age and extent. Thereafter, from the middle of the nineteenth century, this view began to come under increasing pressure, to the point that it has completely lost its domination. For belief in a beginning is once again the majority view of contemporary scientists. Evidence from the red-shift in the light from distant galaxies, the cosmic microwave background and thermodynamics has led scientists to formulate the so-called standard 'Big Bang' model of the universe.

Antipathy to the idea of a beginning

It should at once be said, however, that not all scientists are convinced that the Big Bang model is correct. For example, there are difficulties created by possible alternative interpretations of the red-shift, and by the recently discovered evidence that the expansion of the universe seems to be accelerating – a circumstance which raises the question of the existence of a hitherto unknown force that acts in the opposite direction to gravity.

For some scientists and philosophers, worldview considerations play a role in their antipathy to the idea of a beginning. Engels made a very perceptive comment on the issues at stake. 'Did God create the world, or has the world been in existence eternally? The answers which the philosophers gave to this question split them into two great camps. Those who asserted the primacy of the spirit to nature, and therefore, in the last instance, assumed world creation in some form or other... comprised the camp of idealism. The others, who regarded Nature as primary, belong to the various schools of materialism.'[26] Stephen Hawking adopts a similar view: 'Many people do not like the idea that time has a beginning, probably because it smacks of divine intervention.'[27]

One such was Sir Arthur Eddington (1882–1944), who reacted as follows: 'Philosophically, the notion of a beginning of the present order of Nature is repugnant... I should like to find a genuine loophole.'[28] That repugnance was shared by others. In the mid-twentieth century, for example, Gold, Bondi, Hoyle and Narlikar advanced a series of steady-state theories in which it was argued that the universe had always existed, and that matter was continuously being created in order to keep the density of the admittedly expanding universe uniform. The creation rate they needed was incredibly slow – one atom per cubic metre in ten billion years. This meant, incidentally, that there was no real possibility of testing the theory by observation.

The question of their motivation drew the attention of the prestigious weekly science journal *Nature*,[29] in which well-known science writer John Gribbin pointed out that a great deal of impetus was given to Hoyle and Bondi's steady-state theory by the philosophical and theological problems raised by the idea of a beginning to the universe, in particular, the question of what or who was responsible for it.

Another well-known scientist who found the idea of a beginning repugnant is Sir John Maddox, a former editor of *Nature*. He pronounced the idea of a beginning 'thoroughly unacceptable', because it implied an 'ultimate origin of our world', and gave creationists 'ample justification' for their beliefs.[30] It is rather ironical that in the sixteenth century some people resisted advances in science because they seemed to threaten belief in God; whereas in the twentieth century scientific ideas of a beginning have been resisted because they threatened to increase the plausibility of belief in God.

There is another point to be made about Maddox's statement. One often hears the criticism levelled at those (scientists) who believe in a Creator that they do not have a model of the universe that leads to testable predictions. But Maddox's comment shows that this is simply not true. His antipathy to the idea of a beginning was precisely because a creation-model of the biblical kind clearly predicted a beginning and he did not welcome such confirmation. However, evidence of a space–time singularity in the form of the discovery of the microwave background etc. confirmed the obvious prediction that the biblical account implied. This means that the charge that notions of intelligent design are unscientific because they fail to make any testable predictions is false. Science itself has shown that the hypothesis of creation is testable.

The very beginning

It is important to realize that there are considerable theoretical difficulties surrounding discussion of the very beginning. In the so-called 'standard model', the universe near the beginning was both incredibly massive and incredibly small. At the level of the very small, it is quantum theory that has been developed to describe the behaviour of atoms and their constituents. Physicists have argued, therefore, that we need to think in terms of a quantum cosmology in order to discuss the first split-second of the universe's existence, where 'split' means an almost inconceivably short period of time, the so-called Planck time of 10^{-43} seconds (0.00...001 with 42 zeros between the decimal point and the 1), which gives a theoretical limit to the smallest time interval for which events can be distinguished. The basic idea is that, at the level of the extremely small, there are unavoidable uncertainties and unpredictabilities, governed by Heisenberg's uncertainty principle. In essence, this principle places a limit on our ability to determine the values of measurable quantities, like the position and momentum of atomic and subatomic particles. Thus an element of indeterminacy is introduced, so that although we can give the probability that a certain quantum event will happen, like the radioactive decay of a particle, we cannot fix it precisely. There is a fuzziness in behaviour that cannot be removed. The argument is that, in some way, this fuzziness creates a possibility for the universe to spring into being as a fluctuation in a quantum vacuum.[31]

In their theoretical investigations of this idea, Hawking and Hartle have developed a mathematical model of the early universe which involves the concept of 'imaginary time',[32] which, it is argued, removes the need for singularities, and thus avoids the question of a Creator. But it doesn't. Apart from the admitted highly speculative nature of such explanations, saying that the universe arises from a fluctuation in a quantum vacuum simply pushes the origins question one step further back, to asking about the provenance of the quantum vacuum.

More importantly, it leaves unanswered the question, 'What is the origin of the laws governing such a vacuum?' As for real time, Hawking admits: 'In real time, the universe has a beginning and an end at singularities that form a boundary to space–time and at which the laws of science break down.'[33]

There is, therefore, a remarkable consensus of opinion nowadays, that the universe had a beginning.[34] Attempts to argue that the universe is self-explanatory turn out to be as self-contradictory as the simple acceptance of a beginning as a brute fact is unsatisfactory. The more we get to know about our universe, the more the hypothesis that there is a Creator God, who designed the universe for a purpose, gains in credibility as the best explanation of why we are here. Charles Townes, who won the Nobel Prize for Physics in 1964 for his discovery of the maser, the forerunner of the laser, writes: 'In my view, the question of origin seems to be left unanswered if we explore it from a scientific point of view. Thus, I believe there is a need for some religious or metaphysical explanation. I believe in the concept of God and in his existence.'[35]

The fine-tuning of the universe

Copernicus was responsible for a revolution in scientific thinking. By overturning the idea that the earth was fixed at the centre of the universe he began a process of demoting the earth's significance that has resulted in the widespread view that the earth is a fairly typical planet orbiting a fairly typical sun which is positioned in one of the spiral arms of a fairly typical galaxy which, the multiverse theorists will add, is in a fairly typical universe. This cutting of earth down to size is sometimes known as the Copernican Principle.

However, several avenues of research and thought combine to call this principle into serious question. For, the remarkable picture that is gradually emerging from modern physics and cosmology is one of a universe whose fundamental forces are amazingly, intricately, and delicately balanced or 'fine-tuned' in order for the universe to be able to sustain life. Recent research has shown that many of the fundamental constants of nature, from the energy levels in the carbon atom to the rate at which the universe is expanding, have just the right values for life to exist. Change any of them just a little, and the universe would become hostile to life and incapable of supporting it. The constants are precision-tuned, and it is this fine-tuning that many scientists (and others) think demands an explanation. Of course, by the very nature of things, we can only refer to the current state of affairs in the awareness that there are, as always, disagreements among scientists as to the validity of some of the assumptions that underlie fine-tuning calculations and that some views may well change – scientists do not claim to deliver final truth. Nevertheless, fine-tuning has established itself as an aspect of the universe that merits very serious consideration. Let us look, then, at some examples.

For life to exist on earth an abundant supply of carbon is needed. Carbon is formed either by combining three helium nuclei, or by combining nuclei of helium and beryllium. Eminent mathematician and astronomer, Sir Fred Hoyle, found that for this to happen, the nuclear ground state energy levels have to be fine-tuned with respect to each other. This phenomenon is called 'resonance'. If the variation were more than 1 per cent either way, the universe could not sustain life. Hoyle later confessed that nothing had shaken his atheism as much as this discovery. Even this degree of fine-tuning was enough to persuade him that it looked as if 'a superintellect has monkeyed with physics as well as with chemistry and biology', and that 'there are no blind forces in nature worth talking about'.[36]

However, in terms of the tolerance permitted, this example pales into insignificance when we consider the fineness of the tuning of some of the other parameters in nature. Theoretical physicist Paul Davies tells us that, if the ratio of the nuclear strong force to the electromagnetic force had been different by 1 part in 10^{16}, no stars could have formed. Again, the ratio of the electromagnetic force-constant to the gravitational force-constant must be equally delicately balanced. Increase it by only 1 part in 10^{40} and only small stars can exist; decrease it by the same amount and there will only be large stars. You must have both large and small stars in the universe: the large ones produce elements in their thermonuclear furnaces; and it is only the small ones that burn long enough to sustain a planet with life.

To use Davies' illustration, that is the kind of accuracy a marksman would need to hit a coin at the far side of the observable universe, twenty billion light years away.[37] If we find that difficult to imagine, a further illustration suggested by astrophysicist Hugh Ross may help.[38] Cover America with coins in a column reaching to the moon (380,000 km or 236,000 miles away), then do the same for a billion other continents of the same size. Paint one coin red and put it somewhere in one of the billion piles. Blindfold a friend and ask her to pick it out. The odds are about 1 in 10^{40} that she will.

Although we are now in realms of precision far beyond anything achievable by instrumentation designed by humans, the cosmos still has more stunning surprises in store. It is argued that an alteration in the ratio of the expansion and contraction forces by as little as 1 part in 10^{55} at the Planck time (just 10^{-43} seconds after the origin of the universe), would have led either to too rapid an expansion of the universe with no galaxies forming or to too slow an expansion with consequent rapid collapse.[39]

Yet even this example of precision-tuning is completely eclipsed by what is perhaps the most mind-boggling example of all. Our universe is a universe in which entropy (a measure of disorder) is increasing; a fact which is enshrined in the Second Law of Thermodynamics. Eminent mathematician Sir Roger Penrose writes: 'Try to imagine the phase space... of the *entire* universe. Each point in this phase space represents a different possible way that the universe might have started off. We are to picture the Creator, armed with a 'pin' – which is to be placed at some point in the phase space... Each different positioning of the pin provides a different universe. Now the accuracy that is needed for the Creator's aim depends on the entropy of the universe that is thereby created. It would be relatively 'easy' to produce a high entropy universe, since then there would be a large volume of the phase space available for the pin to hit. But in order to start off the universe in a state of low entropy – so that there will indeed be a second law of thermodynamics – the Creator must aim for a much tinier volume of the phase space. How tiny would this region be, in order that a universe closely resembling the one in which we actually live would be the result?'

His calculations lead him to the remarkable conclusion that the 'Creator's aim' must have been accurate to 1 part in 10 to the power 10^{123}, that is 1 followed by 10^{123} zeros, a 'number which it would be impossible to write out in the usual decimal way, because even if you were able to put a zero on every particle in the universe there would not even be enough particles to do the job'.[40]

Faced with not one, but many such spectacular examples of fine-tuning, it is perhaps not surprising that Paul Davies says, 'It seems as though someone has fine tuned nature's numbers to make the universe... The impression of design is overwhelming.'[41]

Up to this point we have mainly been considering fine-tuning at the large-scale cosmological level. When we think of the specific conditions that are needed nearer home in our solar system and on earth, we find that there are a host of other parameters that must be just right in order for life to be possible. Some of them are obvious to us all. The distance from the earth to the sun must be just right. Too near and water would evaporate, too far and the earth would be too cold for life. A change of only 2 per cent or so and all life would cease. Surface gravity and temperature are also critical to within a few per cent for the earth to have a life-sustaining atmosphere – retaining the right mix of gases necessary for life. The planet must rotate at the right speed: too slow and temperature differences between day and night would be too extreme, too fast and wind speeds would be disastrous. And so the list goes on. Astrophysicist Hugh Ross[42] lists many such parameters that have to be fine-tuned for life to be possible, and makes a rough but conservative calculation that the chance of one such planet existing in the universe is about 1 in 10^{30}.

An intriguing angle on this theme has been opened up in the recent book *The Privileged Planet*, by Guillermo Gonzalez and Jay W Richards.[43] The authors draw attention to the earth's remarkable suitability as a place on which to do science. Their thesis is that, of all possible places in the universe, earth enjoys conditions that not only allow for habitability but simultaneously are extremely congenial to the making of 'a stunning diversity of measurements, from cosmology and galactic astronomy to stellar astrophysics and geophysics'.[44] Once one begins to think about it, examples are abundant, some of them very obvious. We might easily have found ourselves in a part of the universe where we could not see into deep space because of too much starlight; our atmosphere might have been opaque or simply translucent rather than transparent. Others are less obvious: witness the fact that the sizes of the moon and the sun and their distances from the earth are just right that a perfect eclipse is possible. This occurs when the black disc of the moon just barely covers the glowing disc of the sun so that the thin ring of the chromosphere (the 'atmosphere') of the sun is visible and can therefore be investigated scientifically – as a result of which we not only know a great deal more about the sun than we otherwise would, but we were also able to get initial confirmation of the bending of light by gravity predicted by Einstein's theory of general relativity.

Their conclusion is this: 'And yet as we stand gazing at the heavens beyond our little oasis, we gaze not into a meaningless abyss but into a wondrous arena commensurate with our capacity for discovery. Perhaps we have been staring past a cosmic signal far more significant than any mere sequence of numbers, a signal revealing a universe so skilfully crafted for life and discovery that it seems to whisper of an extra-terrestrial intelligence immeasurably more vast, more ancient, and more magnificent than anything we've been willing to expect or imagine.'[45]

Arno Penzias, who used the propitious position of the space-platform of earth to make the brilliant discovery of the 'echo of the beginning', the cosmic background microwave radiation, sums up the position as he sees it: 'Astronomy leads us to a unique event, a universe which was created out of nothing, one with the very delicate balance needed to provide exactly the right conditions required to permit life, and one which has an underlying (one might say 'supernatural') plan.'[46]

We should note that the preceding arguments are not 'God of the gaps' arguments; it is advance in science, not ignorance of science, that has revealed this fine-tuning to us. In that sense there is no 'gap' in the science. The question is rather: How should we interpret the science? In what direction is it pointing?

The anthropic principle

This perception on the part of scientists, that the universe has to be very precisely structured in order to support life, has been called the anthropic principle (Greek: *anthropos* = man). In its weak form (the weak anthropic principle), it runs like this: 'the observable universe has a structure which permits the existence of observers'. Clearly, the precise status of such a statement is open to debate: Is it a tautology? Is it a principle, in the sense that it helps provide explanations etc.? Whatever the answer, at the very least its formulation draws attention to the fact that viable theories of the cosmos must take into account the existence of observers.

Some scientists and philosophers[47] maintain that we ought not to be surprised at the order and fine-tuning we see in the universe around us, since if it did not exist then carbon-based life would be impossible, and we would not be there to observe the fine-tuning. In other words they use the anthropic principle against the inference of design. However, as philosopher John Leslie points out,[48] 'that sounds like arguing that if you faced a firing squad with fifty guns trained on you, you should not be surprised to find that you were alive after they had fired. After all, that is the only outcome you could possibly have observed – if one bullet had hit you, you would be dead. However, you might still feel that there is something which very much needs explanation; namely why did they all miss? Was it by deliberate design? For there is no inconsistency in not being surprised that you do not observe that you are dead, and being surprised to observe that you are still alive.'[49]

Leslie argues that the fine-tuning argument presents us with a choice between, at most, two possibilities. The first of these is that God is real. The only way to avoid that conclusion, according to Leslie, is to believe in the so-called 'many worlds' or 'multiverse' hypothesis (popularized in David Deutsch's book *The Fabric of Reality*[50]), which postulates the simultaneous existence of many, possibly infinitely many, parallel universes in which (almost) anything which is theoretically possible will ultimately be actualized, so that there is nothing surprising in the existence of a universe like ours. This is the view opted for by astronomer Sir Martin Rees, who in his book *Just Six Numbers*[51] discusses the six fine-tuned numbers that he holds to be most significant as controllers of the characteristics of the universe.

Deutsch bases his theory on the interpretation of quantum mechanics due to Hugh Everett III in which the basic idea is that at each act of quantum measurement the universe splits into a series of parallel universes, in which all of the possible outcomes occur. Although the

Everett interpretation holds out certain advantages over other theories – for example, by obviating the necessity of faster than light signalling – many scientists feel that an explanation which involves undetectable universes and represents in addition an extreme violation of the Occam's Razor principle of searching for theories that do not involve unnecessary multiplication of hypotheses, goes well beyond science into metaphysics. There is much speculation and very little evidence.

John Polkinghorne, for instance, himself an eminent quantum theorist, rejects the many-universe interpretation: 'Let us recognize these speculations for what they are. They are not physics, but in the strictest sense, metaphysics. There is no purely scientific reason to believe in an ensemble of universes. By construction these other worlds are unknowable by us. A possible explanation of equal intellectual respectability – and to my mind greater economy and elegance – would be that this one world is the way it is, because it is the creation of the will of a Creator who purposes that it should be so.'[52] Philosopher Richard Swinburne goes even further. 'To postulate a trillion-trillion other universes, rather than one God, in order to explain the orderliness of our universe, seems the height of irrationality.'[53]

Cosmologist Edward Harrison reacts in a very similar way. 'Here is the cosmological proof of the existence of God – the design argument of Paley – updated and refurbished. The fine-tuning of the universe provides *prima facie* evidence of deistic design. Take your choice: blind chance that requires multitudes of universes, or design that requires only one... Many scientists, when they admit their views, incline towards the teleological or design argument'.[54] Arno Penzias puts the argument the other way round: 'Some people are uncomfortable with the purposefully created world. To come up with things that contradict purpose, they tend to speculate about things they haven't seen.'[55]

It should, however, be pointed out that, although Leslie may be correct in suggesting that fine-tuning means that either there is a God or a multiverse, logically these two options are not mutually exclusive, although they are usually presented as such. After all, parallel universes could be the work of a Creator. Furthermore, as philosopher of physics Michael Lockwood has observed, Leslie's firing squad argument for this universe is not actually negated by postulating a multiverse. The element of surprise and need for explanation exists within whichever universe in which the fine-tuning is being observed. After all, the probability that a given person obtains a run of ten sixes in throwing a dice is not altered by the fact that there may be many people throwing dice in the same city at the same time.

In a similar vein Christian de Duve writes: 'Even if the theory turns out to be correct, the deduction drawn from it by Rees and Weinberg strikes me as what is called in French "drowning the fish". Whether you use all the water in the oceans to drown the animal, it will still be there affirming its presence. However many universes one postulates, ours can never be rendered insignificant by the magnitude of this number... what appears to me as supremely significant is that a combination capable of giving rise to life and mind should exist at all.'[56] Therefore the multiverse argument does not in fact weaken the design arguments advanced above.

Finally, Arno Penzias reminds us that the notion that there is a teleological dimension in the universe goes back millennia. He writes: 'The best data we have (concerning the Big Bang) are exactly what I would have predicted, had I nothing to go on but the five books of Moses, the Psalms and the Bible as a whole.'[57]

We notice in passing Penzias' use of the word 'predicted'. Here is another major counter-example to the commonly held notion that there is no element of predictability (and thus no scientific dimension) in the theistic account of creation. For Penzias, as for many other scientists, the majestic words with which Genesis begins have lost none of their relevance or power: 'In the beginning God created the heavens and the earth.'

So much then for the views of physicists and cosmologists. We must presently turn to the biologists. But before doing so we need to emphasise the fact that the arguments we have used from cosmology and physics are arguments based on standard contemporary science that enjoys widespread acceptance. They are not arguments that involve challenging any of the mainstream claims of science, and, as we have pointed out above, they are certainly not 'God of the gaps' arguments: they do not reduce to 'Science can't explain it, therefore God did it.' It is for these two reasons that fine-tuning arguments, for example, gain a ready hearing from most scientists, even though they may agree or disagree with the conclusions we have drawn from them. Such arguments have the ring of being compatible with authentic scientific activity.

When it comes to biology the situation is very different. In that discipline the very mention of God as a designing intelligence, as we shall rapidly see, appears to call in question what is the central pillar of the whole subject – the neo-Darwinian synthesis. Spectres soon arise in many minds of anti-scientific religious obscurantism. Thus, we are about to enter somewhat stormy waters and the reader may wonder why we bother. Why not simply rest content with presenting the case from physics and cosmology that science has not buried God? The answer is not hard to find. There are influential thinkers with a high public profile who insist that it is biology of all the disciplines that gives most support to the contention that science has buried God. For them, biology has strong religious implications. It proves that there is no God. To fail to discuss their arguments would, in their eyes, be to admit defeat. We must therefore take their arguments seriously and so into the stormy waters we must go. It is up to the reader to decide whether we manage to stay afloat – at least, if the waters are stormy, they are surrounded by a fascinating landscape which we might even get a chance to admire.

5

Designer biosphere?

'But suppose I had found a watch upon the ground, and it should be inquired how the watch happened to be in that place... The watch must have had a maker: there must have existed... an artificer... who formed it for the purpose which we find it actually to answer; who comprehended its construction and designed its use... Every indication of contrivance, every manifestation of design, which existed in the watch, exists in the works of nature; with the difference, on the side of nature, of being greater or more, and that in a degree which exceeds all computation.'

William Paley

'No vital forces propel evolutionary change. And whatever we think of God, his existence is not manifest in the products of nature.'

Stephen Jay Gould

'The only watchmaker in nature is the blind forces of physics, albeit deployed in a very special way. A true watchmaker has foresight: he designs his cogs and springs, and plans their interconnections, with a future purpose in his mind's eye. Natural selection, the blind, unconscious, automatic process which Darwin discovered, and which we now know is the explanation for the existence and apparently purposeful form of all life, has no purpose in mind. It has no mind and no mind's eye, it does not plan for the future. It has no vision, no foresight, no sight at all. If it can be said to play the role of watchmaker in nature, it is that of the blind watchmaker.'

Richard Dawkins FRS

The wonder of the living world

We saw in the last section that the universe revealed to us by physics and cosmology is fine-tuned and rationally intelligible; which leads many to think that it has been designed with us in mind – we humans are truly meant to be here. We now turn from the non-living, to the living world, and ask whether biology confirms this impression. And, at first sight, it appears to do so overwhelmingly, revealing to us a world which seems to have 'design' written all over it. In his *Royal Institution Christmas Lectures*, broadcast in 1991, Richard Dawkins says: 'Living objects... look designed, they look overwhelmingly as though they're designed.'

In fact, from the time of the great thinkers of the ancient world, such as Aristotle and Plato, to that of modern biologists, the living world has been a source of never-ending wonder. And the more that science uncovers, the more the wonder grows. Who can fail to be amazed at the homing instinct of the pigeon, the migratory instinct of the Bewick swan, the echo-locator system of the bat, the blood pressure control centre in the brain of a giraffe and the muscles in the neck of a woodpecker, to mention but a few of an unending list that is being added to every day. The living world is simply replete with mechanisms of mind-bending complexity.

So there is no doubt that nature gives an overwhelming *impression* of design. Richard Dawkins even defines biology to be 'the study of complicated things which give the impression of having been designed for a purpose'.[1] But that, say he and many other scientists, is all that it is – an impression of design, admittedly a strong impression of design, but nevertheless not real design. Francis Crick (who won the Nobel Prize jointly with James Watson, for the discovery of the double helix structure of DNA) warns biologists not to mistake that impression for what is, in his estimation, the underlying reality: 'Biologists must constantly keep in mind that what they see was not designed, but rather evolved.'[2]

Such statements provoke the question: Why? After all, if it looks like a duck, waddles like a duck and quacks like a duck, why not call it a duck? Why are such scientists not prepared to draw the obvious inference, and say that living things look as if they are designed precisely because they are designed?

The answer is that the appearance of design is illusory since, in their view, evolutionary processes that involve no intelligent input whatsoever are capable of producing all of the teeming complexity that we see in the universe. And, of course, this view is forced upon them by their presuppositions. Daniel Dennett, in his book *Darwin's Dangerous Idea* puts it this way: 'Darwin was offering a sceptical world... a scheme for creating Design out of Chaos without the aid of Mind.' Dennett regards Darwin's idea as a kind of corrosive acid, which threatens to destroy all pre-Darwinian views of the world; in that, instead of the universe's matter being a product of mind, the minds in the universe are a product of matter. They are nothing more than the results of an undirected, mindless, purposeless process.[3]

We might well wonder at the capacity of this amazing evolutionary engine with its creative power to produce life and consciousness from mere matter, its ability to craft nature's magnificent patterns, and to construct its information processing mechanisms. Not a divine Mind, says Richard Dawkins, but a purely materialistic and unguided mechanism. However tempting it is to think that nature has been designed for a purpose, he claims that there is no need for a divine watchmaker. 'The only watchmaker in nature is the blind forces of physics, albeit deployed in a very special way. A true watchmaker has foresight: he designs his cogs and springs, and plans their interconnections, with a future purpose in his mind's eye. Natural selection, the blind, unconscious, automatic process which Darwin discovered, and which we now know is the explanation for the existence and apparently purposeful form of all life, has no purpose in mind. It has no mind and no mind's eye, it does not plan for the future. It has no vision, no foresight, no sight at all. If it can be said to play the role of watchmaker in nature, it is that of the blind watchmaker.'[4] Dawkins claims that nothing but the laws of physics are needed – a very important point to which we must return later.

Paley and his watch

The watchmaker metaphor has a long history in connection with design arguments. Cicero (106–43 BC) extrapolated from his experience of intelligently designed machines to the ordered movement of the planets and stars: '... when we see some examples of a mechanism... do we doubt that it is the creation of a conscious intelligence? So when we see the movement of the heavenly bodies... how can we doubt that these too are not only the works of reason but of a reason which is perfect and divine?'[5]

Cicero here anticipates by centuries the most famous (or infamous!) classic statement of the design argument, which was made by the eighteenth-century theologian and naturalist, William Paley. 'In crossing a heath, suppose I pitched my foot against a stone, and were asked how the stone came to be there; I might possibly answer, that, for anything I knew to the contrary, it had lain there forever: nor would it perhaps be very easy to show the absurdity of this answer. But suppose I had found a watch upon the ground, and it should be inquired how the watch happened to be in that place; I should hardly think of the answer which I had before given, that for anything I knew the watch had always been there... The watch must have had a maker: there must have existed... an artificer... who formed it for the purpose which we find it actually to answer; who comprehended its construction and designed its use... Every indication of contrivance, every manifestation of design, which existed in the watch, exists in the works of nature; with the difference, on the side of nature, of being greater or more, and that in a degree which exceeds all computation.'[6]

The essence, then, of Paley's argument was that if the complexity of a watch and its evident design, its adaptation to a perceived end, implies the existence of a watchmaker, how much more does a vastly more intricate biological mechanism, like the human eye, demand the existence of an intelligent Divine watchmaker? 'The marks of design are too strong to be got over. Design must have a designer. That designer must have been a person. That person is God.'[7]

Throughout history many people, including scientists, have found this kind of argument very plausible. Darwin, in his student days at Cambridge, was one of them. According to Stephen Jay Gould, Paley was the 'intellectual hero of Darwin's youth'.[8] Darwin himself wrote that Paley's work 'gave me as much delight as did Euclid. The careful study of these works, without attempting to learn any part by rote, was the only part of the Academical Course which, as I then felt and as I still believe, was of the least use to me in the education of my mind. I did not at that time trouble myself about Paley's premises; and taking these on trust I was charmed and convinced of the long line of argumentation.'

However this was all to change. In his autobiography Darwin pinpoints his difficulty: 'The old argument of design in nature, as given by Paley, which formerly seemed to me so conclusive, fails, now that the law of natural selection has been discovered. We can no longer argue that, for instance, the beautiful hinge of a bivalve shell must have been made by an intelligent being, like the hinge of a door by a man.'[9]

So Paley came under attack. So much so that for many today he is simply a figure of fun, a sad and tragic reminder of the absurd and facile attempts that have been made in the past to make belief in God credible by linking it somehow with science. But, as is often the case with figures who have become part of the rhetoric of science in that they stand as icons for a particular constellation of (often extreme) ideas, the reality is much more subtle, and indeed, more interesting, than the myth. Admittedly, Paley attracted legitimate criticism because of his over-concentration on specific adaptations and the fanciful way in which he sometimes embellished the watchmaker argument using 'just-so' stories to explain various specific animal features. For example, his description of the Indian hog (*Babyrussa*) includes an explanation for the long, curved, tusk-like teeth proceeding from the creature's jaw in terms of the fact that it uses them to hook into the branches of trees in order to support its head while sleeping in a standing position.[10] However, it might just be a mistake to write Paley off because of such oddities. Stephen Jay Gould's response is more measured when he says of Paley that 'he presumably read this account of *Babyrussa* in a fallacious travellers report, and can only be charged with insufficient scepticism, not fabrication'.[11]

Paley has also been criticized for over-emphasizing the goodness of nature and failing to take into account its pain, suffering and brutality. However, to cite Gould once more: 'Paley cannot be dismissed as a Panglossian perfectionist. He states explicitly that we cannot use perfection as a criterion for identifying good design, or even as the necessary mark of divinity in craftsmanship.'[12] What Paley actually wrote was: 'It is not necessary that a machine be perfect, in order to show with what design it was made: still less necessary, where the only question is, whether it were made with any design at all.'[13]

Paley's 'Natural Theology' or 'Physical Theology', as it was also called, came in for a different kind of criticism fired, not by the atheists, but by heavyweight theologians such as John Henry Newman: 'Physical theology cannot, from the nature of the case, tell us one word about Christianity proper; it cannot be Christian, in any true sense... this so-called science tends, if it occupies the mind, to dispose it against Christianity.'[14]

There are two points here. To the first Paley might well have agreed. For, in the entire work of over 500 pages Paley scarcely ever mentions Christianity (it is first mentioned on p. 529). He is well aware of the limitations of his objectives and does not claim to establish the characteristic doctrines of Christianity 'proper' directly from nature. He appears to be perfectly content with the fact that natural theology can, at best, give evidence for the existence of God and say something about a certain limited number of his attributes – his power, for example.[15] Clearly he saw this as preparing the way for a consideration of full-blown Christianity, but certainly not as a substitute for it. In his conclusion he writes: 'It is a step to have it proved, that there must be something in the world more than what we see. It is a further step to know, that, amongst the invisible things of nature, there must be an intelligent mind, concerned in its production, order, and support. These points being assured to us by Natural Theology, we may well leave to Revelation the disclosure of many particulars, which our researches cannot reach, respecting either the nature of this Being as the original cause of all things, or his character and designs as a moral governor; and not only so, but the more full confirmation of other particulars, of which, though they do not lie altogether beyond our reasonings and our probabilities, the certainty is by no means equal to the importance. The true theist will be the first to listen to *any* credible communication of Divine knowledge. Nothing which he has learned from Natural Theology, will diminish his desire of further instruction, or his disposition to receive it with humility and thankfulness. He wishes for light: he rejoices in light. His inward veneration of this great Being, will incline him to attend with the utmost seriousness, not only to all that can be discovered concerning him by researches into nature, but to all that is taught by a revelation, which gives reasonable proof of having proceeded from him.'[16]

What makes the situation even more strange is that Newman recognizes (in the very same essay, p. 450) that physical theology has real merit at the level described by Paley: 'Again, this science exhibits, in great prominence and distinctness, three of the more elementary notions which the human reason attaches to the idea of a Supreme Being, that is, three of His simplest attributes, Power, Wisdom and Goodness.' That is, in essence all that Paley claimed for his argument in the first place.

So why should Newman think that it disposed the mind against Christianity? He gives his reason: ' ...because it speaks only of laws and cannot contemplate their suspension, that is, miracles, which are of the essence of the idea of a Revelation. Thus the God of Physical Theology may very easily become an idol; for he comes to the inductive mind in the medium of fixed appointments, so excellent, so skillful, so beneficent, that, when it has for a long time gazed upon them, it will think them too beautiful to be broken, and will at length so contract its notion of Him as to conclude that He never could have the heart (if I may dare use such a term) to undo or mar his own work; and this conclusion will be the first step towards its degrading its idea of God a second time, and identifying Him with his works. Indeed, a Being of Power, Wisdom and Goodness, and nothing else, is not very different from the God of the Pantheist.'

But, to be fair to Paley, nowhere does he suggest that these are the *only* attributes of God: merely that they are the only ones that can be inferred from nature. It is, of course, important to ask questions whose answers go beyond the reach of natural theology and Paley was not the least hesitant to do this. After all, he had already published his *Evidences of Christianity* in 1794.[17] This work contains detailed arguments supporting the miracles claimed in the Gospels, arguments, in fact, that are interestingly directed against the sceptical views of David Hume. Thus it is hard to see how Newman's fears are justified – at least in so much as they apply to Paley himself. One might be forgiven for suspecting a certain rivalry of boat-race proportions between Newman (Oxford, Roman Catholic) versus Paley (Cambridge, Protestant)!

Whatever the answer to this is, it is clear that the net result of criticisms of Paley and his iconic association with all that is regarded as suspect in design arguments, is that his core inference from the nature of a watch to its intelligent origin is itself sometimes dismissed out of hand, even though these criticisms do not really affect it. No less a mind than that of Bertrand Russell, not known for his sympathy to theism, found the design argument logically impressive: 'This argument contends that, on a survey of the known world, we find things which cannot plausibly be explained as the product of blind natural forces, but are much more reasonably to be regarded as evidences of a beneficent purpose. This argument has no formal logical defect; its premises are empirical and its conclusion professes to be reached in accordance with the usual canons of empirical inference. The question whether it is to be accepted or not turns, therefore, not on general metaphysical questions, but on comparatively detailed considerations.'[18,19]

Before we leave Paley, however, we must briefly comment on the oft-repeated claim that it is David Hume's earlier onslaught against design arguments[20] that really demolishes Paley. One element in that attack was the allegation that such arguments tended to be arguments from analogies that did not always hold.[21] Hume's work is cast in the form of a discussion, one protagonist of which was a certain Cleanthes, who is addressed thus: 'If we see a house, Cleanthes, we conclude, with the greatest certainty, that it had an architect or builder; for this is precisely that species of effort that we have experienced to proceed from that species of cause. But surely you will not affirm, that the universe bears such a resemblance to a house, that we can with the same certainty infer a similar cause, or that the analogy is here entire and perfect. The dissimilitude is so striking, that the utmost you can pretend to is a guess, a conjecture, a presumption concerning a similar cause; and how that pretension will be received in the world, I leave you to consider.'[22] For many people Hume's argument still carries the day.

It might just be a trifle premature, however, to conclude that this argument puts the lid on Paley's coffin. Philosopher Elliott Sober has pointed out that 'Although Hume's criticism is devastating if the design argument is an argument from analogy, I see no reason why the design argument should be construed in that way. Paley's argument about organisms stands on its own, regardless of whether watches and organisms happen to be similar. The point of talking about watches is to help the reader see that the argument about organisms is compelling.'[23]

Certainly, Paley's argument about organisms stands on its own; but it is strengthened even more by the observation that Sober is scarcely justified in saying that the analogy fails. For, since Paley's time, developments in science have shown that there are many kinds of systems within living organisms for which the term 'molecular machine' is entirely appropriate and among which are to be found biological clocks that are responsible for the vital molecular timekeeping function within the living cell and which are of vastly greater sophistication than Paley's illustrative watch. Indeed, 'machine' language is ubiquitous in cutting-edge molecular biology.

In any case, Hume might have been astonished to learn that it would one day be possible in laboratories in this world for human intelligence to design biochemical systems and construct proteins, and that, in all probability not that far beyond the present horizon, it will be possible to construct simple organisms from their molecular components. What would Hume have to say then? The design argument has turned out to be very much more robust than Hume thought, though it is important to keep his caution about analogies in mind even though much of the force of his objection has been dissipated by more recent progress in biology.

Hume also argued that, in order to infer that our world had been designed, we would have to have observed other worlds, both designed and not designed, in order to compare. It is clear from this that Hume is formulating his argument against design as an inductive argument dependent for its force on the sample space of observed universes. Thus Hume concludes the argument is very weak since the only universe we have observed is this one. However, as Sober[24] points out, the objection dissolves once we move from the model of inductive sampling to that of likelihood: 'You don't have to observe the processes of Intelligent Design and chance at work in different worlds in order to maintain that the two hypotheses confer different probabilities on your observation.'

The point here is important. Not all science is inductive since we do not always have the luxury of repeated observation or experimentation. We cannot repeat the Big Bang, or the origin of life, or the history of life, or the history of the universe. Indeed what about any historical event? It is not repeatable. Does that mean we can say nothing about these things? It would, if we followed Hume. There is, however, another methodology that can be applied to such situations, well known to historians. It is the method of abduction, or inference to the best explanation, that we described in Chapter 2. Hume's argument leaves abduction untouched. An argument that does explain a given effect is always better than one that does not.

It is important, though sometimes difficult, to separate the design argument from the negative image with which scientific rhetoric about Paley has surrounded it. But there is a further reason, again to do with the rhetoric of science, why design arguments have not been taken seriously in more recent years. This has to do with the fact that the very mention of the word 'design' to some people immediately conjures up the powerful image of clockwork that figured so prominently in older design arguments. The result is that 'design' becomes associated, whether consciously or unconsciously, with the clockwork universe of Newton.[25] Now, likening the workings of the universe to the smooth running of a master-clock had enormous appeal in the heyday of Newtonian mechanics, but its appeal began to wane especially for those engaged in the biological sciences for the simple reason that the biological world did not look much like a clock. It also waned somewhat for the theologians as it could easily be used to support a deistic view of God – the notion that God wound up the universe like a clock and left it to run – rather than the vibrant biblical view of God as Creator and Sustainer of the universe, a God who caused the universe to exist at every moment. Granted all of that, the fact that the biosphere is now known to contain endless sophisticated clocks means that design arguments of this kind cannot so easily be dismissed. However, it would be a mistake to use them with a reductionist spin in order to give the impression that the universe was nothing more than clockwork.[26] Consequently, in order to avoid potentially misleading associations of ideas, it might well be better to talk about arguments inferring intelligent origin, than about design arguments.

To sum up, in the words of John Polkinghorne: 'So where is natural theology today, two centuries after William Paley? The short answer is, "Alive and well, having learned from past experience to lay claim to insight rather than to coercive logical necessity, and to be able to live in a friendly relationship with science, based on complementarity rather than rivalry."'[27]

Does evolution eliminate the need for a Creator?

But now back to our main topic – the widespread contention that evolution eliminates the need for a Creator. Palaeontologist Stephen Jay Gould, a materialist by philosophical conviction, held that after Darwin we know that 'no intervening spirit watches lovingly over the affairs of nature (though Newton's clock-winding God might have set up the machinery at the beginning of time and then let it run). No vital forces propel evolutionary change. And whatever we think of God, his existence is not manifest in the products of nature.'[28]

Indeed, not long after the publication of *The Origin of Species,* the famous American atheist Robert Green Ingersoll wrote that the nineteenth century would be 'Darwin's century' when 'his doctrine of evolution... has removed in every thinking mind the last vestige of orthodox Christianity'.[29]

The point was repeated by Sir Julian Huxley when, at the 1959 Darwin Centennial in Chicago, he summed up the implications of evolution as he saw them: 'In the evolutionary scheme of thought there is no longer either need or room for the supernatural. The earth was not created, it evolved. So did all the animals and plants that inhabit it, including our human selves, mind and soul as well as brain and body. So did religion...'[30] In Huxley's opinion evolution displaces God, giving us a purely naturalistic explanation of the origin, not only of life, but of the higher faculties of consciousness and thought.

This view, that atheism is a logical consequence of evolutionary theory, is not only to be found in popular science books but also in university textbooks. Take, for example, the following statement from a reputable university textbook on evolution by Monroe Strickberger of the Museum of Vertebrate Zoology, Berkeley, California: 'The fear that Darwinism was an attempt to displace God in the sphere of creation was therefore justified. To the question: Is there a divine purpose for the creation of humans? evolution answers No. According to evolution, the adaptations of species and the adaptations of humans come from natural selection and not from design.'[31] Douglas Futuyma agrees: 'By coupling undirected, purposeless variation to the blind uncaring process of natural selection, Darwin made theological or spiritual explanations of the life processes superfluous. Together with Marx's materialistic theory of history and society and Freud's attribution of human behaviour to influences over which we have little control, Darwin's theory of evolution was a crucial plank in the platform of mechanism and materialism – of much of science, in short – that has been the stage of most Western thought.'[32]

It is, therefore, scarcely surprising that there is a widespread feeling that the theory of evolution has swept God away as unnecessary and irrelevant, if not positively embarrassing. Philosopher Roger Scruton is a typical example, giving as his reason: 'I have a scientific mind; I can't just dismiss the evidence of Darwinism – it seems to me to be obviously true.'[33]

So we are confronted with the following rather odd situation. On the one hand, there is the almost instinctive and overwhelming temptation to infer from the existence and nature of biological information that it has an intelligent origin. On the other hand, some of the very people who grant that the temptation is strong resist it because they are convinced that no designer is necessary; unguided, mindless, evolutionary processes can and did do it all.

It goes without saying that this is a critical issue. Indeed, it is no exaggeration to say that the theory of evolution has had the impact of an earthquake on the human quest for significance – an impact that extends to every aspect of human life. If life is the result of a purely naturalistic process, what then of morality? Has it, too, evolved? And if so, of what significance are our concepts of right and wrong, justice and truth? According to William Provine, 'The destructive assumptions of evolutionary biology extend far beyond the assumptions of organized religion to a much deeper and more pervasive belief held by the vast majority of people, that non-mechanistic organizing designs or forces are somehow responsible for the visible order of the physical universe, biological organisms, and human moral order.'[34] Daniel Dennett thinks that we have not yet really taken on board the implications of evolution and he therefore calls evolution 'Darwin's dangerous idea', because it 'cuts much deeper into the fabric of our most fundamental beliefs than many of its sophisticated apologists have yet admitted, even to themselves'.[35]

Dawkins agrees. He has no doubt that, with Darwin, we reach an immensely significant watershed in the history of thought. 'We no longer have to resort to superstition when faced with deep problems: Is there a meaning to life? What are we here for? What is man? After posing the last of these questions, the eminent zoologist G. G. Simpson put it thus: "The point I want to make now is that all attempts to answer that question before 1859 are worthless and that we will be better off if we ignore them completely." ' [36]

Dawkins' argument is that, if evolutionary mechanisms can account for the apparent design in the universe, then the inference to an intelligent origin is false. He tells us that we cannot have both God and evolution. Since everything can be accounted for by evolution, there is no Creator. Evolution implies atheism.

Let us look at the logic of this position. Clearly, Dawkins' argument from evolution to atheism depends on the simultaneous validity of the following two assertions.

Assertion 1   Biological evolution is incompatible with the existence
                    of a Creator.
Assertion 2   Biological evolution accounts for the existence of all of
                    life's complexity.

Many people think that there is nothing to discuss here. For them, both statements are true; the first almost self-evidently and the second as a result of scientific research. Yet two awkward facts insist that things really cannot be quite that simple. Firstly, there are many scientists, indeed in the biological sciences, who deny the first assertion and accept the second: that is, they believe in God as well as in evolution. Secondly, and more controversially, there are *scientific* questions being asked (and not only by believers in God) as to the precise status of the second assertion. This is evidenced by the increasing number of publications on the topic by some of the world's leading academic publishing houses.[37]

Does evolution exclude God?

The idea that God and biological evolution are mutually exclusive alternatives implies first of all that God and evolution belong to the same category of explanation. But this is plainly false – as we have already seen in a different context. A category mistake is being committed. Evolution purports to be a biological mechanism, and those who believe in God regard him as a personal Agent who, among other things, designs and creates mechanisms. We observed before that understanding the mechanism by which a Ford car works is not in itself an argument for regarding Mr Ford himself as non-existent. The existence of a mechanism is not in itself an argument for the non-existence of an agent who designed the mechanism.

With this in mind let us look again at Dawkins' famous description of the evolutionary blind watchmaker: 'The only watchmaker in nature is the blind forces of physics… (*sic*) Natural selection, the blind, unconscious, automatic process which Darwin discovered, and which we now know is the explanation for the existence and apparently purposeful form of all life, has no purpose in mind… If it can be said to play the role of watchmaker in nature, it is that of the blind watchmaker.' Five claims are made here – two for the forces of physics and three for natural selection:

1. The forces of physics are the only watchmaker in nature.
2. The forces of physics are blind.
3. Natural selection is a blind, automatic, process with no purpose in mind.
4. Natural selection is the explanation for the existence of all life.
5. Natural selection is the explanation for the form of all life.

Of course, 'natural selection' here is shorthand for the neo-Darwinian evolutionary synthesis involving natural selection, mutation, genetic drift etc. and not simply natural selection itself.

The first striking thing about these claims is that they take us way beyond Darwin. For the implication of 1 is that natural selection, a process certainly put on the map by Darwin, is reducible to the laws of physics; a claim which Darwin nowhere makes, as far as I am aware. For natural selection by definition assumes that life is there (or at least a system capable of self-replication) to start with. Otherwise natural selection cannot even get going – there is nothing to select from. The danger of sliding rather superficially over the transition from the non-living to the living is such an important matter that we deal with it in greater detail later.

Secondly, Dawkins ascribes creative power to the forces of physics and personifies them. These forces *are* the watchmaker. The rhetoric of personification is important here because it can subtly add a false credibility to an otherwise unsubstantiated thesis: we are more likely to grant that a person has creative powers than an impersonal force. Moreover Dawkins' personified forces are blind. But what does this mean?

For, from one point of view, there is nothing controversial in describing forces or mechanisms as 'blind'. Quite obviously, most are. The strong and weak nuclear forces, electromagnetism and gravity have no eyes to see with, either physical or mental. And most mechanisms are blind – think of a watch, a car, a CD player, a computer hard-disc. Moreover, they are not only blind but also unconscious; indeed, to be even more precise, they are incapable of conscious thought since they have no mind to think with. But those mechanisms, though blind *in themselves*, are all the products of minds that are far from being blind; such mechanisms are intelligently designed. What is more, this holds even for mechanisms that involve an element of randomness in their operation.

The mechanism of a self-winding watch, for example, is blind and automatic and it involves chance processes: it uses the energy from random movements of the arm to wind itself up. But it would be foolish to argue that it had not been designed. Indeed, a self-winding watch is more sophisticated than an ordinary watch and therefore arguably involves more intelligence in its design.

In the field of engineering, computer-implemented genetic algorithms are routinely used for sophisticated engineering optimization purposes – for example, to construct the best possible shape for an aircraft wing. It would be absurd to suggest that the fact that these evolutionary algorithmic optimization processes are themselves blind and automatic constitutes an argument that they do not have an intelligent origin.

It is unfortunately all too easy to miss this point when reading Dawkins, since the subtle rhetorical effect of personifying the evolutionary process is to make the reader think that Dawkins has argued away real personal agency when he has done no such thing. In fact at no point has he even attempted to address the question of whether or not personal agency is involved. It is a very clever sleight of mind.

The lesson here is that we need to be wary of the rhetoric of science in this kind of context, since descriptions of putative evolutionary mechanisms are often loaded with words such as 'blind', 'automatic' and 'purposeless' which, because of their ambiguity in such contexts, tend to convey the impression that the question of the involvement of an intelligent agency has been investigated and rejected when in fact nothing of the kind is the case. Using Dawkins' own terminology, one is tempted to say that he has appeared to deal with the question, but that appearance is an illusion.

The actual logic at issue here is well captured by physicist Sir John Houghton: 'The fact that we understand some of the mechanisms of the working of the universe or of living systems does not preclude the existence of a designer, any more than the possession of insight into the processes by which a watch has been put together, however automatic these processes may appear, implies there can be no watchmaker.'[38]

On the basis of this kind of reasoning there have been and are many leading scientists who accept the evolutionary mechanisms as the Creator's way of producing life's diversity. Darwin himself had such among his supporters, including the distinguished Harvard botanist Asa Gray, a Christian, who was the first person outside England to whom Darwin revealed his theory, and with whom he kept in constant touch.[39]

The novelist Charles Kingsley wrote to Darwin that his theory of natural selection provided 'just as noble a conception of Deity, to believe that He created primal forms capable of self-development... as to believe that He required a fresh act of intervention to supply the lacunas which He Himself had made'. Though Kingsley was not a scientist, Darwin was so impressed by his words that he cited them in the second edition of *The Origin of Species*, possibly with an eye to influencing his more sceptical clerical readers. Kingsley's view of a 'God who was so wise that he could make all things make themselves' is re-expressed by Richard Swinburne: 'Nature... is a machine-making machine... men make not only machines, but machine-making machines. They may therefore naturally infer from nature which produces animals and plants, to a creator of nature similar to men who make machine-making machines.'[40]

In other words, the evolutionary viewpoint, far from invalidating the inference to intelligent origin, arguably does nothing more than moving it back up one level, from the organisms to the processes by which those organisms have come to exist – or, if you like, from primary to secondary causation. Think of a man who, on seeing a car for the first time, supposes that it is made directly by humans only later to discover it is made in a robotic factory by robots which in turn were made by machines made by humans. His initial inference to intelligent origin was not wrong: it was his concept of the nature of the implementation of that intelligence that was inaccurate. To put it another way, direct human activity was not detectable in the robotic factory because it is the existence of the factory itself and its machines that is, ultimately, the result of intelligent human activity.

No less a person than T.H. Huxley, who figures so prominently in the early Darwinian debates, seems to have been well aware of this. Somewhat surprisingly he reminded his contemporaries that 'there is a wider teleology which is not touched by the doctrine of Evolution. This proposition is that the whole world... is the result of the mutual interaction, according to definite laws, of the forces possessed by the molecules of which the primitive nebulosity of the universe was composed. If this be true, it is no less certain that the existing world lay potentially in the cosmic vapour, and that a sufficient intelligence could, from a knowledge of the properties of the molecules of that vapour, have predicted say, the state of the fauna of Britain in 1869, with as much certainty as one can say what will happen to the vapour of the breath on a cold winter's day.' He concluded that the doctrine of evolution 'does not even come into contact with Theism, considered as a philosophical doctrine'.[41]

Thus, even Huxley did not think that the question of God's existence or non-existence could be settled by biology. In an 1883 letter to Charles Watts he wrote: 'Agnosticism is of the essence of science, whether ancient or modern. It simply means that a man shall not say he knows or believes that which he has no scientific grounds for professing to know or believe... Consequently agnosticism puts aside not only the greater part of popular theology, but also the greater part of anti-theology.' It was Huxley, we recall, who invented the term 'agnostic' to describe himself.[42]

Huxley's comment on the potentiality of the 'cosmic vapour' reminds us that the theory of evolution demands the existence of a fine-tuned universe producing exactly the right kind of materials and operating according to complex laws. The fine-tuning arguments from chemistry, physics and cosmology are, of course, left unaffected by the biological theory of evolution. It is therefore surely arguable that the anthropic fruitfulness, both of the fine-tuning of the universe at the physical level and the capacity of its processes to produce organic life by a process of evolution, are, in themselves, strong evidences of a creative intelligence.

Not surprisingly, therefore, such a theistic evolutionary view has commended itself to many scientists from Asa Gray and Richard Owen in Darwin's day to the present. Commenting on this fact, the late Stephen Jay Gould wrote: 'Either half of my colleagues are enormously stupid, or else the science of Darwinism is fully compatible with conventional religious beliefs – and equally compatible with atheism.'[43]

In Britain, for example, Sir Ghillean Prance, FRS, former Director of the world-famous Kew Gardens in London, Sir Brian Heap, FRS, former Vice President of the Royal Society, Bob White, FRS, Professor of Geology at

Cambridge University, Simon Conway Morris FRS, Professor of Palaeobiology, Cambridge University, Sam Berry, Professor of Evolutionary Biology, London University, and Denis Alexander, Director of the Faraday Institute, Cambridge, are all distinguished contemporary evolutionary biologists who are theists, indeed Christians. In the USA there is Francis Collins, Director of the Human Genome Project, who prefers the term Biologos to that of theistic evolution. They would all vigorously reject as invalid any attempt to deduce atheism from evolutionary theory. As Alister McGrath points out: 'There is a substantial logical gap between Darwinism and atheism which Dawkins seems to prefer to bridge by rhetoric, rather than evidence.'[44] Denis Alexander goes even further in saying that the 'Darwinian theory of evolution, whatever may have been the various ideological uses to which it has been put since 1859, is essentially devoid of either religious or moral significance, and those who try to derive such significance from it are mistaken',[45] a conclusion with which Richard Dawkins, among others, would radically disagree.

Similarly, Stephen Jay Gould says that 'science simply cannot (by its legitimate methods) adjudicate the issue of God's possible existence. We neither affirm it nor deny it; we simply can't comment on it as scientists.'[46]

Those scientists who think that there is simply no case to be made for evolutionary biology having any implications for theism or atheism maintain that there is no need to consider evolution any further in this connection, although they do not deny that science can make a contribution to the science–religion debate. For example, the theists among them tend to support the fine-tuning arguments advanced earlier. And indeed in many ways it would be a comfortable place for us to stop and draw our conclusions. We now must make clear why we do not think that we can indulge in that particular luxury, in spite of the perils that may lie in wait for us if we proceed any further.

Undesigned designers

Why, then, the insistence that evolution implies atheism? The argument that the existence of mechanism does not preclude the activity of intelligent agency seems logically compelling to many scientists and it therefore puzzles them, especially in the light of cautionary statements such as those made by Huxley and Gould, why so many scientists nonetheless still tenaciously maintain the line that evolution implies atheism.

As a case in point, let us consider the explanation given by Daniel Dennett. He maintains that, granted that the existence of a mechanism does not *in general* logically preclude the existence of a designer, nevertheless the *particular* evolutionary mechanism that Darwin found is of such a kind that it does not in fact need a designer. Indeed, according to Dennett, to think that it does need a designer shows a failure to appreciate the evolutionary mechanism for what it actually is. Dennett admits that 'automatic processes are themselves often creations of great brilliance… we can see that the inventors of the automatic transmission and the automatic door-opener were no idiots, and that their genius lay in seeing how to create something that could do something 'clever' without having to think about it'.[47] He then goes on to say how it might have seemed to some people (like Charles Kingsley, mentioned above) that God did his work of creation by designing an automatic design-maker. But Dennett then claims, and this is his key point, that what Darwin found was a different sort of process (natural selection), which distributed the 'designing' work over a long period of time, and conserved what had been accomplished at each stage. That is, natural selection somehow designs without either itself being designed or having any purpose in view. Dennett characterizes this process as 'mindless, motiveless, mechanicity'.[48]

We note once more that the language here is, at first sight, ambiguous. However, Dennett goes on to make it clear that he means that the Darwinian mechanism is mindless and motiveless in the sense that it has neither mind nor motive behind it. It is an agentless mechanism. 'Love it or hate it, phenomena like this [DNA] exhibit the heart of the power of the Darwinian idea. An impersonal, unreflective, robotic, mindless little scrap of molecular machinery is the ultimate basis of all agency, and hence meaning, and hence consciousness in the universe.'[49] To use the language of Aristotle, Dennett claims that it is the very nature of the efficient cause (evolution) that rules out the very existence of a final cause (divine intention).

Consequently, Assertion 1 carries no weight at all with Dennett. This, of course, does not mean that it has no weight. Nevertheless, we must ask if Dennett's analysis is correct.

The question that dare not be asked

In other words we must now query Assertion 2, which boils down to the question of whether the evolutionary mechanism can bear all the weight that is put on it. In particular, is Dawkins' claim true that natural selection accounts not merely for the *form* of life but for its *existence*?

Now asking this question is very risky. Even doing something as revolutionary as questioning the constancy of the velocity of light provokes nothing like the hurricane that is unleashed against the person who dares to query the validity of certain aspects of the neo-Darwinian synthesis. Indeed the question provokes Dawkins so severely as to proclaim his (rather unexpected) belief in an absolute: 'It is absolutely safe to say that if you meet somebody who claims not to believe in evolution, that person is ignorant, stupid or insane (or wicked, but I'd rather not consider that).'[50] Even the formulation '*claims* not to believe in evolution' shows Dawkins' utter incredulity that anyone could really have doubts – maybe there is still a faint possibility that their claim does not match what they actually believe or that they do not understand what they are saying.

So I now face the momentous decision whether to risk a Dawkins' Certificate of Lunacy by continuing. Why not rest content with the argument so far? Well, apart from the reason just given above, the sheer vehemence of the protest fascinates me. Why is it so strong? Furthermore, why is it only in connection with this area of intellectual endeavour that I have ever heard an eminent scientist (with a Nobel Prize to his name, no less) say in a public lecture in Oxford: 'You must not question evolution'? After all, scientists have dared to question even Newton and Einstein. Indeed, most of us were (rightly – dare I say?) brought up to believe that questioning standard wisdom was one of the most important ways in which science grows. All science, however well established, benefits from being periodically questioned. So why is there such a taboo on questioning evolution? Why is this, and only this, particular area of science a no-go area, fenced off from being questioned?

A leading Chinese palaeontologist Jun-Yuan Chen ran into this problem when visiting the USA in 1999. His work on the remarkable discoveries in Chengjiang of strange fossil creatures led him to question the orthodox evolutionary line. In true scholarly fashion he mentioned his criticisms in his lectures but they elicited very little response. This lack of reaction surprised him and so he eventually asked one of his hosts what was wrong. He was told that scientists in the USA did not like to hear such criticism of evolution. To this he gave the delightful reply that it seemed to him that the difference between the USA and China was: 'In China we can criticize Darwin, but not the government; in America you can criticize the government, but not Darwin.'

So I have decided to take the risk. For me it is a double risk, in fact, since I am a mathematician and not a biologist. However, I take comfort in the fact that, from Darwin to Dawkins, biologists have been kind enough to write for the general intelligent public on the basis that they assumed that ordinary thinking people were quite capable of understanding their ideas. The concomitant of that, surely, is that moderately intelligent people are entitled to bleat when they do not find the ideas put to them satisfactory. And, one might add, they are encouraged in their bleating when they come across evaluations of neo-Darwinism like the following by the distinguished biologist Lynn Margulis: 'Like a sugary snack that temporarily satisfies our appetite but deprives us of more nutritious foods, neo-Darwinism sates intellectual curiosity with abstractions bereft of actual details – whether metabolic, biochemical, ecological, or of natural history.'[51]

But before I take the risk of asking the question that dare not be asked let me encourage the reader not to put the book down just yet by saying in advance that I have no intention of denying that natural selection has an important role to play in the variations that we see in the living world all around us, as Darwin brilliantly observed. The questions I shall be raising have to do with whether evolution can carry *all* the weight put upon it. That it can carry some weight, I do not doubt.

However, since, in the view of many, even this modest level of questioning is nothing short of suicidal, I might as well begin by assuring the reader that, should I naturally select my own demise, I have already composed my own brief epitaph:

Here lies the body of John Lennox.
You ask me why he's in this box?
He died of something worse than pox,
On Darwinism – heterodox.

So, from beyond my own potential grave as it were, let me first of all indicate why I think the protest against questioning evolution is as strong as it is, in the hope that this will clear the ground for meaningful discussion.

We start with something that we alluded to earlier – the unusual, if not unique, relationship of evolutionary theory to philosophical and worldview assumptions.

The relationship between evolution and philosophy

Reflecting on Strickberger's admission, cited above, that, in his opinion at least, part of the motivation behind evolutionary theory lies in an attempt to remove God,[52] we are lead to the question of just what the relationship is between evolutionary theory and metaphysics. That there seems to be a connection is stated by Michael Ruse, a leading evolutionary philosopher, in a keynote lecture to the American Association for the Advancement of Science in 1993 which claimed that, for many evolutionists, evolution has played the role of a secular religion. Colin Patterson reminds us[53] of Popper's caution, that even a scientific theory may become an intellectual fashion, a substitute for religion, an entrenched dogma, adding: 'this has certainly been true of evolutionary theory'. Phillip Johnson of the University of California, Berkeley, who has done much to stir up debate (and high-level debate at that) on the subject, has pointed out: 'The danger here is that a methodological premise which is useful for limited purposes has been expanded to form a metaphysical absolute.'[54]

Donald McKay, an expert in research on the communication networks in the brain, has long since described the way this happened: ' "Evolution" began to be invoked in biology, apparently as a substitute for God. And if in biology, why not elsewhere? From standing for a technical hypothesis... the term was rapidly twisted to mean an atheistic metaphysical principle whose invocation could relieve a man of any theological shivers at the spectacle of the universe. Spelt with a capital E and dishonestly decked in the prestige of the scientific theory of evolution (which in fact gave it no shred of justification), "Evolutionism" became the name for a whole anti-religious philosophy, in which "Evolution" played the role of a more or less personal deity, as the "real force in the universe".'[55]

C.S. Lewis saw the issue even earlier. In a prescient essay entitled 'The Funeral of a Great Myth', he explains that 'we must sharply distinguish between Evolution as a biological theorem, and popular Evolutionism... which is certainly a myth'. Lewis grounds this assertion, first of all, in chronology. 'If popular evolutionism were (as it imagines itself to be) not a myth but the intellectually legitimate result of the scientific theorem on the public mind, it would arise after that theorem had become widely known.'[56] But, he goes on to say, it did not. Historically, the philosophy of evolutionism appeared long before the biological theory of evolution.

Secondly, Lewis offers internal evidence of his claim. 'Evolutionism... differs in content from the evolution of the real biologists. To the biologist, evolution is a hypothesis. It covers more of the facts than any other hypothesis on the market, and is therefore to be accepted unless or until some new proposal can cover still more facts with even fewer assumptions. At least that is what I think most biologists would say. Professor D. M. S. Watson would not go so far. According to him, evolution "is accepted by zoologists, not because it is observed to occur or... can be proved by logically coherent evidence to be true, but because the only alternative, special creation, is clearly incredible". This would mean that the sole ground for believing it is not empirical but metaphysical – the dogma of an amateur metaphysician who finds special creation incredible. I do not think it has come to that.' One wonders what Lewis would have to say today.

The logical implications of naturalism: evolution as a philosophical necessity

Lewis' observation brings us directly to the heart of the matter. We argued above that naturalism does not follow from biological evolution (remember Assertion 1); but what about the reverse deduction? Suppose that naturalism is true. Then, *merely as a matter of sheer logical necessity*, it follows that some kind of evolutionary account must be given for life, apart altogether from any evidence which may be offered to support it. For, what other possibility can there be? If, for example, we start off with the materialistic hypothesis that all we have is matter/energy and the forces of physics, then there is only one option – matter/energy together with the forces of nature over time have produced life, that is, evolution of some sort.

The fact that, from the naturalistic and materialistic perspectives, evolution appears as a philosophical necessity is nothing new. It was perceived centuries, indeed millennia, before Dawkins and Darwin. The ancient Greek materialist philosopher Epicurus used precisely this logic to produce an evolutionary theory from the atomic theory of Democritus. The most powerful expression of the Epicurean theory is to be found in the Latin poem *De Rerum Natura* ('On the Nature of Things' or 'On the Nature of the Universe' as it is often translated), written around the middle of the first century BC by the Roman poet Lucretius. Benjamin Wiker in his recent detailed study of Lucretius calls him 'the first Darwinian' and claims that Lucretius, whose philosophy was enthusiastically revived at the time of the Renaissance, should be regarded as the intellectual progenitor of contemporary naturalistic philosophy.[57]

In the contemporary scientific world we thus have the very unusual situation that one of science's most influential theories, biological macro-evolution, stands in such a close relationship to naturalistic philosophy that it can be deduced from it directly – that is, without even needing to consider any evidence, as the ancient arguments of Lucretius plainly show. This circumstance is extraordinary since it is very difficult to think of another scientific theory that is in a similar position. Think, for example, of trying to deduce Newton's theory of gravitation or Einstein's theory of relativity or the theory of Quantum Electrodynamics from a philosophical principle or worldview, whether materialistic, naturalistic or, even, theistic. There is no obvious way that it could be done. And yet, as Lucretius saw, and as anyone who thinks about it can readily see, it can be done with evolution.

Paradigm pressure

Of course, unusual closeness of relationship between a scientific theory and a worldview does not determine whether that theory is true or false. What it does mean, however, is that there may be so much *a priori* philosophical pressure from the reigning naturalistic or materialistic paradigm, that aspects of the theory may not be subjected to the wide-ranging, rigorous, self-critical analysis which is, or should be, characteristic of all science.[58] Thomas Kuhn warned of paradigms that produced a box-like structure so rigid that things that did not fit into it were often simply overlooked. If something has simply got to be true, then conflicting evidence can easily be ignored or superficially dismissed as irrelevant. To avoid this danger, Richard Feynman emphasized that one should always be careful to record all the evidence against one's theories; indeed, one should bend over backwards to consider it, since the easiest person to fool is oneself.

Sadly, Kuhn and Feynman's warnings seem often to go unheeded, with the result that the questioning of evolution, *even on scientific grounds*, is fraught with risk. It can be highly dangerous to think outside the evolutionary box. For, to question evolution is, in the eyes of many, to question what is, to them, sheer fact by virtue of philosophical necessity; and thus the questioner runs the risk of being classified – if not certified – as a member of the lunatic fringe. But that kind of attitude, ironically, is precisely the one that Galileo faced. There is a luminous parallel between the Aristotelianism of his day and the naturalism of our own. Galileo ran the risk of questioning Aristotle, and we all know what happened to him. We also know who was right. The question is: Will we learn anything from it? Must Darwin be protected in the same way that Aristotle was? After all, it was a clear fact, was it not, that the earth did not move?

In a similar vein to Dawkins, geneticist Richard Lewontin confidently asserts the facthood of evolution: 'It is time... to state clearly that evolution is fact, not theory... Birds arose from non-birds and humans from non-humans. No person who pretends to any understanding of the natural world can deny these facts any more than she or he can deny that the earth is round, rotates on its axis and revolves around the sun.'[59]

Of course, granted Lewontin's admitted *a priori* materialism (see Chapter 2), we can now put his protest in context: no other option is open to him. However, there is reason to suspect that at least part of the vehemence of this kind of protest arises from ambiguity in the very definition of the term 'evolution'.

6

The nature and scope of evolution

'Nothing makes sense in biology except in light of evolution.'

Theodosius Dobzhansky

___

'Large evolutionary innovations are not well understood. None has ever been observed, and we have no idea whether any may be in progress. There is no good fossil record of any.'

Paul Wesson

___

'Well, as common sense would suggest, the Darwinian theory is correct in the small, but not in the large. Rabbits come from other slightly different rabbits, not from either [primeval] soup or potatoes. Where they come from in the first place is a problem yet to be solved, like much else of a cosmic scale.'

Sir Fred Hoyle

___

The definition of evolution

Thus far we have been using this term as if it had a single, agreed meaning. But this is manifestly not the case. Discussion of evolution is frequently confused by failure to recognize that the term is used in several different ways, some of which are so completely non-controversial that rejection of them might indeed evidence some kind of ignorance or stupidity (but, even then, scarcely wickedness).

What, then, is evolution? Here are some of the ideas for which the term 'evolution' is used:

1. Change, Development, Variation

Here the word is used to describe change, without any implication for the kind of mechanism or intelligent input (or lack of it) involved in bringing about the change. In this sense we speak of the 'evolution of the motor car', where, of course, a great deal of intelligent input is necessary. We speak of the 'evolution of a coastline', where the natural processes of sea and wind, flora and fauna shape the coastline over time, plus possibly steps taken by engineers to prevent erosion. When people speak of the 'evolution of life' in this sense, all they mean is that life arose and has developed (by whatever means). Used in this way, the term 'evolution' is neutral, innocuous and uncontroversial.

2. Microevolution: variation within prescribed limits of complexity, quantitative variation of already existing organs or structures

Such processes were observed by Darwin in connection with the Galapagos finch species (see also Jonathan Weiner's detailed study[1]). This aspect of the theory is scarcely controversial as such effects of natural selection, mutation, genetic drift etc. are constantly being recorded.[2] One classic example with which we are, sadly, all too familiar right round the world is the way in which bacteria develop resistance to antibiotics.

It is worth recording that the changes in average finch beak lengths, which had been observed during the drought period of 1977, were reversed by the rains of 1983; so that this research is more an illustration of cyclical change due to natural selection than it is of permanent improvement (or even change). This reversal is, however, not always mentioned in textbooks.[3]

However, one of the main studies that has been copied from textbook to textbook and heralded as one of the main proofs of evolution has come in for very serious criticism in recent years. It concerns the occurrence of industrial melanism in the peppered moth (*Biston betularia*). The claim is that natural selection produced a variation of the relative numbers of light moths to dark moths in a population. Light moths were more easily seen by predators than dark ones, against the dark, polluted surfaces of tree trunks, and so eventually the population would become dominated by dark moths. Of course, if this account were true, it would at best only be an example of microevolution and that only in the sense of cyclical change (no new moths were created in the process since both kinds existed to start with). Therefore it would not be controversial except insofar as examples of microevolution are frequently cited as sufficient evidence for macroevolution. However, according to Michael Majerus, a Cambridge expert on moths, 'the basic peppered moth story is wrong, inaccurate or incomplete, with respect to most of the story's component parts'.[4] In addition, there appears to be no evidence that peppered moths rest on tree trunks in the wild. Many photographs in textbooks, showing them doing so, have apparently been staged. In the *Times Higher Educational Supplement*,[5] biologist Lynn Margulis is puzzled by the fact that Steve Jones still used the peppered moth in his book update of Darwin, entitled *Almost like a whale*,[6] even though, according to her, he must know of the dubious nature of the research. When University of Chicago biologist Jerry Coyne learned of the difficulties with the peppered moth story, he wrote: 'My own reaction resembles the dismay attending my discovery, at the age of six, that it was my father and not Santa who brought the presents on Christmas Eve.'[7,8]

3. Macroevolution

This refers to large-scale innovation, the coming into existence of new organs, structures, body-plans, of qualitatively new genetic material; for example, the evolution of multicellular from single-celled structures. Macroevolution thus involves a marked increase in complexity. This distinction between micro and macroevolution is the subject of considerable dispute since the gradualist thesis is that macroevolution is to be accounted for simply by extrapolating the processes that drive microevolution over time, as we shall see below.

4. Artificial selection, for example, in plant and animal breeding

Breeders have produced many different kinds of roses and sheep from basic stocks, by very careful selective breeding methods. This process involves a high degree of intelligent input; and so, although often cited, in particular by Darwin himself, who argued that what humans can do in a relatively short time nature could do in a long time, provides in itself no real evidence for evolution by *unguided* processes.

5. Molecular evolution

Some scientists argue that, strictly speaking, evolution presupposes the existence of self-replicating genetic material. For instance, Dobzhansky's view was that, since natural selection needed mutating replicators, it followed clearly that 'prebiological natural selection is a contradiction in terms'.[9] However, the term 'molecular evolution' is now commonly used to describe the emergence of the living cell from non-living materials.[10] This language usage can easily obscure the fact that the word 'evolution' here cannot mean a Darwinian process in the strict sense.

Of course, the term 'evolution' also covers the theories about how these things happened; the most widespread being the neo-Darwinian synthesis, which involves natural selection operating on the variations that arise through mutation, genetic drift, and so on.

In light of these ambiguities in the meaning of evolution, Lewontin's and Dawkins' accusations become more understandable. If 'questioning evolution' means questioning it in senses 1, 2 or 4, then an accusation of stupidity or ignorance might be understandable. As we have already said, no one seriously doubts the validity of microevolution and cyclic change as examples of the operation of natural selection.

Confusion can easily arise, therefore, particularly when evolution is defined as microevolution. Take, for instance, the following statement about evolution by E.O. Wilson: 'Evolution by natural selection is perhaps the only one true law unique to biological systems, as opposed to non-living physical systems, and in recent decades it has taken on the solidity of a mathematical theorem. It states simply that if a population of organisms contains multiple hereditary variants in some trait (say, red versus blue eyes in a bird population), and if one of those variants succeeds in contributing more offspring to the next generation than the other variants, the overall composition of the population changes, and *evolution has occurred*. Further, if new genetic variants appear regularly in the population (by mutation or immigration), *evolution never ends*. Think of red-eyed and blue-eyed birds in a breeding population, and let the red-eyed birds be better adapted to the environment. The population will in time come to consist mostly or entirely of red-eyed birds. Now let green-eyed mutants appear that are even better adapted to the environment than the red-eyed form. As a consequence the species eventually becomes green-eyed. Evolution has thus taken two more small steps' [italics original].[11]

Quite so. But this seems to be no more than a description of microevolution – indeed, since we have red-eyed birds and blue-eyed birds in the initial population, Wilson is only describing the kind of uncontroversial cyclic change mentioned above in connection with Darwin's finches. Thus Wilson completely bypasses the question as to whether the mechanism described can bear all the extra weight that is put upon it in any full-blown understanding of evolution – for example, answering the question, 'Where did the birds come from in the first place?' Yet he claims elsewhere in his article that natural selection does bear that weight. For instance he says, 'all biological processes arose through evolution of these[12] physicochemical systems through natural selection'; or again, humans are 'descended from animals by the same blind force that created those animals'.

Furthermore, it has been repeatedly noted that, at the level discussed in Wilson's definition, natural selection itself is no more than a tautology and is therefore essentially self-evident. Colin Patterson, FRS, in his standard text on evolution,[13] presents it in the form of the following deductive argument:

- all organisms must reproduce
- all organisms exhibit hereditary variations
- hereditary variations differ in their effect on reproduction
- therefore variations with favourable effects on reproduction will succeed, those with unfavourable effects will fail, and organisms will change.

Thus natural selection is a description of the process by which the strain in a population that produces the weaker progeny eventually gets weeded out, leaving the stronger to thrive.

Patterson argues that, formulated this way, natural selection is, strictly speaking, not a scientific theory, but a truism. That is, if we grant the first three points, then the fourth follows as a matter of logic, an argument similar to that advanced by Darwin himself in the last chapter of *The Origin of Species*. Patterson observes that 'this shows that natural selection must occur but it does not say that natural selection is the only cause of evolution,[14] and when natural selection is generalized to be the explanation of all evolutionary change or of every feature of every organism, it becomes so all-embracing that it is in much the same class as Freudian psychology and astrology'.[15] By this Patterson seems to be suggesting that it fails to satisfy Popper's criterion of falsifiability, just as the Freudian statement that adult behaviour is due to trauma in childhood is not falsifiable.[16] Patterson is warning us of the danger of simply slapping the label 'natural selection' in this generalized sense on some process, and thinking that we have thereby explained that process.

Patterson's description highlights something very easily overlooked – the fact that natural selection is not creative. As he says, it is a 'weeding out process' that leaves the stronger progeny. The stronger progeny must be already there: it is not produced by natural selection. Indeed the very word 'selection' ought to alert our attention to this: selection is made from already existing entities. This is an exceedingly important point because the words 'natural selection' are often used as if they were describing a creative process, for instance, by capitalizing their initial letters. This is highly misleading as we see from the following illuminating statement by Gerd Müller, an expert on EvoDevo, an increasingly influential theory integrating evolutionary theory and developmental biology that aims to fill some of the gaps in standard neo-Darwinism. Müller writes: 'Only a few of the processes listed above are addressed by the canonical neo-Darwinian theory, which is chiefly concerned with gene frequencies in populations and with the factors responsible for their variation and fixation. Although, at the phenotypic level, it deals with the modification of existing parts, the theory is intended to explain neither the origin of parts, nor morphological organization, nor innovation. In the neo-Darwinian world the motive factor of morphological change is natural selection, which can account for the modification and loss of parts. But selection has *no innovative capacity*: it eliminates or maintains what exists. The generative and ordering aspects of morphological evolution are thus absent from evolutionary theory' [italics mine].[17]

Müller thus confirms what logic and even language would tell us: natural selection, by its very nature, does not create novelty. This flatly contradicts Richard Dawkins' bold assertion cited earlier that natural selection accounts for the form and existence of all living things. Such polar opposition of views on the central thesis of neo-Darwinism raises disturbing questions as to the solidity of its scientific basis and prompts us to explore a bit further.

We now turn to the fact that the hereditable variations on which natural selection acts are random mutations in the genetic material of organisms. However, Dawkins and others are careful to inform us that evolution itself is not a purely random process. He is sufficiently impressed by calculations of mathematical probabilities to reject any notion that, say, the human eye evolved by pure chance in the time available. In his inimical way he writes: 'It is grindingly, creakingly, crashingly obvious that, if Darwinism were really a theory of chance, it couldn't work. You don't need to be a mathematician or a physicist to calculate that an eye or a haemoglobin molecule would take from here to infinity to self-assemble by sheer higgledy-piggledy luck.'[18] What then is the answer? That natural selection is a law-like process that sifts the random mutations so that evolution is a combination of necessity and chance. Natural selection, we are told, will find a faster pathway through the space of possibilities. The idea here is, therefore, that the law-like process of natural selection increases the probabilities to acceptable levels over geological time.

Putting it simply, the essence of the argument is this. Natural selection favours the strong progeny over the weak in a situation where resources are limited. It helps preserve any beneficial mutation. Organisms with that mutation survive and others do not. But natural selection does not cause the mutation. That occurs by chance. The quantity of resources (food) available is one of the variable parameters in the situation. It occurred to me as a mathematician that it would be interesting to see what happens if this parameter is allowed to increase. I invite you to do a thought experiment. Imagine a situation in which resources increase so that, in the limiting case, there is food for all, the strong and the weak. As resources increase, there would seem to be less and less for natural selection to do, since most progeny would survive. What would neo-Darwinists say to this? Would they say on the basis of their chance arguments that evolution would now be less and less likely? For it would now seem that chance is doing all the work: and the neo-Darwinists have ruled that possibility out of court.

When I thought of this I was sure that it must have occurred to someone earlier, and not surprisingly it has. Indeed, in 1966, British chemist R.E.D. Clark drew attention to the fact that Darwin had been disturbed by a letter from the eminent botanist Joseph Hooker in 1862 in which Hooker argued that natural selection was in no sense a creative process.[19] However, Clark had to reconstruct Hooker's argument from Darwin's reply as he thought Hooker's original letter had been lost. Hooker's letter has not been lost, however. It reads: 'I am still very strong in holding to impotence of crossing with respect to [the] origin of species. I regard Variation as so illimitable in {animals}. You must remember that it is neither crossing nor natural selection that has *made* so many divergent human individuals, but simply *Variation* [Hooker's emphasis]. Natural selection, no doubt has hastened the process, intensified it (so to speak), has regulated the lines, places etc., etc., etc., in which, and to which, the races have run and led, and the number of each and so forth; but, given a pair of individuals with power to propagate, and [an] infinite [time] span to procreate in, so that not one be lost, or that, in short, Natural Selection is not called upon to play a part *at all*, and *I maintain that after n generations you will have extreme individuals as totally unlike one another as if Natural Selection had extinguished half.*

'If once you hold that natural selection can *make* a difference, i.e. *create* a character, your whole doctrine tumbles to the ground. Natural Selection is as powerless as physical causes to make a variation; the law that "like shall *not* produce like" is at the bottom of [it] all, and is as inscrutable as life itself. This it is that Lyell and I feel you have failed to convey with force enough to us and the public: and this is the bottom of half the infidelity of the scientific world to your doctrine. You have not, as you ought, begun by attacking old false doctrines, that "*like does produce like*". The first chapter of your book should have been devoted to this and nothing else. But there is some truth I now see in the objection to you, that you make natural selection the *Deus ex machina* for you do somehow seem to do it by neglecting to dwell on the *facts* of infinite incessant variation. Your eight children are really all *totally* unlike one another: they agree *exactly in no one property*. How is this? You answer that they display the inherited differences of different progenitors – well – but go back, and back and back in time and you are driven at last to your original pair for origin of differences, and logically you must grant, that the differences between the original [MALE] & [FEMALE] of your species were equal to the sum of the extreme differences between the most dissimilar existing individuals of your species, or that the latter varied from some inherent law that had them. Now am not I a cool fish to lecture you so glibly?'[20]

It is interesting to note the force with which Hooker writes in ascribing 'half the infidelity of the scientific world' against Darwin to his failure to deal with this argument. Darwin's reaction came in a letter (after 26 November but actually dated 20 November 1862). 'But the part of your letter which fairly pitched me head over heels with astonishment; is that where you state that every single difference which we see might have occurred without any selection. I do and have always fully agreed; but you have got right round the subject and viewed it from an entirely opposite and new side, and when you took me there, I was astounded. When I say I agree, I must make proviso, that under your view, as now, each form long remains adapted to certain fixed conditions and that the conditions of life are in [the] long run changeable; and second, which is more important that each individual form is a self-fertilizing hermaphrodite, so that each hairbreadth variation is not lost by intercrossing. Your manner of putting [the] case would be even more striking than it is, if the mind could grapple with such numbers – it is grappling with eternity – think of each of a thousand seeds bringing forth its plant, and then each a thousand. A globe stretching to furthest fixed star would very soon be covered. I cannot even grapple with the idea even with races of dogs, cattle, pigeons or fowls; and here all must admit and see the accurate strictness of your illustration. Such men, as you and Lyell thinking that I make too much of a Deus of natural selection is conclusive against me. Yet I hardly know how I could have put in, in all parts of my Book, stronger sentences. The title, as you once pointed out, might have been better. No one ever objects to agriculturalists using the strongest language about their selection; yet every breeder knows that he does not produce the modification which he selects. My enormous difficulty for years was to understand adaptation, and this made me, I cannot but think rightly, insist so much on natural selection. God forgive me for writing at such length; but you cannot tell how much your letter has interested me, and how important it is for me with my present Book in hand to try and get clear ideas.'[21]

Darwin clearly feels the force of Hooker's argument to the extent of agreeing with it though astonished at the way in which it was put. The argument seems rather important because it raises very serious questions about the kind of argument that purports to render probabilities of macro (or molecular) evolution acceptable within the timescale constraints supplied by contemporary cosmology.

Hooker's argument, however, is not the only difficulty lying in the path of arguments invoking the law-likeness of natural selection. Completely independently of Hooker's argument, in Chapter 10 we shall investigate from a mathematical perspective some of the scenarios developed by

Dawkins and others to simulate the way in which such law-likeness might be realized, and we find them wanting for very different reasons.

Of course, Hooker's argument does not affect the kind of (microevolutionary) variations of the kind that Darwin observed. Thus the next question one might ask is:

What is the extent of microevolution?

Although some biologists resist differentiating between microevolution and macroevolution, the terms are increasingly used to distinguish, roughly speaking, between evolution below and beyond species level, there being debate on just where the line should be drawn.[22] Resistance to this distinction often arises because the evolutionary process is regarded as one seamless whole; that macroevolution is simply what results from microevolutionary processes operating over long periods of time. This is the view of 'gradualists' like Dawkins and Dennett. It begs the key question as to whether evolution really is one seamless whole or not; whether, for example, the selection mechanisms which can, say, reasonably account for variations in finch beak-lengths or the development of antibiotic resistance in bacteria can account for the existence of finches and bacteria in the first place.

A statement that exemplifies the value of the distinction between micro and macroevolution is made by Paul Wesson. 'Large evolutionary innovations are not well understood. None has ever been observed, and we have no idea whether any may be in progress. There is no good fossil record of any.'[18] By contrast, microevolutionary variations due to mutation and natural selection have been and are observed.

It seems to the intelligent outsider looking in that there is considerable difficulty here. A.P. Hendry and M.T. Kinnison put it as follows: 'Evolution is often considered in two categories: microevolution and macroevolution. The former obviously implies a small amount of change and the latter a large amount. The difficulty comes in deciding where the boundary between the two should fall, whether or not they represent the same processes (acting over different timescales), and whether or not the dichotomy is even useful or valid... Are macroevolutionary events (large morphological changes or speciation) simply the cumulative outcome of microevolutionary mechanisms (micromutation, selection, gene flow, genetic drift) or does macroevolution require some qualitatively different mechanism? The history of this debate is long, convoluted and sometimes acrimonious.'[23]

One problem here is clearly that extrapolating from the observed to the unobserved is fraught with danger. S.F. Gibbert, J.M. Opitz and R.A. Raff maintain that: 'Microevolution looks at adaptations that concern only the survival of the fittest, not the arrival of the fittest. As Goodwin (1995) points out, "the origin of species – Darwin's problem – remains unsolved",[24] thus echoing the verdict of geneticist Richard Goldschmidt: "the facts of microevolution do not suffice for an understanding of macroevolution".'[25] Convinced Darwinists, John Maynard Smith and E. Szathmary, take a similar line: 'There is no theoretical reason that would permit us to expect that evolutionary lines would increase in complexity with time; there is also no empirical evidence that this happens.'[26]

Siegfried Scherer of the Technical University in Munich suggests that living things can be classified in certain basic types – a classification slightly broader than that of species. A 'basic type' is defined to be a collection of living things connected either directly or indirectly through hybridization, without regard for whether the hybrids are sterile or not.[27] This definition incorporates both genetic and morphological concepts of species, and, according to Scherer, research so far indicates that 'in the whole experimentally accessible domain of microevolution (including research in artificial breeding and in species formation), all variations have certainly remained within the confines of basic types'.[28]

Such comments lend weight to the view of biologist and philosopher Paul Erbrich: 'The mutation-selection mechanism is an optimization mechanism.'[29] That is, it enables an already existing living system to adapt selectively to changing environmental conditions much in the same way as genetic algorithms facilitate optimization in engineering. It does not, however, create anything radically new.

More muscle is added to the argument by the fact that *the vast majority of mutations observed in the laboratory have deleterious effects*. This is not at all surprising in view of the digital nature of the genetic code that we shall have occasion to explore in some detail later. After all, one would hardly expect a computer programme to be improved by random changes in its code! Even the tiniest of changes is usually disastrous. But for the moment we simply record that cell biologist E.J. Ambrose of the University of London argued that it is unlikely that fewer than five genes could ever be involved in the formation of even the simplest new structure, previously unknown in the organism. He then points out that only one in 1,000 mutations is non-deleterious, so that the chance of five non-deleterious mutations occurring is 1 in a million billion (1 in 10^{15}) replications. After showing that this is only the beginning of the problems, in having such beneficial mutations integrated into the development of the entire organism and passed on in the gene pool, he concludes 'that recent hypotheses about the origin of species fall to the ground, unless it is accepted that an intensive input of new information is introduced at the time of isolation of the new breeding pair'.[30] The question of such inputs of information must be considered later.

It was on this same kind of evidential ground that Pierre Grassé of the Sorbonne in Paris, who was President of the Académie Française and editor of the definitive 28-volume work *Traité de Zoologie*, rejected neo-Darwinism. The great geneticist Theodosius Dobzhansky held Grassé in high esteem: 'Now one can disagree with Grassé, but not ignore him... his knowledge of the living world is encyclopaedic' (ibid). He described Grassé's book, *L'évolution du vivant*,[31] as 'a frontal attack on all kinds of Darwinism. Its purpose is "to destroy the myth of evolution, as a simple, understood and explained phenomenon", and to show that evolution is a mystery about which little is, and perhaps can be, known'.[32] In his book Grassé observed that fruit flies remain fruit flies in spite of the thousands of generations that have been bred and all the mutations that have been induced in them. In fact, the capacity for variation in the gene pool seems to run out quite early on in the process, a phenomenon called genetic homeostasis. There appears to be a barrier beyond which selective breeding will not pass because of the onset of sterility or exhaustion of genetic variability. If there are limits even to the amount of variation the most skilled breeders can achieve, the clear implication is that *natural* selection is likely to achieve very much less. It is not surprising that he argued that microevolution could not bear the weight that is often put upon it.

More recent work on the E. coli bacterium backs this up. In this research no real innovative changes were observed through 25,000 generations of E. coli bacteria.[33]

It is therefore surely clear on the basis of considerable scientific authority that macroevolution is, to say the least, not unequivocally in the category to which Lewontin, Dennett and others assign it. We now have two important reasons showing that macroevolution is not a 'fact' that has the same status as the fact that the earth orbits the sun. Firstly, the claim that the earth orbits the sun is a matter established by observation. That is manifestly not the case for Lewontin's claim that 'birds arose out of "non-birds"' (whatever the latter might have been). That process has never been observed. Secondly, the fact that the earth orbits the sun is not only a matter of observation, it is a matter of repeated observation. Lewontin's claim about the origin of birds concerns an unrepeatable, unobserved past event. To put an unobservable and unrepeatable phenomenon in the same category as an observable and repeatable one would seem to be such an elementary blunder, that one cannot help wondering if his aforementioned fear of a divine footprint is playing a key role, and that materialistic prejudice is overriding common (scientific) sense.

Microevolution concerns observable phenomena and so is open to the methods of inductive science; and it remains an important scientific question to try to understand more thoroughly what the limits of variation and adaptability are and what determines them. But macroevolution is not directly open to such methods; nor is molecular evolution. Because they are largely concerned with claims about unrepeatable past events, we have to approach them, as mentioned in Chapter 2, using methods appropriate to historical science; principally, the method of inference to the best explanation, or 'abduction', which methodology by definition does not carry the same kind of authority as that rightly enjoyed by inductive science.

What say the mathematicians?

Mathematicians are becoming increasingly interested in biology, especially since the revolution in molecular biology. Mathematical biology has become a burgeoning discipline. One of the first significant attempts at high-level debate between a group of eminent biologists and mathematicians who were interested in biology took place at the Wistar Institute in Philadelphia in 1966. An attempt to quantify the probabilities for the likelihood of gradualist evolution by the accumulation of micromutations led to a fascinating interchange between mathematician Stanley Ulam and biologists Sir Peter Medawar and the chairman of the conference, C.H. Waddington. Ulam argued on the basis of his mathematical calculations that it was highly improbable that the eye could have evolved by numerous small mutational changes since the available time was simply not available. Sir Peter Medawar replied: 'I think the way that you have treated this is a curious inversion of what would normally be a scientific process of reasoning. It is, indeed, a fact that the eye has evolved; and that, as Waddington says, shows that this [i.e. Ulam's] formulation is, I think, a mistaken one.' Biologist Ernst Mayr later commented: 'So all I am saying is that we have so much variation in all of these things that somehow or other by adjusting these figures we will come out all right. We are comforted by knowing that evolution has occurred.'[34]

This astonishing interchange is very revealing. It is surely a 'curious inversion' of the normal scientific process to assume the truth of what you want to prove and on that basis discredit evidence that is brought against it. What the interchange showed was that, for the biologists present, there could be no question of the mathematical evidence even getting them to consider that there might be flaws in their evolutionary assumptions.

Ulam's calculations were supported by Marcel-Paul Schützenberger, a Professor of Mathematics from Paris and a Member of the French Academy of Sciences. He objected to what he considered to be the too easy acceptance of evolution on the part of the biologists and was challenged by Waddington: 'Your argument is simply that life must have come about by special creation' – to which Schützenberger, along with a number of others, cried 'No.' Two things are clear from this interchange: firstly that the mathematicians were insisting that their thinking was not motivated by anything other than science; and secondly that the arguments they used were consistent with the view that there was a Creator – at least their biologist colleagues thought so.

Astrophysicist and mathematician Sir Fred Hoyle did some calculations that led him also to doubt the validity of extrapolating from micro to macroevolution: 'As it became clear that the Darwinian theory could not be broadly correct a question still remained, however, for I found it difficult to accept that the theory would be wholly incorrect. When ideas are based on observations, as the Darwinian theory certainly was, it is usual for them to be valid at least within the range of the observations. It is when extrapolations are made outside the range of observations that troubles may arise. So the issue that presented itself was to determine just how far the theory was valid and exactly why beyond a certain point it became invalid.'[35]

Fred Hoyle's conclusion to his mathematical arguments is characteristically blunt: 'Well, as common sense would suggest, the Darwinian theory is correct in the small, but not in the large. Rabbits come from other slightly different rabbits, not from either [primeval] soup or potatoes. Where they come from in the first place is a problem yet to be solved, like much else of a cosmic scale.'[36]

Hoyle, then, rejected Assertion 2. He did not believe that evolution accounts for the existence of all of life's complexity.

The fossil record

The impression that microevolution is limited in its scope is confirmed by the comments of Wesson and others to the effect that the fossil record gives no good examples of macroevolution. This will sound surprising to many people since it is a widespread public impression that one of the most powerful evidences for evolution comes from the fossil record. And yet this impression does not correspond to all that is to be found in the scientific literature. Indeed, at the outset, some of Darwin's strongest objectors were palaeontologists. He himself gives us the reason for this; it concerns the absence of the transitional forms in the fossil record, which his theory led him to expect. He wrote in *The Origin of Species*: 'The number of intermediate varieties, which have formerly existed on the earth, [should] be truly enormous. Why then is not every geological formation and every stratum full of such intermediate links? Geology assuredly does not reveal any such graduated organic chain; and this, perhaps is the most obvious and gravest objection which can be urged against my theory.'[37] Zoologist Mark Ridley comments on the situation: 'The fossil record of evolutionary change within single evolutionary lineages is very poor. If evolution is true, species originate through changes of ancestral species: one might expect to be able to see this in the fossil record. In fact it can rarely be seen. In 1859 Darwin could not cite a single example.'[38]

What, then, is the result of nearly a century and a half of intensive activity, since Darwin's time? Palaeontologist David Raup of the Field Museum of Natural History, which houses one of the largest fossil collections in the world, said: 'We are now about 120 years after Darwin and the knowledge of the fossil record has been greatly expanded. We now have a quarter of a million fossil species, but the situation hasn't changed much. The record of evolution is still surprisingly jerky and, ironically, we have even fewer examples of evolutionary transition than we had in Darwin's time.'[39]

Stephen Jay Gould said, 'The extreme rarity of transitional forms in the fossil record persists as the trade secret of palaeontology.'[40] His fellow palaeontologist, Niles Eldredge of the American Museum of Natural History, adds: 'When we do see the introduction of evolutionary novelty, it usually shows up with a bang, and often with no firm evidence that the fossils did not evolve elsewhere. Evolution cannot forever be going on somewhere else. Yet that's how the fossil record has struck many a forlorn palaeontologist looking to learn something about evolution.'[41]

In fact, Eldredge makes an astonishing admission. 'We palaeontologists have said that the history of life supports [the story of gradual adaptive change] knowing all the while it does not.'[42] But why? What conceivable reason could there be for members of an academic community to suppress what they know to be the truth – unless it were something which supported a worldview, which they had already decided was unacceptable?

What, then, does the fossil record reveal? Gould wrote: 'The history of most fossil species includes two features particularly inconsistent with the idea that they gradually evolved:

1. Stasis. Most species exhibit no directional change during their tenure on earth. They appear in the fossil record looking pretty much the same as when they disappear; morphological change is usually limited and directionless.
2. Sudden appearance. In any local area a species does not arise gradually by the steady transformation of its ancestors; it appears all at once and "fully formed".'[43]

Gould and Eldredge's reading of the fossil record as revealing short periods of rapid change, followed by long periods of stasis, led to their development of the theory of 'punctuated equilibrium' to attempt to explain it. The idea is that the long periods of stasis are broken sporadically by sudden large macroevolutionary 'jumps'. As a spectacular example of such a jump Gould, in his best selling book *Wonderful Life*,[44] describes how all the major phyla (taxonomic ranks) we have today – plus a good many more which have become extinct – appeared very suddenly in the so-called Cambrian Explosion. Of course, the question of what caused such sudden 'jumps' is another matter and increases the difficulties of those who wish to argue that microevolutionary processes are an adequate engine for large-scale evolution.

It is interesting and perhaps somewhat ironic that the theory of punctuated equilibrium was embraced by Marxist thinkers long before it had any basis in biology, since it seemed to fit into their dialectical way of thinking. They argued that, when thesis and antithesis clash, the new synthesis occurs rapidly in the form of a jump rather than a long, gradual process. This is another example of how worldviews and ideologies can influence science.

Simon Conway Morris, FRS, of Cambridge University, is more tempered in his approach to the Cambrian Explosion than Gould, but nonetheless thinks that such an explosion took place: 'Forms transitional between species can be observed today, and can be inferred to have existed in the past. Nevertheless, the net result is very far from a seamless tapestry of form that would allow an investigator to read the Tree of Life simply by finding the intermediates – living and extinct – that in principle connect all species. On the contrary, biologists are much more impressed by the discreteness of organic form, and the general absence of intermediates.'[45]

The theory of punctuated equilibrium stands in complete contrast to the gradualist approach of the 'ultra-Darwinians', such as John Maynard Smith, Richard Dawkins and Daniel Dennett. Indeed, the battle between the two groups has been vitriolic at times. The gradualists, as we have seen, hold that microevolution over time becomes macroevolution. They therefore believe that the very slow accumulation of tiny evolutionary steps over aeons of time can add up to a large innovatory step. Niles Eldredge accuses them of being weak on palaeontology. His argument is that the gradualists are concerned to understand how genetic information comes to be modified over the course of time, and then they simply assert that 'evolutionary history is the outcome of natural selection working on available genetic variation'.[46] In other words, they simply extrapolate from what they observe in the present, backwards through geological time. 'And that,' Eldredge continues, 'to my palaeontological eyes is just not good enough. Simple extrapolation does not work. I found that out back in the 60s as I tried in vain to document examples of the kind of slow directional change we all thought ought to be there ever since Darwin told us that natural selection should leave precisely such a tell-tale signal... I found instead that once species appear in the fossil record they tend not to change very much at all. Species remain imperturbably, implacably resistant to change as a matter of course – often for millions of years.'

This verdict, which is so strikingly at odds with the popular understanding of fossils, is supported by Colin Patterson, FRS: 'I will lay it on the line – there is not one such fossil [a fossil which is ancestral or transitional] for which one could make a watertight argument.'[47] It is additionally interesting that Patterson said this in connection with the Archaeopteryx, whose fossilized remains were actually under his care in the Natural History Museum and which is often cited as an example of a transitional species between reptiles and birds.

Now it is frequently argued in the literature that the fossil record is liable to be incomplete, in particular because soft body parts do not easily fossilize for obvious reasons. However, palaeontologists are very well aware of this and yet think nevertheless that the incompleteness of the fossil record cannot be the whole story. James Valentine in a major study *On the Origin of Phyla*[48] writes: 'Many of the branches [of the Tree of Life], large as well as small, are cryptogenic (cannot be traced into ancestors). Some of these gaps are surely caused by the incompleteness of the fossil record (chap. 5), but that cannot be the sole reason for the cryptogenic nature of some families, many invertebrate orders, all invertebrate classes, and all metazoan phyla.'

It should also be pointed out in this connection that, although soft body parts are rarely preserved, there are some spectacular recent finds of preserved sponge embryos in the Precambrian near Chengjiang in China. Their existence, according to marine palaeobiologist Paul Chien and his colleagues, creates a real problem: If the Precambrian strata are capable of preserving soft-bodied embryos of organisms why do they not also contain the precursors to the Cambrian animals? Does not the preservation of soft embryos make more likely the preservation of the fully mature animal?[49]

It should of course also be said that interpretation of the fossil record may well be complicated by genetic considerations. Intensive studies are being made of the connection between genes and morphology (particularly the Hox genes), and there are suggestions made, for example, by Simon Conway Morris, that once animals that have a sufficiently high degree of complexity are in existence, then relatively small genetic changes may trigger fairly large morphological changes. But even here he advises caution: 'While few doubt that the development of form is underwritten by the genes, at the moment we have almost no idea how form actually emerges from the genetic code.'[50] His observations serve to emphasize just how important, for the whole debate, is the question of the origin of the genetic code itself – a matter to which we devote Chapter 8.

What shall those of us who are not experts in the field make of the fossil record? Surely the fact that such leading thinkers as those we have cited are publicly expressing concerns about foundational aspects of the theory, in particular about the extrapolation from the present to the past, would indicate, at the very least, that the fossils do not offer the strength of support to the neo-Darwinian theory at the macro level that is often claimed.

Common descent

To these comments on the difficulties involved in extrapolating microevolution to macroevolution it will be objected that there is another, much more powerful technique of establishing the common ancestry of all living things. That is the way in which, quite independently of the fossil record or comparative anatomy, a genealogical tree can be constructed by a computer on the basis of comparing the structure of the DNA sequences in a collection of organisms.

This is widely interpreted as evidence of full common ancestry of all living things, and hence of evolution in its broadest sense. Zoologist Mark Ridley makes a very important observation: 'the simple fact that species can be classified hierarchically into genera, families, and so on, is not an argument for evolution. It is possible to classify any set of objects into a hierarchy, whether their variation is evolutionary or not.'[51] Cars, for instance, can be arranged in a hierarchy. But all cars have similar parts, because those parts are essential for their operation; and because they are constructed according to a common design, not because they have descended from each other.

Thus similarities in the DNA sequences could logically equally well be read as evidence of common design. Indeed, the common ancestry might have been designed, so that the concepts are not mutually exclusive. For instance, Francis Collins suggests that, although from our perspective 'evolution could appear to be driven by chance, from God's perspective the outcome would be entirely specified'.[52]

However, one could have common design without necessarily having common ancestry; except, of course, to the degree determined by the scope of microevolutionary processes. Consider, for example, what a fossil hierarchy of all dogs might look like – even if one restricted consideration to the dogs known to have been obtained by selective breeding from a single original type.

Thus similarities, both genetically and morphologically, are to be expected whatever hypothesis one adopts – whether design or common descent. Stephen Meyer argues that the hypothesis of common ancestry is methodologically equivalent to that of common design in the sense that any accusations of being scientific or unscientific which can be made against one, can be made equally against the other. For example, postulating an unobserved designer is no more unscientific than postulating unobserved macroevolutionary steps.[53]

This is one reason why some think it important and useful to distinguish conceptually between intermediate forms and transitional forms. An intermediate form would be precisely that – a form that could, on the criteria of some given scheme of classification, be placed 'between' two entries A and B of that classification, without any necessary implication of whether it had descended from A and was an ancestor of B. An intermediate form would only be transitional if it could be shown to have descended from A and was an ancestor of B and, to establish that, some mechanism would have to be demonstrably adequate for the task.

It would seem, however, that some evolutionary biologists are critical of the idea of a universal common ancestor. For instance, Carl Woese of the University of Illinois holds on the basis of his research that, in all probability, life had not only one but many independent starting points.[54] In addition to this one runs into another complicating factor in the path of common ancestry which is that the genetic code does not appear to be fully universal.[55]

We have argued in this chapter that natural selection acting on random mutation, though it helps us understand many things about the 'variations on a theme' present in the living world, may not fare so well in accounting for the transitions between the different levels of life. But *even if we allow for the sake of argument that the difficulties are not insuperable*, there is a far more formidable challenge on the horizon – the existence of life itself. Biogenesis is the subject of our next chapter.

The origin of life

'Anyone who tells you that he or she knows how life started on the earth some 3.45 billion years ago is a fool or a knave. Nobody knows.'

Stuart Kaufmann

'It has become inordinately difficult even to begin to think about constructing a naturalistic theory of the evolution of that first reproducing organism.'

Anthony Flew

The complexity of the living cell

Our first objective in this chapter is to get some idea of the vast complexity of the living cell and then to concentrate our attention on one aspect of it – the nature of the complexity of DNA.

According to geneticist Michael Denton, the break between the non-living and the living world 'represents the most dramatic and fundamental of all the discontinuities of nature. Between a living cell and the most highly ordered non-biological systems, such as a crystal or a snowflake, there is a chasm as vast and absolute as it is possible to conceive.'[1] Even the tiniest of bacterial cells, weighing less than a trillionth of a gram, is 'a veritable microminiaturized factory containing thousands of exquisitely designed pieces of intricate molecular machinery, made up altogether of 100 thousand million atoms, far more complicated than any machine built by man and absolutely without parallel in the non-living world'.[2]

Furthermore, according to Denton, there seems to be little evidence of evolution among cells: 'Molecular biology has also shown us that the basic design of the cell system is essentially the same in all living systems on earth from bacteria to mammals. In all organisms the roles of DNA, mRNA and protein are identical. The meaning of the genetic code is also virtually identical in all cells. The size, structure and component design of the protein synthetic machinery is practically the same in all cells. In terms of their basic biochemical design, therefore, no living system can be thought of as being primitive or ancestral with respect to any other system, nor is there the slightest empirical hint of an evolutionary sequence among all the incredibly diverse cells on earth.'[3]

This view is supported by Nobel Prize-winner Jacques Monod, whom Denton cites. 'We have no idea what the structure of a primitive cell might have been. The simplest living system known to us, the bacterial cell... in its overall chemical plan is the same as that of all other living beings. It employs the same genetic code and the same mechanism of translation as do, for example, human cells. Thus the simplest cells available to us for study have nothing "primitive" about them... no vestiges of truly primitive structures are discernible.'[4]

Thus the cells themselves exhibit a similar kind of 'stasis' to that referred to in the previous chapter in connection with the fossil record.

Irreducible complexity

'We have always underestimated cells,' says Bruce Alberts, President of The National Academy of Sciences of the USA. 'The entire cell can be viewed as a factory that contains an elaborate network of interlocking assembly lines, each of which is composed of a set of large protein machines... Why do we call the large protein assemblies that underlie cell function, protein machines? Precisely because, like machines invented by humans to deal efficiently with the macroscopic world, these protein assemblies contain highly co-ordinated moving parts.'[56]

It is hard for us to get any kind of picture of the seething, dizzyingly complex activity that occurs inside a living cell, which contains within its lipid membrane maybe 100 million proteins of 20,000 different types and yet the whole cell is so tiny that a couple of hundred could be placed on the dot in this letter 'i'.

The cell is restlessly productive as its many micro-miniature assembly lines produce their unending quotas of protein machines. The existence of these exquisitely constituted molecular machines is powerful evidence for some scientists of a designing intelligence. Prominent among them is biochemist Michael Behe, who studies such machines in a book that has generated a lot of critical discussion.[7] One example he gives is that of the tiny acid-driven motor (discovered in 1973) that powers the bacterial flagellum – a propeller-like device that enables bacteria to swim – and he shows that this motor, so small that 35,000 laid end to end would take up only 1 mm (0.04 in), consists of some forty protein parts including a rotor, a stator, bushings and a drive-shaft. Behe argues that the absence of any one of these protein parts would result in complete loss of motor function. That is, the motor is *irreducibly complex* – it is a 'single system composed of several well-matched, interacting parts that contribute to the basic function, wherein the removal of any one of the parts causes the system to effectively cease functioning'.[8] A simple illustration of this concept is provided by the humble mousetrap. All of its five or six components must be present for it to function. This means, as Behe points out, 'that no irreducibly complex system can be produced directly (that is, by continuously improving the initial function, which continues to work by the same mechanism) by slight, successive modifications of a precursor system, because any precursor to an irreducibly complex system that is missing a part, is by definition non-functional'.

Now it is obvious that the existence of irreducibly complex biological machines would present a formidable challenge to evolutionary theory, as Darwin himself saw when he wrote: 'If it could be demonstrated that any complex organ existed which could not possibly have been formed by numerous, successive, slight modifications, my theory would absolutely break down.'[9] The point is repeated by Dawkins in *The Blind Watchmaker*,[10] who says that if such an organism is found he will 'cease to believe in Darwinism'.[11]

Behe responds to Darwin's challenge by arguing that there exist many irreducibly complex molecular machines – like the flagellum. Now it is clear from the definition that establishing that any particular system is irreducibly complex involves proving a negative; and this, as is well known, is notoriously difficult. Not surprisingly, therefore, Behe (who, it should be noted, appears to have no quarrel with the Darwinian idea of descent with modification) has provoked a storm of controversy[12] with his claim that 'molecular evolution is not based on scientific authority. There is no publication in the scientific literature – in prestigious journals, specialty journals, or books – that describes how molecular evolution of any real, complex, biochemical system either did occur, or even might have occurred. There are assertions that such evolution occurred, but absolutely none is supported by pertinent experiments or calculations... despite comparing sequences and mathematical modelling, molecular evolution has never addressed the question of how complex structures came to be. In effect, the theory of Darwinian molecular evolution has not published, and so it should perish.'[13]

James Shapiro, a biochemist at the University of Chicago, also admits that there are no detailed Darwinian accounts for the evolution of any fundamental biochemical or cellular system; only a variety of wishful speculations. Even the highly critical review of Behe by Cavalier-Smith concedes Behe's point that no detailed biochemical models exist.

Stephen Jay Gould, who had no known sympathy with Behe's argument, nonetheless recognized the importance of the concept of irreducible complexity: 'Classical science, with its preferences for reduction to a few controlling factors of causality, was triumphantly successful for relatively simple systems like planetary motion and the periodic table of the elements. But irreducibly complex systems – that is, most of the interesting phenomena of biology, human society and history – cannot be so explained. We need new philosophies and models, and these must come from a union of the humanities and the sciences as traditionally defined.'[14] It is interesting here that Gould speaks of new philosophies and not simply of new scientific methods, a point that is also of interest to Behe.

For Behe the inadequacy of the neo-Darwinian synthesis consists in the fact that it cannot *even in principle* explain the origin of irreducible complexity. He argues that the existence of irreducible complexity at the molecular machine level points unmistakably to intelligent design: 'To a person who does not feel obliged to restrict his search to unintelligent causes, the straightforward conclusion is that many biochemical systems were designed. They were designed not by the laws of nature, not by chance and necessity; rather, they were planned. The designer knew what the systems would look like when they were completed, then took steps to bring the systems about. Life on earth at its most fundamental level, in its most critical components, is the product of intelligent activity.'[15] In addition Behe emphasizes that his conclusions are inferred naturally from the data, and not from sacred books or sectarian beliefs. They require no new principles of logic or science, but flow from the evidence provided by biochemistry combined with a consideration of the way in which we normally make design inferences. This is such a far-reaching claim that we shall have to look at it in more detail later.

But first, while the battle still rages over whether Behe has established his point or not (and, in light of what is at stake, that battle is likely to rage for a long time), we turn to look at what lies behind the complex structure of molecular machines. This leads us at once to the question of the origin of life itself.

The building blocks of life

Molecular machines like the flagellum are made from proteins, which are in turn made out of what are often called the basic building blocks of living systems – the amino acids, twenty of which occur in living organisms. One of the key questions in biology is: How did they arise?

The famous Russian biochemist A. I. Oparin suggested in the 1920s that the atmosphere of the primeval earth was composed essentially of methane, ammonia, hydrogen and water vapour; and that life had arisen as a result of chemical reactions occurring between this atmosphere and the chemicals found in the earth with the aid of ultraviolet radiation from the sun and other naturally occurring sources of energy such as lightning. In 1952, 22-year-old graduate student Stanley Miller conducted a famous experiment to test Oparin's suggestion in the laboratory by passing electrical discharges through a chemical mixture simulating what was thought to be the atmosphere of the early earth. After two days Miller found a 2 per cent yield of amino acids. Subsequent experimentation has produced all but one of the twenty amino acids necessary for life.[16]

Such experiments were understandably hailed with great enthusiasm as a solution for the problem of life's origin. It seemed as if the building blocks of life could be relatively easily obtained by natural, unguided processes. However, the euphoria has subsided in the face of subsequent major difficulties raised by deeper understanding of the chemistry involved.

First of all, the consensus of opinion among geochemists as to the composition of the earth's early atmosphere has changed. They now think that it did not contain significant amounts of ammonia, methane or hydrogen that were needed to produce a strongly reducing atmosphere as required by the Oparin hypothesis, but was much more likely to have consisted of nitrogen, carbon dioxide and water vapour. There is also evidence of significant amounts of free oxygen.[17] This alters the picture completely, for there are theoretical and practical reasons why amino acids could not be formed in such an atmosphere, as has been confirmed experimentally. The presence of oxygen, for example, would inhibit the production of the crucial biomolecules, and indeed even degrade such that did exist. In short then, the evidence suggests that the atmosphere of the early earth would actually have been hostile to the formation of amino acids.[18]

Now suppose that we want to make a protein that involves 100 amino acids (this would be a short protein – most are at least three times as long). Amino acids exist in two chiral forms that are mirror images of each other, called L and D forms. These two forms appear in equal numbers in prebiotic simulation experiments, so that the probability of getting one or other of the forms is roughly 1/2. However, all of the proteins found in nature contain only the L-form. The probability of getting 100 amino acids of L-form is, therefore, $(1/2)^{100}$, which is about 1 chance in 10^{30}. Next, our amino acids have to be joined together. Functional protein requires all the bonds to be of a certain type – peptide bonds – in order for it to fold into the correct 3-dimensional structure. Yet in prebiotic simulations no more than half of the bonds are peptide bonds. So the probability of a peptide bond is about 1/2, and again the probability of getting 100 such bonds is 1 in 10^{30}. Thus the probability of getting 100 L-acids at random with peptide bonds is about 1 in 10^{60}. In all known forms of life, the chirality of the molecules and the peptide bonds are maintained by the genetic machinery. In the absence of such complex information processing molecules in the prebiotic state, variable chirality, bonding and amino acid sequence would not lead to reproducible folded states which are essential to molecular function.

Of course a short protein is much less complicated than the simplest cell – for that the probabilities would be very much smaller. However, already in this section, the small probabilities we have just obtained are strikingly similar to those we listed in the section on the fine-tuning of the universe. The very building blocks of life show the kind of evidence from which we might well infer that our bodies are fine-tuned for life.

Physicist Paul Davies points out that there are immense thermodynamic problems in producing the peptide chains of amino acids. The Second Law of Thermodynamics describes the natural tendency of closed systems to degenerate, to lose information, order and complexity; that is, to increase their entropy. Heat flows from hot to cold, water flows downhill, cars rust, etc. Now the second law has a statistical character – it does not absolutely forbid physical systems going against the flow 'uphill', but it stacks the odds very much against it. Davies says, 'It has been estimated that, left to its own devices, a concentrated solution of amino acids would need a volume of fluid the size of the observable universe, to go against the thermodynamic tide, and create a single small polypeptide spontaneously. Clearly, random molecular shuffling is of little use when the arrow of directionality points the wrong way.'[19]

In addition there is a major problem with time since the time available for such 'random molecular shuffling' to occur is much shorter than many people think. According to current estimates there is relatively little time – less than a billion years after the formation of the earth roughly 4.5 billion years ago – for life to emerge (however it did so), since remains of single-celled organisms have been found in the very oldest rocks.

The major problem: the origin of protein structure

But even these difficulties (and they are major difficulties) seem relatively minor, indeed almost trivial, in comparison with what is by far the biggest problem of all. This has to do with the *way* in which proteins are built out of amino acids. For proteins are not made simply by mixing the right amino acids together in the correct proportions, as we might mix an inorganic acid with an alkali to produce a salt and water. Proteins are immensely specialized and intricate constructions of long chains of amino acid molecules and cannot be produced simply by injecting energy into the raw materials needed for their construction.

Paul Davies puts it more graphically: 'Making a protein simply by injecting energy is rather like exploding a stick of dynamite under a pile of bricks and expecting it to form a house. You may liberate enough energy to raise the bricks, but without coupling the energy to the bricks in a controlled and ordered way, there is little hope of producing anything other than a chaotic mess.'[20]

It is one thing to produce bricks; it is an entirely different thing to organize the building of a house or factory. If you had to, you could build a house using stones that you found lying around, in all the shapes and sizes in which they came due to natural causes. However, the organization of the building requires something that is not contained in the stones. It requires the intelligence of the architect and the skill of the builder. It is the same with the building blocks of life. Blind chance just will not do the job of putting them together in a specific way. Organic chemist and molecular biologist A.G. Cairn-Smith puts it this way: 'Blind chance... is very limited... he can produce exceedingly easily the equivalent of letters and small words, but he becomes very quickly incompetent as the amount of organization increases. Very soon indeed long waiting periods and massive material resources become irrelevant.'[21]

Cairns-Smith uses the analogy of letters and words here and this is exactly right since the crucial feature that characterizes proteins is that *the amino acids which comprise them must be in exactly the right places in the chain*. Think of the amino acids as the twenty 'letters' of an 'alphabet'. Then the protein is an incredibly long 'word' in that alphabet in which every amino acid 'letter' must be in the right place. That is, the order in which the amino acids are arranged in the chain is the vital thing, not simply the fact that they are there – just as the letters in a word, or the keystrokes in a computer programme, must be in the correct order for the word to mean what it should mean, or for the programme to work. A single letter in the wrong place, and the word could become another word or complete nonsense; a single incorrect keystroke in a computer programme, and it will probably cease to function.

The point of this argument is made very clear from simple-minded, probabilistic considerations. Among the many different kinds of amino acids there are twenty involved in making proteins, so that if we had a pool consisting of all twenty the probability of getting the correct amino acid at a specific site in the protein would be 1/20. Thus the probability of getting 100 amino acids in the correct order would be $(1/20)^{100}$, which is about 1 in 10^{130}, and therefore vanishingly small.[22]

But that is only the start – and a very modest start at that. For these calculations concern only a single protein. Yet life as we know it requires hundreds of thousands of proteins, and it has been calculated that the odds against producing these by chance is more than $10^{40,000}$ to 1. Sir Fred Hoyle famously compared these odds against the spontaneous formation of life with the chance of a tornado sweeping through a junkyard and producing a Boeing 747 jet aircraft.[23]

This is but an updated version of an observation made by Cicero around 46 BC. He saw the immense difficulties associated with the chance-origin of something language-like very clearly: 'If a countless number of copies of the one-and-twenty letters of the alphabet, made of gold or what you will, were thrown together into some receptacle and then shaken out on to the ground, [would it] be possible that they should produce the *Annals of Ennius*? I doubt whether chance could possibly succeed in producing a single verse.'[24] Precisely. Blind chance simply will not do, a sentiment that finds fairly universal agreement among scientists whether or not they are naturalists, but one about which more needs to be said below.

Self-organization scenarios

There is increasing interest in the idea that the solution to the problem of the origin of life lies with the fascinating concept of *self-organization*. For instance, Nobel Laureate Ilya Prigogine and Isabelle Stengers argue that order and organization can arise spontaneously out of chaos and disorder.[25] The kind of chaos they are interested in is that exhibited by thermodynamic systems that are driven far from equilibrium and begin to exhibit non-linear behaviour of such a kind that a very small change in input can trigger disproportionately large consequences. The most famous example of this is the so-called 'butterfly effect' in which the flapping of a butterfly's wings in one part of the world sets of a chain of events that trigger a tropical storm somewhere else. Such systems, like the weather, that are exceedingly sensitive to changes in initial conditions and are therefore inherently unpredictable are called chaotic systems. Prigogine shows that unexpected ordered patterns can be unexpectedly produced. One of the best examples is that of Rayleigh-Bénard convection, in which heat flowing smoothly through a liquid suddenly changes into a convection current that reorganizes the liquid so that a honeycomb pattern made up of hexagonal cells appears, looking just like the famous rock formations at the Giant's Causeway in Northern Ireland.

Another frequently cited example is the Belousov-Zhabotinski reaction which exhibits temporal, rather than spatial, symmetry breaking. This phenomenon occurs, for example, when malonic acid is being oxidized by potassium bromate with the aid of two catalysts, cerium sulphate and ferroin, for instance. If the mixture is kept at about 25°C (77°F) and continuously stirred it will repeatedly change colour from red to blue[26] at approximately one minute intervals so that the reaction functions like a kind of chemical clock with a remarkably regular period. This reaction is so fascinating that a short and extremely simplified descriptive explanation is in order.

Let us therefore imagine a reaction in which a substance A is being converted to a substance B. We represent this diagrammatically as:

1.   A >> B

Suppose then that this is followed by a second reaction, called an *autocatalytic* reaction:

2.   A+B >> 2B

Here B is acting as a catalyst since each molecule of B on the left reappears on the right. But there is more of B than we started with so that the rate of reaction 2 depends on the amount of product formed and so we have a positive feedback loop that speeds up the reaction – hence the term autocatalytic. Now we complicate the situation and simultaneously make it much more interesting by introducing two further reactions:

3.   B+C >> 2C
4.   C >> D

Reaction 3 is a further autocatalytic reaction, but this time it has the effect of reducing the amount of B and so it works in the opposite direction to 2. We can imagine the fourth reaction as producing a waste product D. The final ingredients we need to complete the picture are an indicator that turns red in the presence of B and blue in the presence of C. We now start the reaction with proportionately more in terms of concentration of A than C.

Then, since reaction rates are proportional to the concentrations of reactants, reaction 2 will initially dominate reaction 3. Thus the concentration of B will rise and the mixture will be red. But autocatalytic reaction 3 will eventually take over and reduce the concentration of B and the colour will change to blue because of the domination of C. But now reaction 4 comes into play and eats away at C, and so B eventually dominates once more and we get another colour change. Eventually the process will stop as A gets used up, or D clogs the system. We could clearly keep it going – that is, maintain the system far from equilibrium – by supplying more A and removing D.

Thus, in each of these systems, order is generated and it is thought by some that in some way these processes give us an idea of how life may have started.[27]

However, the view that this kind of process gives insight into the origin of life runs into serious difficulties that have to do with the nature of the complexity exhibited by the structure of the proteins that we mentioned at the end of the last section. For the core problem is *not* that of producing the kind of order that is to be seen in a crystal, honeycomb, or even a Belousov-Zhabotinski reaction. It is that of producing the qualitatively different, language-type of structures formed by the complex ordering of the amino acids that form a protein. Paul Davies puts the difference very clearly: 'Life is actually *not* an example of *self*-organization. Life is in fact *specified*, i.e. genetically directed, organization. Living things are instructed by the genetic software encoded in their DNA (or RNA). Convection cells form spontaneously by self-organization. There is no gene for a convection cell. The source of order is not encoded in software, it can instead be traced to the boundary conditions in the fluid... In other words, a convection cell's order is imposed *externally*, from the system's environment. By contrast, the order of a living cell derives from *internal* control... The theory of self-organization as yet gives no clue how the transition is to be made between spontaneous, or self-induced organization – which in even the most elaborate non-biological examples still involves relatively simple structures – and the highly complex, information-based, genetic organization of living things.'[28]

Stephen Meyer puts the issue this way: 'Self-organizational theorists explain well what does not need to be explained. What needs explaining is not the origin of order... but the origin of information.'[29] It is the concept of information that lies at the heart of the problem, to the understanding of which we must now devote our attention for most of the rest of this book.

One of the most eminent scientists working on the origin of life, Leslie Orgel, summed up the position as follows: 'There are several tenable theories about the origin of organic material on the primitive earth, but in no case is the supporting evidence compelling. Similarly, several alternative scenarios might account for the self-organization of a self-replicating entity from prebiotic organic material, but all of those that are well formulated are based on hypothetical chemical syntheses that are problematic.[30]

Orgel therefore echoes the view of Klaus Dose, also a prominent worker in origin of life research, who ten years earlier made the following assessment: 'More than thirty years of experimentation on the origin of life in the fields of chemical and molecular evolution have led to a better perception of the immensity of the problem of the origin of life on earth rather than to its solution. At present all discussions on principal theories and experiments in the field either end in stalemate or in a confession of ignorance.'[31]

Sir Francis Crick, not known to be sympathetic to the miraculous, nevertheless wrote: 'The origin of life seems almost to be a miracle, so many are the conditions which would have had to have been satisfied to get it going.'[32]

All of which leads one to think that the verdict of Stuart Kaufmann of the Santa Fe Institute is valid: 'Anyone who tells you that he or she knows how life started on the earth some 3.45 billion years ago is a fool or a knave. Nobody knows.'[33] More recently, Francis Collins has said the same: 'But how did self-replicating organisms arise in the first place? It is fair to say that at the present time we simply do not know. No current hypothesis comes close to explaining how in the space of a mere 150 million years, the prebiotic environment that existed on planet earth gave rise to life. That is not to say that reasonable hypotheses have not been put forward, but their statistical probability of accounting for the development of life still seems remote.'[34]

8

The genetic code and its origin

'What lies at the heart of every living thing is not a fire, warm breath, nor a "spark of life". It is information, words, instructions... Think of a billion discrete digital characters... If you want to understand life think about digital technology.'

Richard Dawkins

'The concept of information is central both to genetics and evolutionary theory.'

John Maynard Smith

Information in the cell

In order to grasp even more clearly the issues involved in thinking about the origin of life, we must now move beyond the proteins to the molecular level, to what determines the order of the links in the chain of amino acids in the proteins. That leads us at once to one of the greatest scientific discoveries of all time: the nature and meaning of the information-bearing DNA macromolecule. For a living cell is not merely matter. It is matter replete with information. According to Richard Dawkins, 'What lies at the heart of every living thing is not a fire, warm breath, nor a "spark of life". It is information, words, instructions... Think of a billion discrete digital characters... If you want to understand life think about digital technology.'[1,2]

The information content of DNA is fundamental to life – but there is clearly more to life than DNA. For a start, DNA is not itself alive. But Dawkins is nonetheless right that we need to think about information as playing a fundamental role in the whole business of life. The information-bearing DNA is contained in the cell's nucleus and it stores the instructions needed to build the proteins in the functional organism. It is the molecule of heredity containing those characteristics that is passed on to our children. Like a computer hard disc, DNA contains the database of information and the programme to produce a specified product. Every one of the 10 to 100 trillion cells in the human body contains a database larger than the *Encyclopaedia Britannica*. What we have witnessed in the last few decades is at first a somewhat reluctant, but then a wholesale acceptance on the part of molecular biologists of the language and methodology of information technology forced on them by the recognition of the nature and function of the genetic code. We now talk quite happily about a living cell as an information processing machine since that is precisely what it is – a molecular structure with an information processing capacity.[3] This is an exciting intellectual development because it means that the nature of biological information can be explored using the concepts and results of information theory.

However, let us not rush to investigate this before having some picture in our minds of what the DNA molecule is and how it carries information.

What is DNA?

The letters are an acronym for Deoxyribose Nucleic Acid. This is a very long molecule with a double helix structure the discovery of which gained the Nobel Prize for Crick and Watson. It resembles a spiral ladder made up of a very long chain of much simpler molecules called nucleotides. There are ten of these in each full twist of the spiral. The nucleotides consist of a sugar called ribose together with a phosphate group from which one oxygen atom has been removed (thus accounting for the prefix *deoxy-*) and a base. The bases, as they are called, are the four chemicals Adenine, Guanine, Cytosine and Thymine, or A,G,C,T for short, and they (alone) distinguish one nucleotide from the next. The first two bases are purines and the second two are pyrimidines. The rungs of the ladder are formed out of the base pairs, where the two base-pair molecules forming the ends of any given rung are held together by hydrogen bonds. There is a rule that A is invariably paired with T and C with G, that is, a purine always bonds to a pyrimidine. Thus if one strand of the double helix starts AGGTCCGTAATG... then the other strand will start TCCAGGCATTAC... The two strands are therefore complementary – if you know one strand, you can work out the other. We shall see the importance of this in a moment.

Of course, the labelling of the nucleotides on the strands is arbitrary in the sense that we could, for example, assign four numbers to them, say 1,2,3,4 or 2,3,5,7 (or indeed any four distinct symbols), and we would then get for the start of the first strand mentioned above 133422341143... or 255733572275..., respectively. Thus a unique number could be assigned to each DNA molecule (usually an extremely long number, as we shall see below) from which its sequence of bases could be read off.

Just as a sequence of letters from the ordinary alphabet of one of the world's written languages can carry a message that depends on the precise ordering of the letters, so the sequence of bases on the spine of DNA (the sequence of rungs in the ladder, if you like) carries a precise message written in the four-letter alphabet consisting of the letters A,C,G,T. A *gene* is a long string of these letters carrying the information for a protein so that a gene can be interpreted as a set of instructions, like a program, for making that protein. The way the coding works is that each group of three nucleotides, called a codon, codes for an amino acid. Since there are four nucleotides there are 4^3 = 64 possible triples available for coding the twenty amino acids. It turns out that one and the same amino acid can have more than one (up to six in fact) different triples coding for it. It is this coding that gives rise to the concept of the genetic code.

The *genome* consists of a complete set of genes. Genomes are generally very large: the DNA of an E. coli bacterium is about four million letters long and would fill 1,000 pages in a book, whereas the human genome is over 3.5 billion letters long and would fill a whole library.[4] As a matter of interest the actual length of the DNA tightly coiled in a single cell of the human body is roughly 2 metres. Since there are about 10 trillion (= 10^{13}) cells in the human body the total length of DNA is a mind-boggling 20 trillion metres.

For the sake of accuracy it should be pointed out that, although we often think of the DNA in a given organism as the genome, strictly speaking, the genome actually occupies only a part of the DNA, a relatively small part, in fact – in humans 3 per cent. The remaining 97 per cent of the DNA, so-called non-coding DNA, has been described as 'junk DNA', but it is becoming clear that it is far from being junk as it turns out to be responsible not only for the regulation, maintenance and reprogramming of genetic processes but it also contains highly mobile segments of DNA called transposons that can fabricate copies of themselves and then move to different sites on the genome with varying effects, including possibly disabling genes and activating hitherto inactive genes.[5] Another interesting use to which non-coding DNA has been put is the forensic technique of genetic fingerprinting discovered by Alec Jeffreys in 1986.

How does the DNA give rise to the proteins?

The DNA resides in the nucleus of the cell, which is protected by a membrane. In order for anything to happen, for the cell to 'live', the information contained in the DNA must be transported to the cytoplasm, the area of the cell outside the nucleus where the cellular machinery is working – the factory floor of the cell, if you like. That information is needed, for example, for the construction of enzymes in the cytoplasm by molecular machines called ribosomes. So how does the information on the DNA get to the ribosomes to make an enzyme? It is done by means of another long nucleic acid molecule called ribonucleic acid (RNA) which is very similar to DNA except that it is not usually double stranded, though it does possess the extra oxygen atoms that are missing in DNA. Like DNA it has four bases: three of them are our old friends A, G and C but the fourth is a newcomer, Uracil (U), which replaces DNA's T. What happens first is that the DNA inside the nucleus 'unzips' down the middle separating the two strands. This is facilitated by the fact that the hydrogen bonds between the strands are weak compared with the bonds that connect the bases in each strand of the DNA. Next a strand of RNA called messenger RNA (mRNA) transcribes one of the DNA strands resulting in the production of something very like the complementary strand of DNA with U replacing T throughout. Sometimes there are errors (usually very few) in the copying process giving rise to mutations. The mRNA then travels through the wall of the nucleus to the cytoplasm where the stunningly intricate process of translation takes place.

The mRNA strand can be thought of as something like a magnetic computer tape and the ribosome a machine that constructs a protein from the information contained on that tape. In order to do so the ribosome moves along the mRNA strand 'reading' the information contained in it as it goes. It is just like a magnetic tape-recording head in a computer, or the scanning head of a Turing machine, though there we tend to think of the head as fixed and the tape as moving, an insignificant difference for our purposes. Computer-like it reads the codons, which we recall are groups of three consecutive characters, in the order they appear on the tape – so, for example, AAC UGC UUG... The next task for the ribosome is to find the amino acids that correspond to these codons (in this case, Asparagine, Cysteine and Leucine). They turn out to be swimming around in the neighbourhood of the ribosome attached by weak hydrogen bonds to molecules (called transfer RNA, tRNA) that look like crosses. If, for example, Asparagine is attached to one arm of such a molecule then the other end of that arm is attached to what is called the anticodon corresponding to the codon AAC, that is, CCA. When the ribosome reads any particular codon it fishes around for the corresponding anticodon, nets it and then removes the amino acid attached to it. The ribosome then joins that amino acid to those it has already assembled. Thus the new protein gradually emerges.

These tiny mechanisms, so small that it takes very powerful microscopes to see them, are of a bewildering order of sophistication, as a glance at any textbook on molecular biology will confirm. The nature of their complexity is such that even convinced evolutionary biologists such as John Maynard Smith and Eörs Szathmary confess that: 'The existing translational machinery is at the same time so complex, so universal, and so essential, that it is hard to see how it could have come into existence, or how life could have existed without it.'[6] Nearly ten years later we find microbiologist Carl Woese lamenting that even humans with all their intelligence cannot construct such mechanisms: 'We don't understand how to create novelty from scratch – that's a question for biologists of the future.'[7]

Is it all in the genes?

We need to pause here since, in talking about the complexity of information-rich biomolecules like DNA and the genetic code, it is easy to give the impression that the genes tell us everything about what it means to be human. Indeed for many years molecular biologists have regarded it as a 'central dogma', as Francis Crick called it, that the genome accounts completely for an organism's inherited characteristics. This inevitably fuelled the kind of biodeterminism that held individual genes responsible for a whole variety not only of human diseases but also of all manner of characteristics from predisposition to violence or obesity to mathematical ability.

A hierarchy of complexity

However, evidence is rapidly mounting that this is very unlikely to be the case. For the human genome turns out to contain only 30,000 to 40,000 genes. This came as a great surprise to many people – after all human cellular machinery produces somewhere around 100,000 different proteins so one might have expected at least that number of genes to encode them. There are simply too few genes to account for the incredible complexity of our inherited characteristics, let alone for the great differences between, say, plants and humans. For this reason geneticist Steve Jones sounds a strong cautionary note: 'A chimp may share 98 per cent of its DNA with ourselves but it is not 98 per cent human: it is not human at all – it is a chimp. And does the fact that we have genes in common with a mouse, or a banana say anything about human nature? Some claim that genes will tell us what we really are. The idea is absurd.'[8]

Take, for example, the fact that genes can be switched on or off – and that at certain stages in the development of an organism. The control of such switching is mainly undertaken by sequences called 'promoters', which are usually to be found near to the start of the gene. Let us now imagine an organism with n genes, each of which can be in one of two states, on or off, expressed or unexpressed, in genetic terminology. Then there are clearly 2^n possible expression states. Suppose now we have organisms A and B with 32,000 and 30,000 genes, respectively. Then the number of expression states for A is $2^{32,000}$ and for B is $2^{30,000}$. Hence A has 2^{2000} times as many expression states as B – and 2^{2000} is a very large number, larger in fact by far than the number of elementary particles there are estimated to be in the universe (about 2^{80}).

Thus a relatively small difference in the number of genes could account for the very large differences in the phenotype (observable characteristics) of the organism. But that is only a beginning since the base assumption in our last calculation that genes are either on or off is too simplistic by far, especially if we are thinking of the more complex organisms. The genes of such organisms tend to be 'smarter' in the sense that they have a much wider range of molecular machines they can build and control. For instance, they may be partly expressed, that is, neither completely on nor completely off. Such control mechanisms are capable of responding to the cellular environment in determining to what extent a gene should be switched on. Thus they are like miniature control computers in their own right. And, since the degree to which they are on or off varies, the above calculations must be drastically revised upwards. The effect of proteins working on proteins means that we are now entering a hierarchy of sharply increasing levels of complexity even the lowest level of which is difficult to grasp.

But there is very much more in the way of complexity yet in store since it is now evident that a large collection of genes may be involved in any one particular trait or function – their correspondence is many-to-one rather than one-to-one. The reasons for this are beginning to emerge. Barry Commoner, Senior Scientist and Director of the Critical Genetics Project at the Center for the Biology of Natural Systems at Queens College, City University of New York, in his article 'Unravelling the DNA Myth'[9] lists three discoveries that support the contention that there is more to life than DNA.

1. Alternative splicing

Commoner suggests that one of the key tenets of the 'central dogma', Crick's sequence hypothesis – that the nucleotide sequence of a single gene encodes the amino acid sequence of a single protein – may be in need of considerable revision. For it has been shown that a single gene can give rise to many protein variants by means of a process called alternative splicing, which may occur when the nucleotide sequence of a gene is being transferred to messenger RNA. In other words, there is not a one-to-one correspondence between genes and proteins. What happens is that a special group of up to 150 proteins together with five molecules of RNA known as a spliceosome assemble at various sites in the mRNA and form a molecular machine that cuts the mRNA into segments, which are then recombined in various different orders. Sometimes some pieces may be removed and others added. Any such recombined material therefore carries a sequence differing from the original one. In this way, by the cut-and-paste technique of alternative splicing, a single gene can give rise to many different proteins: there is, for example, such a gene in the inner ear of chicks and humans which can give rise to 576 variant proteins.[10] There is also a gene in the fruit fly that is known to give rise to 38,016 different proteins.

Commoner points out the devastating implications of this discovery for the belief that the genetic information which comes from an original DNA sequence terminates unchanged in the amino acid sequence of the protein. Crick had asserted that 'the discovery of just one type of present day cell' in which genetic information passed from protein to nucleic acid or from protein to protein 'would shake the whole intellectual basis of molecular biology'.[11] But that is just what is happening here – novel genetic information is being produced in the RNA by the splicing process, a process that involves the proteins of the spliceosome. Thus one simply cannot predict the effect of a single gene simply by specifying the instructions in its nucleotide sequence. The splicing process has the effect of editing those instructions and thus enabling them to give rise to a multiplicity of meanings. And errors in the splicing has been shown by Shin Kwak of the University of Tokyo in 2002 to be the most likely cause of amyotrophic lateral sclerosis, a fatal paralytic disease.

The splicing process used to be considered rare. However, it has been observed that the frequency of incidence of alternative splicing increases with the complexity of the organism in question and it is now estimated that up to 75 per cent of human genes are subject to the process. It is clear that the amount of additional information added by alternative splicing is enormous and so it is no longer surprising that there can be vast differences between organisms with very similar sets of genes.

2. Error-correction

The incredibly precise duplication of DNA is not accomplished by the DNA alone: it depends on the presence of the living cell. In its normal surroundings in the cell the DNA replicates with roughly one error in 3 billion nucleotides (remember the human genome is about 3 billion nucleotides long). However, on its own in a test tube the error rate rises dramatically to about 1 in 100. When, still in a test tube, appropriate protein enzymes are added, the error rate sinks to about 1 in 10 million. The final low error rate depends on the addition of yet more proteins in the form of 'repair' enzymes that detect and correct errors.[12]

The process of nucleic acid replication therefore depends on the presence of such protein enzymes, and not simply on the DNA itself. An interesting comment on the repair system is made by James Shapiro, who writes: 'It has been a surprise to learn how thoroughly cells protect themselves against precisely the kinds of accidental genetic change that, according to conventional theory, are the sources of evolutionary variability. By virtue of their proofreading and repair systems, living cells are not the passive victims of the random forces of chemistry and physics. They devote large resources to suppressing random genetic variation and have the capacity to set the level of background localized mutability by adjusting the activity of their repair systems.'[13]

Which came first – the chicken or the egg?

One very important implication of the existence of alternative splicing and error repair mechanisms is that DNA would appear to depend on life for its existence, rather than life on DNA, thus calling in question the common notion that life originated in an RNA to DNA to life sequence (the RNA-world scenario). Commoner puts it bluntly: 'DNA did not create life; life created DNA.' Miller and Levine expand on this: 'The largest stumbling block in bridging the gap between non-living and living still remains. All living cells are controlled by information stored in DNA, which is transcribed in RNA and then made into protein. This is a very complicated system and each of these three molecules requires the other two – either to put it together or to help it work. DNA, for example, carries information but cannot put that information to use, or even copy itself without the help of RNA and protein.'[14]

There seems to be an irreducible symbiosis here that simplistic models of origins cannot reflect. Another similar example is provided by Leslie Orgel of the Salk Institute for Biological Studies: 'There is no agreement on the extent to which metabolism could develop independently of a genetic material. In my opinion, there is no basis in known chemistry for the belief that long sequences of reactions can organize spontaneously – and every reason to believe they cannot. The problem of achieving sufficient specificity, whether in aqueous solution or on the surface of a mineral, is so severe that the chance of closing a cycle of reactions as complex as the reverse citric acid cycle, for example, is negligible.'[15]

3. The geometry of proteins

When proteins are made they fold into a precise three-dimensional geometric configuration on which their subsequent biochemical activity depends. It used to be assumed that, once its amino acid sequence was determined, the protein 'knew' how to fold into the correct shape. However, it is now known that some proteins need other 'chaperone' proteins to help them fold correctly – otherwise they would remain biochemically inactive.

Furthermore, there exist proteins – the prions, which are nucleic acid free – that are involved in degenerative brain diseases like 'mad cow' disease. Research has shown that a prion penetrates a normal brain protein which it proceeds to refold in conformity with the three-dimensional structure of the prion. This process makes the refolded protein infectious and sets up a fatal chain reaction. Now the strange and very interesting thing is that the prion and the brain protein it acts upon have the same amino acid sequence and yet one is fatally infectious and the other is normal and healthy. This strongly suggests that the folded structure must to some extent at least be independent of the amino acid sequence. This would of course mean that in estimating the information content of the protein the three-dimensional geometry of the folding would have to be taken into account – a problem of mind-boggling proportions.

In light of the fact that much of this has been known to scientists for some time, Commoner asks why the central dogma has continued to stand. His answer is: 'To some degree the theory has been protected from criticism by a device more common to religion than science: dissent, or merely the discovery of a discordant fact, is a punishable offence, a heresy that might easily lead to professional ostracism. Much of this bias can be attributed to institutional inertia, a failure of rigour, but there are other, more insidious, reasons why molecular geneticists might be satisfied with the status quo; the central dogma has given them such a satisfying, seductively simplistic explanation of heredity that it seemed sacrilegious to entertain doubts. The central dogma was simply too good not to be true.' It would therefore appear that there is very much more to what it means to be human than what is in the genes.

Proteomics

The hierarchy of levels of complexity does not stop with the translation of the genetic code into proteins. For proteins can be modified in many ways and even cut and spliced in the same way as mRNA molecules can. This has led to the burgeoning discipline of proteomics, where the proteome is a complete set of all the proteins and variants of proteins that can arise out of a given genome. Elucidating its staggering complexity, far greater than that of the genome, is one of the greatest intellectual challenges facing science.

Information processing in the cell

Thus, the more the living cell is studied, the more aspects it appears to have in common with one of the most sophisticated high-technology products of human intelligence: computers. Except that the cell's information processing capacity far outstrips anything present-day computers can do. The founder of the Microsoft Corporation, Bill Gates, said that 'DNA is like a computer programme, but far, far more advanced than any software we've ever created.'[16]

In his book *Gödel, Escher, Bach – an Eternal Golden Braid*[17] mathematician Douglas Hofstadter writes: 'A natural and fundamental question to ask on learning of these incredibly, intricately interlocking pieces of software and hardware is: "How did they ever get started in the first place?"... from simple molecules to entire cells, is almost beyond one's power to imagine. There are various theories on the origin of life. They all run aground on this most central of central questions: "How did the Genetic Code, along with the mechanisms for its translation, originate?" ' The question is not made any easier by the fact that this code is viewed as being extremely ancient. Werner Loewenstein, who has won world renown for his discoveries in cell communication and biological information transfer, says: 'This genetic lexicon goes back a long, long way. Not an iota seems to have changed over two billion years; all living beings on earth, from bacteria to humans, use the same sixty-four word code.'[18]

Let us think of one aspect of this complex of problems – the origin of the genetic software DNA. It is sometimes suggested that the generation of genetic information is facilitated by certain chemical affinities between the molecules that carry that information. However, there is a simple logical reason that this cannot be so. Think of the alphabet. In English there is a rule that a 'q' must be followed by a 'u'. Now imagine that there are similar 'affinities' between other pairs of letters. It is immediately clear that the more such 'affinities' you have between the letters of an alphabet, the fewer expressions you can write down. The freedom to write the letters in almost any order you like is crucial to having a rich linguistic store of words. It is the same with DNA. The whole point about the nucleotide bases (A,C,G,T) is that they may be positioned essentially randomly. If there were any affinities between them, their information-carrying potential would be drastically reduced.

Now the two base-pair molecules forming the ends of any given rung in the DNA ladder are held together by weak chemical bonds. But the rungs themselves, whose sequence in the ladder codes the information necessary to build a protein, have no chemical bonds between them. Michael Polanyi explains the implication of this: 'Suppose that the actual structure of the DNA molecule were due to the fact that the bindings of its bases were much stronger than the bindings would be for any other distribution of bases, then such a DNA molecule would have no information content. Its code-like character would be effaced by an overwhelming redundancy... Whatever may be the origin of a DNA configuration, it can function as a code only if its order is not due to the forces of potential energy. It must be as physically indeterminate as the sequence of words is on a printed page.'[19] The operative word here is 'physically'. As we saw earlier, the message is not derivable from the physics and chemistry of paper and ink.

Hubert Yockey, author of the influential text *Information Theory and Biology*,[20] confirms this judgement: 'Attempts to relate the idea of order... with biological organization or specificity must be regarded as a play on words which cannot stand careful scrutiny. Informational macromolecules can code genetic messages and therefore carry information because the sequence of bases or residues is affected very little, if at all, by physico-chemical factors.'[21] The genetic text is not generated by the chemistry of the bonding between molecules.

If explanations in terms of chemical bonds do not work, what other possibilities are there? A simple-minded appeal to Darwinian-like processes is very unlikely to provide a solution since we are talking about biogenesis, the origin of life and, whatever Darwinian processes can do, it is very hard to see how they could even get going in the absence of life. For in order for natural selection to do anything it needs the existence of a mutating replicator. We have already cited the well-known dictum of Theodosius Dobzhansky: 'Prebiotic evolution is a contradiction in terms.' Though seeming 'old-hat' to many now, it cautions us in our use of terms like 'molecular evolution' which could be understood to imply that we are covertly assuming that we have at our disposal the very process (replication, about which alone it makes sense to talk of natural selection acting upon it) whose existence we are trying to explain. As John Barrow points out, James Clerk Maxwell had observed as early as 1873 that atoms were 'populations of identical particles whose properties were not acted on by natural selection and whose properties determined whether life could exist'.[22]

Nevertheless attempts continue to be made to solve the origin of life problem using Darwinian type arguments that rely solely on chance and necessity. To put them into context we now need to consider some further mathematical contributions to the debate.

Matters of information

'Life is digital information.'

Matt Ridley

'The problem of the origin of life is clearly basically equivalent to the problem of the origin of biological information.'

Bernd-Olaf Küppers

'Our task is to find an algorithm, a natural law that leads to the origin of information.'

Manfred Eigen

'A machine does not create any new information, but it performs a very valuable transformation of known information.'

Leonard Brillouin

What is information?

So far in this book we have been freely using the word 'information'. But the time has come to look at this fundamental concept more closely.

In ordinary language we use the word 'information' to describe something that we now know which we did not know before – we say that we have received information. There are many methods of transmitting information: verbally, in plain writing, in sign language, in cryptic code, etc.

The problem comes when we try to quantify information. However, the theory of information has made considerable progress which is of great importance in our consideration of the nature of what we have called genetic information.

Let's start by exploring the intuitive notion that information decreases our uncertainty. For example, we arrive at a small hotel where we have made a reservation and find that there are only eight rooms. Then, on the assumption that all the rooms are similar and that we have not requested any particular room there is a probability of 1 in 8 that we will be assigned any particular room. That probability is a clear measure of our uncertainty. On being given the information that we have been assigned room 3, say, that uncertainty disappears. One of the ways in which we might measure the information we have received is to work out the least number of yes or no questions we would have to ask in order to find out which room we have been assigned. A little thought should convince us that that number is three. We say that we have received three *bits* of information or that we need three bits of information in order to specify our room. We notice that 3 is the power to which we have to raise 2 to get 8 (that is, $8 = 2^3$) or, putting it the other way round, 3 is the logarithm of 8 in base 2, (that is $3 = \log_2 8$). It is easy to generalize this argument to see that if there are n rooms in the hotel, then the amount of information needed to specify a particular room is $\log_2 n$.

Think now of a text message written in English, which we shall regard as a language written in sentences consisting of words and spaces so that our 'alphabet' consists of 26 letters plus a space so that 27 symbols are needed. If we are waiting for a message on our mobile phone then the probability of receiving any symbol (letter or space) is 1/27. The information added by each text symbol is $\log_2 27$ (= 4.76 approx). So the information conveyed by a text m symbols long will be $m\log_2 27$ (4.76m approx).

We notice here that the amount of information conveyed is *relative* to the known size of the 'alphabet'. For example, if we know that our text message may contain numbers as well as letters and spaces then our 'alphabet' has now got 37 letters. Hence the information represented by each symbol received is now $\log_2 37$ (= 5.2 approx).

In all of this the number 2 obviously plays a special role. In fact the symbol 'alphabet' used in computing consists of the two symbols 0 and 1. It is easy to see that 2 is the minimum number of symbols necessary in order to encode any alphabet whatsoever. For example, if we think of English as needing 26 letters plus a space then binary strings of length at most 5 ($2^5 = 32 > 27$) will suffice to encode it all with room to spare: we could encode the space symbol as 00000 and put A = 00001, B = 00010, C = 00011, etc.

Syntactic and semantic information

We now introduce a very important idea that is sometimes a little tricky to get our heads around at first. Suppose we get the following 'message' on our mobile phone: ZXXTRQ NJOPW TRP. This message is 16 symbols long and so, doing the usual calculation, we get an information content of $16\log_2 27$ bits. But you say: 'Hang on a minute: that is absurd since I have not received any message at all. There is no information in this gibberish.' Well of course, the message might be in code, it might have a hidden message. Let us assume that this is not the case. What then? We have now reached the fact that 'information' in the sense we have just been discussing has actually got nothing to do with 'meaning' at all. We call it *syntactic information*.

At first sight this seems counter-intuitive from the perspective of our daily experience; and so it needs spelling out in more detail. Suppose that you are told to expect a 'message' on your mobile phone. You are also told that there are four possible symbols you may receive ($\sim$ # * ^) and that the message will be five symbols long. You look at the screen and what you see is: ^ ^ # ~ *. How much 'information' have you received? Well, none in the sense that you have no idea what it means; indeed, you do not know if it means anything at all. But in the syntactic sense you have received information. There are four possible symbols. So the probability you will get a particular one of them is ¼ and the information supplied by each symbol received is two bits. The total 'message' consisting of five symbols contains ten bits. Putting it another way: if we count up how many possible 'messages' (that is strings of five symbols) you might receive, we see that it is 2^{10}. You now know what the message is (not what it means!). You did not know before. So, in that sense, you have received information.

Think again of everyday electronic communications across a channel, for example, an ordinary telephone line. At any given moment various kinds of 'information' may be flowing down it: voice communication, fax communication, data communication – all kinds of streams of electronic 'symbols'. Some of it will carry meaning for some people and not for others (for instance, a person speaking Chinese will convey no information in the semantic sense to someone who speaks no Chinese), and some of it could be strings of random symbols representing noise on the line generated by random electronic effects, carrying no meaning whatsoever.

Now a communications engineer is not interested in the meaning of what is going through the channel. She is not really interested in the specific sequences that are being transmitted but rather in things such as:

the capacity of the channel – how many symbols (of whatever kind) can be sent through it in a second; the reliability of the channel – what is the probability that a symbol will be sent in error, for example, because of noise on the channel; the possibility of error correction etc. And these things affect all of us – many of us have been frustrated with the slowness of data communication in homes that have no broadband access.

So measuring syntactic information is very important and the theory associated with it is called the *Shannon Theory of Information*, after Claude Shannon who developed it and proved certain mathematical results about the capacity of a noisy channel that are the foundation of the theory of communication upon which our society depends today.

Let's look at another everyday example just to make sure we have got the idea. You go into a library and ask for a book on nephrology. The library assistant may never have heard of nephrology. But, as a string of symbols, the word 'nephrology' contains $10 \log_2 27$ bits of information and if you give the library assistant those bits of information she can type them into her computer index system and come up with the fact that you should look in the section of the library labelled MedSci 46, say, where you will find three books on the subject. That is, she acts as a 'channel' to communicate the information to her index system even though, for her, the symbol string 'nephrology' has no semantic connotation at all.[1]

In this example, the word 'nephrology' is treated by the library assistant at the purely syntactic level – she neither knows nor needs to know what the word means. The only information she needs is the string of letters of which it is composed: she simply treats the word as a meaningless string of letters from an alphabet. However for you as a medical doctor the word 'nephrology' has a meaning – it conveys not only syntactic information but *semantic information* ('semantic' derives from the Greek word for a sign, hence 'semiotics' meaning the theory of signs).

Measuring semantic information is a much more difficult problem to get a grip of mathematically and no successful way has yet been discovered. That this is hardly surprising has to do with the well-known fact that the meaning of a text is highly dependent on its context. If you see me receiving on my cell phone the message YES you may well guess that it is the answer to a question I have asked, but you will not know whether that question is 'Have you a ticket for the football game tonight?' or 'Will you marry me?'. The meaning of the message just cannot be determined without prior knowledge of the context. In other words a great deal more information is necessary to interpret any given piece of information.

DNA and information

Now let us apply some of this thinking to molecular biology. Think of the string of 'letters' that we find in the chemical alphabet of the DNA molecule. Suppose you are a molecular biologist and know (something about) what the string of letters 'means' in the sense that you can divide them up into genes and say what proteins are coded for, etc. That is, for you, the string has a semantic dimension. For you DNA exhibits precisely the same kind of specified complexity as language since the order of the letters in a gene specifies the order of the sequence of amino acids in the protein.[2]

But not for me: I see the string as nothing but a lengthy list of 'meaningless' symbols ACGGTCAGGTTCTA... But it still makes perfect sense to talk of my knowing the information content of the symbol string in the syntactical or Shannon sense. Indeed, in spite of the fact that I do not understand the 'meaning' of the string, I can work out precisely how much syntactic information you need to give me in order that I can reproduce the string accurately. The genetic alphabet consists of four letters so each letter you read out to me (or send me by computer) involves two bits of information. Thus, for example, the DNA in a human genome which is roughly 3.5 billion letters long contains about 7 billion bits of information. If I am given them I can write out the DNA without having any idea whatsoever of the 'meaning' of what I have written.

A very important aspect of research on the genome is that of finding specific patterns that may be repeated in a given genome or of finding specific sequences that are common to several genomes. Now the reason for looking for a specific sequence may well be motivated by semantic considerations, but the actual computer search for it in the large database that is formed by the genome proceeds at the level of syntactical information.

Complexity

Thus far in this chapter we have not mentioned the concept of complexity. However, we can see at once that saying that the human genome contains 7 billion bits of information is giving us some idea of its complexity. But only some. Think, for example, of the following binary string: 001001001001001001001001... Let us assume that it goes on like this to total 6 billion digits (we shall want a number divisible by three). Then we can see that, from our perspective so far, it contains 6 billion bits of information. Is it therefore (nearly) as complex as the human genome?

Clearly not. For we see at once that it consists of a repeated pattern – the triple 001 is repeated again and again. Thus, in a sense, all of the information contained in the string is contained in the statement 'repeat the triple 001 two billion times'. This mechanical process of repetition is an example of what mathematicians call an algorithm[3] – the kind of process that computer programmes are designed to implement. In this case we could, for example, write a simple programme as follows: 'For n = 1 to 2 billion, write 001. Stop.' Now I needed only 39 keystrokes to type this programme and it is at once obvious that if we think of 39 as the 'length' of the programme, this gives us a much more accurate impression of the amount of information contained in the string of binary digits than does its actual length of 6 billion digits.

Another example that will convey this idea intuitively is as follows: consider the string of letters ILOVEYOUILOVEYOUILOVEYOUILOVEYOU… and suppose the string contains 2 billion repetitions of the three words I LOVE YOU. Clearly the information (in the semantic sense this time) contained in the string is already contained in the first three words (although it might well be argued that the repetition carries emphasis!). In any case the full syntactic information is given by the programme 'For n = 1 to 2 billion, write ILOVEYOU. Stop' and we could therefore get a much better measure of the information content simply by counting the number of bits of syntactic information contained in the (short) programme rather than in the (long) text.

Algorithmic information theory

This 'compressing' a given string of symbols (binary digits, letters, words etc.) into a (much) shorter space by means of a computer programme is the fundamental idea behind what is called the algorithmic theory of information. The word 'algorithm' derives from the name of the mathematician Mohammed Ibn-Musa Al-Khwarizmi, who worked in the famous House of Wisdom in Baghdad in the ninth century. An algorithm is an effective procedure, a way of getting something done in a finite number of steps. For example the formula $x = (-b \pm \sqrt{(b^2 - 4ac)})/2a$ gives us an effective procedure for calculating the roots of the quadratic equation $ax^2 + bx + c = 0$, where a, b, c are numbers. It is, therefore, an algorithm. Similarly, computer programmes (software) are algorithms that enable the computer hardware to do its information processing. In general, computer programmes will involve many algorithms, each directing its own bit of effective computation. Algorithmic information theory (AIT) was developed by Kolmogorov and Chaitin as a way of getting a grip on complexity, in particular, on the information content or complexity of a specific sequence, by considering the size of algorithm needed to generate that sequence.[4]

According to AIT, then, the information content of X (where X is, for example, a string of binary digits, or a string of ordinary digits or letters in any alphabet, etc.) is the size H(X) in bits of the shortest programme that can generate X.

Now consider a second string generated by a monkey playing with a computer keyboard: Mtl3(#8HJD[;ELSN29X1TNSP]\@... And suppose that it, too, is 6 billion letters long, i.e. the same length as the strings just considered. Then it is clear that, since the string is essentially random, any programme written to generate it will be of essentially the same length as the string itself. That is, this string is algorithmically incompressible. Indeed, algorithmic incompressibility is a very good way of defining what randomness means. Also, this string is maximally complex on the basis of our criterion of complexity.

Finally, if we take as our third string the first 6 billion letters of the books on the shelves of a library of English books, then, although we might achieve a little algorithmic compression, it will be negligible compared with the length of the string. That is, this string is just as algorithmically incompressible as the second string (and so, from a mathematical point of view, it is random). By the same token it is very complex. Yet its complexity is somehow different from that of the string generated by the monkey. For it had no meaning that we could read. This third string by contrast contains semantic information – we can understand the meaning of the words in the books. And the reason that the third string has meaning for us is that we have *independently* learned English and so we recognize the words formed by the letters in the string. Such a string is not only complex but also exhibits what is called *specified complexity*, the kind of special complexity associated with language. This term *specified complexity* was first used by Leslie Orgel in his book *The Origins of Life*[5] and also by Paul Davies in *The Fifth Miracle*,[6] but in neither place is it made precise. It has been investigated in a thoroughgoing fashion by mathematician William Dembski in *The Design Inference: Eliminating Chance through Small Probabilities*.[7]

Now there clearly are great differences between the highly compressible string represented by the crystal type order of our first example above and each of the virtually incompressible strings of the second two examples. Those differences make the kind of ordering processes exhibited in Rayleigh-Bénard convection or the Belousov-Zhabotinski reaction unlikely to be of much relevance to the origin of life.

Again, the fact that strings are algorithmically incompressible means (by definition, in fact) that they cannot arise as an 'emergent' property of some relatively simple algorithmic process, in the same way as beautiful fractal pictures can arise from quite simple equations. There has been much fascination with the intricate self-symmetry of the famous Mandelbrot set, computer-generated images of which adorn many a coffee-table book. Yet this set is traceable back to a relatively simple mathematical function of the form $f(z) = z^2 + k$ of the complex variable z. Can we not say that the complex fractal 'emerges' from the simplicity of this equation?

In one sense it does, that is, if we are thinking of the fact that we can use the equation to plot the fractal curve (on a computer screen, say). But we need to be careful, even here. For, if we ask how the image on the screen 'emerges' from the equation we find that there is a lot more involved than simply writing down the Mandelbrot equation. Many different iterations of the function must be calculated; colours must be assigned to corresponding pixels on the screen according to whether the trajectory of a given iteration satisfies certain properties (like local-boundedness), so that each trajectory has to be checked for this property. Thus the 'emergent' picture is only derived from the simple equation by the cost of a considerable additional input of information in terms of programming effort and intelligently designed hardware. It does not come 'free'.

A more obvious argument applies to the illustration of emergence offered by Dawkins in a public lecture in Oxford[8] that we mentioned earlier. Dawkins claimed that the capacity to do word-processing is an 'emergent' property of computers. It is; but only at the expense of the input of the information contained in an intelligently designed software package like Microsoft Word. One thing is certain: no blind-watchmaker process gives rise to the word-processing capacity of a digital computer.

To fix in our minds the importance of the difference between the second and third kinds of complexity, we give another example. If ink spills on paper a complex event occurs in the sense that, of all possible inkblots, the chance of getting just that one is infinitesimally small. But the complexity of the inkblot is unspecified. On the other hand, if someone writes a message in ink on paper we get specified complexity. Incidentally, we ascribe the inkblot to chance and the writing to intelligent agency without a moment's thought, do we not?

Now let us apply some of these ideas to the genome. The A's, C's, G's and T's on the DNA molecule may occupy any given position and so they are capable of representing expressions that are essentially algorithmically incompressible and so, we emphasize, from a mathematical point of view, they are random. We should not of course think that this mathematical randomness implies that the DNA sequences are completely arbitrary. Far from it. Indeed only a very tiny proportion of all possible sequences on the

DNA molecule will exhibit the specified complexity of biologically significant molecules, very much in the same way as only a very small proportion of all possible sequences of letters in the alphabet, or indeed words of any human language, exhibit the specified complexity of meaningful statements in the words of that language. For example, Professor Derek Bickerton gives us an interesting insight into linguistics by explaining how even a single sentence presents a prodigious problem: 'Try to rearrange any ordinary sentence consisting of ten words. There are, in principle, exactly 3,628,800 ways in which you could do this, but for the first sentence of this [quote] only one of them gives a correct and meaningful result. That means 3,628,799 of them are ungrammatical.' Bickerton then asks the obvious question: 'How did we learn this? Certainly, no parent or teacher ever told us. The only way in which we can know it is by possessing, as it were, some recipe for how to construct sentences, a recipe so complex and exhaustive that it automatically rules out all 3,628,799 wrong ways of putting together a ten word sentence and allows only the right one. But since such a recipe must apply to all sentences, not just the example given, that recipe will, for every language, rule out more ungrammatical sentences than there are atoms in the cosmos.'[9] But we must not get diverted into the fascinating (and indeed related issue) of the origin of the human language faculty!

To give some idea of the numbers involved in the biological situation we note that the smallest proteins possessing biological function that we know of involve at least 100 amino acids and so the DNA molecules corresponding to them have as many as 10^{130} sequence alternatives, only a minute proportion of which will have biological significance. The set of all possible sequences is therefore unimaginably large. Moreover, under equilibrium conditions, since there are no chemical affinities between the bases, it follows that all sequences of a given length exist with essentially the same probability. This fact, incidentally, entails that the probability of a purely random origin for a specified sequence of biological significance is so small as to be negligible.

And that is not all. Proteins exhibit a high degree of molecular sensitivity in the sense that even the substitution of a single amino acid in a viable protein can mean catastrophic failure.[10] It could therefore be argued that the molecular biology of the cell shows the same order of fine-tuning that we saw earlier in connection with physics and cosmology.

The key point here is that a DNA sequence that actually codes for a functional protein *at one and the same time* exhibits the specified complexity necessary for it to code for that protein and is consequently algorithmically incompressible, and thus random from the mathematical point of view. Paul Davies writes: 'Can specific randomness be the guaranteed product of a deterministic, mechanical, law-like process, like a primordial soup left to the mercy of familiar laws of physics and chemistry? No it couldn't. No known law of nature could achieve this.'[11] Elsewhere he writes: 'We conclude that biologically relevant macromolecules simultaneously possess two vital properties: randomness and extreme specificity. A chaotic process could possibly achieve the former property but would have a negligible probability of achieving the latter.'

His next statement is fascinating: 'At first sight this appears to make the genome an impossible object, unattainable by either known laws or chance.' Quite so. Nevertheless Davies asserts: 'Clearly Darwinian evolution by variation and natural selection has what is needed to generate both randomness (information richness) and tightly specified biological functionality in the same system'.[12] But this is begging the question: for precisely what is at issue is whether natural processes of any kind (including Darwinian evolution, of course) have got that capacity, or whether the very thing that his argumentation is piling up evidence for is that they have not got it. Indeed, since the whole passage is about biogenesis, Davies appears to contradict what he has just said by adding: 'The problem as far as biogenesis is concerned is that Darwinism can only operate when life (of some sort) is already going. *It cannot explain how life starts in the first place*' (italics mine).[13]

But what other possibility is there beyond chance and necessity? Well, as Sherlock Holmes might have told us, if chance and necessity, either separately or together, are not capable of biogenesis, then we must consider the possibility that a third factor was involved. That third possibility is the input of information.

This suggestion will be met by a chorus of protest that we are not talking about a detective story and that it is in any case anti-scientific and intellectually lazy to propose what is essentially an 'intelligence of the gaps', that is, a 'God of the gaps'-type solution. Now although the charge must be taken seriously – it is, after all, possible for a theist to be intellectually lazy and say in effect 'I can't explain it, therefore God did it' – it is important to say that sauce for the goose is sauce for the gander. It is also very easy to say 'evolution did it' when one has not got the faintest idea how, or has simply cobbled up a speculative just-so story with no evidential basis. Indeed, as we have seen, a materialist *has* to say that natural processes were solely responsible, since, in his or her book, there is no admissible alternative. As a result it is just as easy to end up with an 'evolution of the gaps' as with a 'God of the gaps'. One might even say that it is easier to end up with an 'evolution of the gaps' than a 'God of the gaps' since the former suggestion is likely to attract far less criticism than the former.

To make sure this point is not forgotten we record a warning by an expert on the origin of life, Nobel Laureate physicist Robert Laughlin, whose research is on those properties of matter that make life possible (and who is not an advocate of intelligent design): 'Much of present day biological knowledge is ideological. A key symptom of ideological thinking is the explanation that has no implications and cannot be tested. I call such logical dead ends anti-theories because they have exactly the opposite effect of real theories: they stop thinking rather than stimulate it. Evolution by natural selection, for instance, which Darwin conceived as a great theory has lately come to function as an anti-theory called upon to cover up embarrassing experimental shortcomings and legitimize findings that are at best questionable and at worst not even wrong. Your protein defies the laws of mass action – evolution did it! Your complicated mess of chemical reactions turns into a chicken – evolution! The human brain works on logical principles no computer can emulate? Evolution is the cause!'[14]

How can we, then, avoid the charge of intellectual laziness or 'God of the gaps' thinking? For it does seem at first sight that the charge might be justified. In order to explain the next step in the argument we turn to the realm of pure mathematics. If a conjecture (say, the famous conjecture from antiquity that any angle can be trisected using only a straight-edge and compasses) has been thought about for many years and all attempts to prove it true have failed, then, though mathematicians will not necessarily give up trying to prove it true, they may also mount an attempt to see if it is *provably false* – as indeed turned out to be the case with the trisection of the angle, as all students of pure mathematics (should) know.

In other words, when mathematicians fail to prove a conjecture true, they do not necessarily either give up their efforts or keep going doggedly on in the same direction as before: they may well decide alternatively (or additionally) to mount a *mathematical* attempt to *prove* that the conjecture is false. Now it seems to me that this is precisely the kind of thinking that we need to introduce in the physical and biological sciences in connection with the question we are discussing. I said we need to introduce it. That is not quite correct. Not only is it already here, but most of us are aware of it – at least in the physical sciences.

I refer, of course, to the seemingly endless search for perpetual motion machines. Every year articles are written by people who think they have discovered the secret of perpetual motion by inventing devices that will remain in continual motion once they have been started without any additional input of energy.[15] But such articles are not taken seriously by scientists familiar with the fundamentals of thermodynamics. In fact most of them are never even read, and that is not because the scientists who receive them are intellectually lazy and not prepared to consider new arguments. It is because scientists believe that there is strong evidence to support the law of conservation of energy. This law is a *proscriptive* law and it directly implies that perpetual motion machines are impossible. Consequently, scientists know that if they did examine the detail of any putative perpetual motion machine, they would invariably discover that it would eventually need an injection of energy from outside to keep it running. Hence, and this is the key point for our purposes, it is *science* that has shown that perpetual motion machines do not exist. Intellectual laziness does not come into it. Indeed, it would be intellectually perverse to reject this argument and keep on searching for perpetual motion.

Why should we not apply the same kind of logic to the question of the origin of genetic information? Might not the difficulties involved in all attempts so far to give a naturalistic explanation for the origin of genetic information be sufficient reason to expend at least some of our intellectual energy enquiring if there is something like an information-theoretic parallel to the law of energy conservation? Such an investigation might lead to *scientific* evidence against the validity of any explanation of biogenesis that did not involve an input of information from an external intelligent source.

Admittedly, the issues at stake here are clearly of a different order of magnitude than those involved in the existence of perpetual motion machines. For, if there was adequate scientific reason for thinking biogenesis cannot be adequately explained without factoring in an information input then interest would inevitably focus on finding out what the source of that information is. But it should be noted that the latter is a completely separate issue – however hard it may be to keep the two apart in our thinking. Whether or not the source of the information can be determined is logically irrelevant to the question of whether an external input of information is necessary. After all, if we went to Mars and discovered a long sequence of piles of titanium cubes receding towards the Martian horizon where the piles each consisted of a prime number of cubes and the piles were in the correct ascending order 1,2,3,5,7,11,13,17,19,... then we would surely immediately conclude that this arrangement involved an intelligent input even if we had no idea whatsoever of the nature of the intelligence behind it. But if we discovered something much more complex – say a DNA molecule – then naturalistic scientists would presumably conclude that it was a result of chance and necessity!

Is information conserved?

Our question now reads: Is there any scientific evidence that information is conserved in some meaningful sense of the term? If the answer turned out to be positive, then a lot of valuable research time and effort in connection with the origin of life could be saved by giving up the fruitless search for an information-theoretic equivalent of a perpetual motion machine.

We should also observe that it is no longer adequate to object to machine-type language when referring to organisms. Nowadays, as we have repeatedly seen, machine language is ubiquitous in molecular biology for the simple reason that proteins, flagella, cells etc. *are* molecular machines. They may well be *more* than machines but, at the level of their information processing capability, they are certainly (digital processing) machines.

This carries with it the implication, already exploited scientifically in myriad different ways in recent years, that biological machines are open to mathematical analysis in general and information-theoretic analysis in particular. It is to this analysis that we now therefore turn to pick up ideas on the question of whether molecular machines (of whatever kind) can generate novel information. Leonard Brillouin, in his classic work on information theory, has no doubt where the answer lies. He says that 'A machine does not create any new information, but it performs a very valuable transformation of known information.'[16]

Twenty years later, no less a scientist than Nobel Laureate Peter Medawar wrote: 'No process of logical reasoning – no mere act of mind or computer-programmable operation – can enlarge the information content of the axioms and premises or observation statements from which it proceeds.'[17] He deduced from this observation that some kind of law of conservation of information must hold. Medawar did not attempt any demonstration of such a law, contenting himself with challenging his readers 'to find a logical operation that will add to the information content of any utterance whatsoever'. He did, however, give a mathematical example to illustrate what he meant. He points out that Euclid's famous geometric theorems are simply a 'spelling out, or bringing out into the open, of information already contained in the axioms and postulates'. After all, he adds, philosophers and logicians since the time of Bacon had no difficulty in perceiving that the process of deduction merely makes explicit information that is already there; it does not create any new information whatsoever.

Putting it another way, the theorems of Euclid are reducible to his axioms and postulates, a circumstance that should remind us of our discussion in Chapter 3 of the limits to mathematical reduction imposed by Gödel's Theorem. And, indeed, Gödel, who ranks as one of the greatest mathematicians of the twentieth century, indicated that he also thought that some kind of conservation of information was characteristic of living things. He said that 'the complexity of living bodies has to be present in the material [from which they are derived] or in the laws [governing their formation]. In particular, the materials forming the organs, if they are governed by mechanical laws, have to be of the same order of complexity as the living body'. Gödel's own formulation (in the third person) runs as follows: 'More generally, Gödel believes that mechanism in biology is a prejudice of our time which will be disproved. In this case, one disproval, in Gödel's opinion, will consist in a mathematical theorem to the effect that the formation within geological times of a human body by the laws of physics (or any other laws of a similar nature), starting from a random distribution of the elementary particles and the field, is as unlikely as the separation by chance of the atmosphere into its components.'[18]

The fascinating thing here is that Gödel expected that there would one day be a mathematical proof of this – in other words that mathematics would contribute decisively to the resolution of the biological problem of the origin of information. There is a delightful irony here. For it was Gödel himself who blazed the trail for subsequent developments on this very problem. Using the theory of algorithmic information, mathematician Gregory Chaitin found proofs of even stronger results related to Gödel's that bear on the question of whether algorithms generate novel information and hence, by implication, on biogenesis.

The first thing to note is that it is well established that there is *some* kind of informational limit to what algorithms can accomplish. In an important work Gregory Chaitin has established that you cannot prove that a specific sequence of numbers has a complexity greater than the programme required to generate it.[19]

But Chaitin's work has further implications. Leading origin of life researcher Bernd-Olaf Küppers deduces from it the following interesting consequence: 'In sequences that carry semantic information the information is clearly coded irreducibly in the sense that it is not further compressible. Therefore there do not exist any algorithms that generate meaningful sequences where those algorithms are shorter than the sequences they generate.'[20] Küppers points out that this is, of course, a conjecture, since the very work of Chaitin he is discussing shows that it is impossible to prove, for a given sequence and algorithm, that there is no shorter algorithm that could generate the sequence.

Chaitin's arguments are based on the concept of a Turing machine. This is an abstract mathematical construct named after its inventor, the brilliant mathematician Alan Turing, who worked at Bletchley Park in the UK during the Second World War and led the team that cracked the famous Enigma code. The upshot of Chaitin's work is to make plausible the idea that no Turing machine can generate any information that does not either belong to its input or its own informational structure.

Why is this important? Because, according to the Church-Turing Thesis, any computational device whatsoever (past, present or future) can be simulated by a Turing machine. On this basis, any result obtained for Turing machines can be at once translated into the digital world. One implication of this might then be that no molecular device is capable of generating any information that does not either belong to its input or its own informational structure.

More recently, William Dembski has argued for a non-deterministic law of conservation of information in the sense that, although natural processes involving only chance and necessity can effectively transmit complex specified information, they cannot generate it.[21]

Much interesting and difficult work remains to be done in this developing area. However, at least we are already in a position to have a shot at testing these ideas on origin of life simulations. For, if information is conserved in some sense, then we might logically expect that any origin of life simulations that claim to get information 'for free' by purely natural processes must somehow, in spite of their claim, be smuggling that information in from outside. Thus, if we can establish the latter, then we at least have a plausibility argument that an information input is necessary for the origin of life.

In light of this we shall now try to analyze one of the most famous attempts to simulate the genesis of the specified complexity of DNA by means of natural processes. Bring on the typing monkeys!

The monkey machine

Arthur Dent to Ford Prefect: 'Ford!' he said, 'there's an infinite number of monkeys outside who want to talk to us about this script for *Hamlet* they've worked out.'

Douglas Adams

'You don't need to be a mathematician or a physicist to calculate that an eye or a haemoglobin molecule would take from here to infinity to self-assemble by sheer higgledy-piggledy luck.'

Richard Dawkins

Typing monkeys

Richard Dawkins contends that unguided natural processes can account for the origin of biological information – no external source of information is necessary. In *The Blind Watchmaker* he uses an analogy whose roots lie in an argument alleged to have been used by T.H. Huxley in his famous debate with Wilberforce in Oxford in 1860. Huxley is said[1] to have argued that apes typing randomly, and granted long life, unlimited supplies of paper and endless energy, would eventually type out one of Shakespeare's poems or even a whole book, by chance. Well, it is hardly likely that Huxley said such a thing for the simple reason that typewriters were not available on the market until 1874.[2] But no matter. It is a nice story and, within the limit now set for the age of the universe, let alone that set for the earth, it is easy to see that it is mathematical nonsense. The eminent mathematician Gian-Carlo Rota in a book on probability (unfinished at the time of his death) wrote: 'If the monkey could type one keystroke every nanosecond, the expected waiting time until the monkey types out *Hamlet* is so long that the estimated age of the universe is insignificant by comparison... this is not a practical method for writing plays.'

The calculations are not hard to do. For example, Russell Grigg, in his article 'Could Monkeys Type the 23rd Psalm?',[3] calculates that if a monkey types one key at random per second, the average time to produce the word 'the' is 34.72 hours. To produce something as long as the 23rd Psalm (a short Hebrew poem made up of 603 letters, verse numbers and spaces) would take on average around 10^{1017} years. The current estimate of the age of the universe lies somewhere between four and fifteen times 10^9 years. According to Dawkins' definition, this calculation certainly makes the 23rd Psalm a complex object: it possesses 'some quality, specifiable in advance, that is highly unlikely to have been acquired by random chance alone'.[4]

Since 1 July 2003 there has been a monkey typewriting random number generator simulator operating which simulates monkeys typing one key per second. They started with 100 monkeys and this number *doubles every few days* – and of course there is an unlimited supply of bananas. The current record is 24 consecutive letters from Shakespeare's *Henry IV* produced in around 10^{40} monkey years (the age of the universe is estimated at less than 10^{11} years)[5].

Calculations of this kind have long since persuaded most scientists – Dawkins included – that purely random processes cannot account for the origin of complex information-laden systems. Dawkins cites Isaac Asimov's estimate of the probability of randomly assembling a haemoglobin molecule from amino acids.[6] Such a molecule consists of four chains of amino acids twisted together. Each of the chains consists of 146 amino acids and there are 20 different kinds of amino acid found in living beings. The number of possible ways of arranging these 20 in a chain 146 links long is 20^{146}, which is about 10^{190}. (There are only about 10^{70} protons in the entire universe.)

We remind the reader of Dawkins unequivocal conclusion: 'It is grindingly, creakingly, crashingly obvious that, if Darwinism were really a theory of chance, it couldn't work. You don't need to be a mathematician or a physicist to calculate that an eye or a haemoglobin molecule would take from here to infinity to self-assemble by sheer higgledy-piggledy luck.'[7]

Sir Fred Hoyle and astrophysicist Chandra Wickramasinghe share Dawkins' view – on the capabilities of pure chance processes, that is. 'No matter how large the environment one considers, life cannot have had a random beginning. Troops of monkeys thundering away at random on typewriters could not produce the works of Shakespeare, for the practical reason that the whole observable universe is not large enough to contain the necessary monkey hordes, the necessary typewriters and certainly not the waste paper baskets required for the deposition of wrong attempts.

The same is true for living material. The likelihood of the spontaneous formation of life from inanimate matter is one to a number with 40,000 noughts after it... It is big enough to bury Darwin and the whole theory of evolution. There was no primeval soup, neither on this planet nor on any other, and if the beginnings of life were not random, they must therefore have been the product of purposeful intelligence.'[8,9]

Is Mount Improbable climbable?

All seem agreed, then, that the chance origin of the constituents of life seems to be dead in the primeval soup. So how can the origin of such complexity be explained? Dawkins attempts to solve the difficulty of the origin of systems whose highly specified complexity rules out a chance origin by 'breaking the improbability up into small manageable parts, smearing out the luck needed, going round the back of Mount Improbable and crawling up the gentle slopes, inch by million year inch'.[10]

Let's try, then, to follow Dawkins up his mountain, and try to reduce the improbability of producing, say, a haemoglobin molecule (described above) by breaking the process up into small steps. Let us say 1,000 steps to the top of the mountain, and let us look at a very simplified situation where there are only two choices at every step. One leads to something viable, and the other does not; so that natural selection will eliminate it; and each step is independent. What is the probability of finding the right path up the mountain? 1 in 2^{1000}, that is about 1 in 10^{300}. But this is smaller than the probability of the random assembly of the haemoglobin molecule in the first place. Dawkins' mountain climb is improbable in more senses than one.

Nobel Prize-winning physicist, Brian Josephson of Cambridge, points out another hidden assumption in Dawkins' attempt to climb his mountain: 'In such books as *The Blind Watchmaker*, a crucial part of the argument concerns whether there exists a continuous path, leading from the origins of life to man, each step of which is both favoured by natural selection, and small enough to have happened by chance. It appears to be presented as a matter of logical necessity that such a path exists, but actually there is no such logical necessity; rather, commonly made assumptions in evolution require the existence of such a path.'[11]

The only way out of the probabilistic impasse is to try to drastically increase the probabilities, and this is precisely what Dawkins does in *The Blind Watchmaker*. He claims that the origin of life was far from a purely chance process although, according to him, it must have begun with something simple enough to have arisen by chance. But then, instead of having a purely one-step 'sieving' process, like that of jumbling together all the amino acid constituents of haemoglobin and hoping to get that molecule by chance, he suggests that the process was a kind of cumulative sieving or 'selection'[12] in which the results of one sieving process are fed into the next. According to Dawkins this introduces a measure of law-likeness into the process so that it can be thought of as a combination of chance and necessity. To illustrate this, he uses a computer simulation of a variant of Huxley's typing monkeys analogy and gives us an algorithm based on it.[13] He now imagines that the monkeys have a target phrase, his chosen example being the Shakespearean phrase 'Methinks it is like a weasel', which is taken from *Hamlet*. This phrase is 28 'letters' long (we count spaces as 'letters' and we take the alphabet to consist of 26 letters and one space). So the situation is that we have 28 monkeys (one corresponding to each letter of the target sequence) sitting in a row and typing.[14] Each monkey, therefore, has a target letter in the target phrase. We first calculate the probability of them producing the target phrase by random typing. The chance of getting the first letter of the phrase right by random typing (the analogue of a mutation) is 1 in 27: two letters right 1 in 27 x 27, etc. So the probability of getting it right by random hitting of keys at one attempt is 1 in 27^{28}, that is, approximately 1 in 10^{40} – again unimaginably small, less than one in a trillion-trillion-trillion. To put it another way, the target phrase is a particular isolated point in a space of a trillion-trillion-trillion other points – a point that we have to find by some efficient process.

Let us now work out the probability of hitting the target, that is, landing on that point in n attempts. This is best calculated as follows. Consider the first attempt. The probability of the monkeys all getting it wrong is $1 - 1/(27^{28})$. And so in n attempts the probability of getting it wrong is $(1 - 1/(27^{28}))^n$. Hence the probability of getting it right in n attempts is $1 - (1 - 1/(27^{28}))^n$. If we take n to be a billion, this probability is still incredibly small – approximately 1 in 10^{31} – and this is so even though the sequence of letters under consideration is trivial compared with the length of a mammalian genome (in the human it is over 3 billion letters).

What, then, is Dawkins' purported solution to the problem of increasing these tiny probabilities to more manageable proportions? It is this. Each time a monkey hits a letter, the letter it types is compared with its target letter – a highly non-random process. This comparison, of course, has to be done by some mechanism, a computer (or by a Head Monkey, as mathematician David Berlinski delightfully suggests). If the monkey has typed its target letter the comparison mechanism retains that letter – another highly non-random process – and the monkey stops typing, its job done. Otherwise the monkey is allowed to go on randomly typing until it gets its target letter.

The net result of this is that the target phrase is reached very rapidly indeed – in 43 steps in the case of Dawkins' actual version of the simulation. So, what in the pure chance situation would have only a chance of 1 in roughly 10^{31} of occurring in a billion attempts, now takes only 43. We note that Dawkins' model involves both chance (the typing monkeys) and necessity (the law-like algorithm that does the comparing of an attempt with the target phrase). His algorithm measures what is called the 'fitness' of a solution by calculating the difference or 'distance' of that solution from the target phrase.

We have now reached the heart of Dawkins' argument. Remember what it claims to show – that natural selection – a blind, mindless, unguided process – has the power to produce biological information. But it shows nothing of the kind. Dawkins has solved his problem, only by introducing the two very things he explicitly wishes at all costs to avoid. In his book he tells us that evolution is blind, and without a goal. What, then, does he mean by introducing a target phrase? A target phrase is a precise goal which, according to Dawkins himself, is a profoundly un-Darwinian concept. And how could blind evolution not only see that target, but also compare an attempt with it, in order to select it, if it is nearer than the previous one? Dawkins tells us that evolution is mindless. What, then, does he mean by introducing two mechanisms, each of which bears every evidence of the input of an intelligent mind – a mechanism that compares each attempt with the target phrase, and a mechanism which preserves a successful attempt? And, strangest of all, the very information that the mechanisms are supposed to produce is apparently already contained somewhere within the organism, whose genesis he claims to be simulating by his process. The argument is entirely circular.

It should be noted that it is this feature that distinguishes Dawkins' mechanism from an evolutionary algorithm. Evolutionary algorithms are well known from engineering and other applications as excellent, well-tried ways of finding a solution to a complex problem. For instance, Rechenberg[15] demonstrated an evolutionary strategy whereby the electrical resistance of a complex system could be minimized by successive applications of random variations. At each 'evolutionary step' the systems parameters are varied arbitrarily and the resistance measured. If the variation leads to increased resistance it is reversed; if to decreased resistance it is retained and used as the starting position for the next step. Such an evolutionary strategy assumes that a measurable parameter exists which one wishes to optimize – for instance, one might wish to minimize electrical resistance. With the objective of minimizing the resistance, the model tests all possible forms reached by chance variation and eventually produces the previously unknown optimal form.

Thus, and this is the important point here, at the beginning of the process the solution is not known. In the Dawkins scenario the exact opposite is the case, as we have just seen. So it would be rather naive to argue that Dawkins' simulation is plausible because of the success of evolutionary algorithms.

Indeed, mathematician David Berlinski in a much-discussed article rather trenchantly comments: 'The entire exercise is... an achievement in self-deception. A target phrase? Iterations which resemble the target? A computer or Head monkey that measures the distance between failure and success? If things are sightless how is the target represented, and how is the distance between randomly generated phrases and the targets assessed? And by whom? And the Head Monkey? What of him? The mechanism of deliberate design, purged by Darwinian theory on the level of the organism, has reappeared in the description of natural selection itself, a vivid example of what Freud meant by the return of the repressed.'[16]

Oddly, Dawkins admits that his analogy is misleading, precisely because cumulative natural selection is 'blind to a goal'. He claims that the programme can be modified to take care of this point – a claim that, not surprisingly, is nowhere substantiated, since it cannot be. Indeed such a claim, even if it were true, would serve to establish the exact opposite of what Dawkins believes, since modifying a programme involves applying yet more intelligence to an intelligently designed artefact – the original programme. Dawkins' more sophisticated biomorph programme – a computer package in which the computer generates certain shapes to be displayed on the screen, which the computer operator can select for their elegance, etc., leading to increasingly complex patterns called biomorphs – similarly involves an intelligently designed filtering principle. Remove the filtering principle, the target and the Head Monkey, and you end up with gibberish. For their plausibility, then, Dawkins' analogies depend on introducing to his model the very features whose existence in the real world he denies.

What Dawkins has really shown is that sufficiently complex systems such as languages of any type, including the genetic code of DNA, are not explicable without the pre-injection of the information sought into the system.

A simpler example of what is going on here is provided by a self-winding watch. Such a device uses the random movements of wrist and arm to wind itself up. How does it do that? An intelligent watchmaker has designed a ratchet that allows a heavy flywheel to move in only one direction. Therefore, it effectively selects those movements of wrist and arm that cause the flywheel to move, while blocking others. The ratchet is a result of intelligent design. Such a mechanism, according to Dawkins, cannot be Darwinian. His blind watchmaker has no foresight. To quote Berlinski again: 'The Darwinian mechanism neither anticipates nor remembers. It gives no directions and makes no choices. What is unacceptable in evolutionary theory, what is strictly forbidden, is the appearance of a force with the power to survey time, a force that conserves a point or a property because it will be useful [like the ratchet in the watch]. Such a force is no longer Darwinian. How would a blind force know such a thing? And by what means could future usefulness be transmitted to the present?'

Irreducibly complex machines

But there are yet more problems with Dawkins' analogy. Especially if we try to apply it to the origin of one of the irreducibly complex machines described by Michael Behe, which we discussed earlier. The problem here is best illustrated by Elliott Sober's version of Dawkins' analogy, in which he imagines a combination lock that can be opened only by the combination METHINKSITISAWEASEL. The combination lock is composed of [19] discs placed side by side, each containing the 26 letters of the alphabet and equipped with a window through which a single letter of the alphabet can be seen. We imagine that the discs are randomly spun and a disc is stopped by some mechanism when the letter in the viewing window matches the target combination. The remaining discs are randomly spun and the process repeated. So the system is essentially that of Dawkins.

Michael Behe points out that the analogy 'purports to be an analogy for natural selection which requires a function. But what function is there in a lock combination that is wrong? Suppose that, after spinning the discs for a while, we had half the letters right, something like the sequence MDTUIFKQINIOAFERSCL (every other letter is correct). The analogy asserts that this is an improvement over a random string of letters, and that it would somehow help us open the lock. ... If your reproductive success depended on opening the lock, you would leave no offspring. Ironically for Sober and Dawkins, a lock combination is a highly specified, irreducibly complex system which beautifully illustrates why, for such systems, function cannot be approached gradually.'[17]

In Dawkins' original typing monkeys version, selection would only retain attempts at the target that had some function; which, in terms of the analogy, would mean that what the monkeys typed at every intermediate step in the process would have to form words that made sense. On such terms, by simply looking at the output of Dawkins' simulation, the process could not even start. Dawkins' ideas simply cannot begin to cope with irreducible complexity. 'Instead of an analogy for natural selection acting on random mutation, the Dawkins-Sober scenario is actually an example of the very opposite: an intelligent agent directing the construction of an irreducibly complex system.'[18]

And there is more. Dawkins' monkeys appear to be generating complexity. But are they? Let us do some more calculating. Imagine the 28 monkeys of the first scenario above to be simultaneously typing. Let us choose a monkey and ask: What is the probability he will get the right letter in the target phrase corresponding to his position in n attempts? The easiest way to do this calculation is first to consider what is the probability of the monkey *not* getting the right letter in any one attempt. This is 26/27. Thus by Bernouilli's Theorem the number of incorrect letters after one attempt is on average 28(26/27). Since all correct letters are retained, we now repeat the process but starting only with the monkeys who have not yet got the correct letter, and so on. This is the essence of *cumulative* selection. In this way we shall have on average $28(26/27)^n$ incorrect letters remaining to be selected after n attempts. This number is about 5 after 43 attempts (so Dawkins did quite well). The average number of incorrect letters is 3 after 60 attempts, and the average is close to 0 after about 100 attempts (one actual calculation gave 0.64286).

What is happening here? We have used an intelligently programmed device to remove the real problem we originally set out to solve, which was not the generation of the building blocks or letters, but getting them in the right order. The superficial impression given is that we have generated all the information contained in the string METHINKS IT IS LIKE A WEASEL. But we have not. All we have done is generated a *known* string in a partially random manner. No new information is obtained.

To put it another way: Dawkins' mechanism claims to be a mechanism for increasing probability. But the effect of increasing probability in this way is to reduce complexity. For something to be complex, as we have seen, there must be many other real options that could take its place. But Dawkins' algorithm can only produce one outcome – his target phrase – and that with probability 1. So, the information added in the process is precisely 0.

It should also be noted in passing that the fact that a correctly typed key is retained, never to be lost again, is equivalent to making the assumption that advantageous mutations are always preserved in the population. But, as evolutionary biologist Sir Ronald Fisher showed in his foundational work, this is not the case in nature.[19] Most beneficial mutations get wiped out by random effects, or by the likely much larger number of deleterious mutations. This contradicts the idea commonly held since Darwin, that natural selection would preserve the slightest beneficial variation until it took over the population. It also gives further evidence for the irreducible complexity argument – as illustrated earlier by Behe's combination lock: an 'advantageous' mutation is only advantageous if it occurs simultaneously with a large number of other 'advantageous' mutations – which is the fatal flaw in the 'target phrase' argument for the typing monkeys.

Another way to see the fundamental weakness of Dawkins' analogy is to replace the phrase METHINKS IT IS LIKE A WEASEL by the complete human genome, more than 3 billion (3×10^9) letters long, where each letter is either A, C, G, or T. Dawkins' scenario would lead to us imagining that there are 3 billion typing monkeys, and that we have the usual mechanism for retaining a correct letter in the sequence. Then the probability of any monkey hitting the wrong letter is 3/4. After n attempts the number of incorrect letters will be about $3 \times 10^9 (3/4)^n$, which is less than one after about 80 attempts. So, on average, you would get the human genome in 80 tries.

It could also be pointed out that it is reckoned that only about 1 to 5 per cent of the DNA is actively used, and if we incorporate this into our model by making our sequence only 5 per cent of its original length, then, on average, the whole sequence would be generated in less than 65 tries.

What does this mean? That Dawkins' model is useless as a simulation of how complexity, in the sense of getting the letters in the right order, can be built up from a random sequence by an *undirected* evolutionary process. For, the postulation of the existence of a mechanism to compare an attempt with the target sequence and retain it means that the real problem of getting the letters in the right order has simply been solved before you start. It has been factored out of the problem completely by being built into the system with the effect that, not surprisingly, you now can reach the target sequence in a very small number of steps since you are aiming at it from the start.

This is the key to the analysis from the perspective of the algorithmic theory of information introduced in the preceding chapter. Dawkins' machine fails and it fails in exactly the way that Küppers' result would lead us to expect, namely that the information contained in the output of Dawkins' algorithmic machine is already contained either in the input or in the informational structure of the machine. Küppers is right. It is in the latter.

Dawkins' whole proposal thus turns out to be nothing but a further example of assuming what you claim to be proving. Philosopher Keith Ward's comment is highly apposite: 'Dawkins' strategy for reducing amazement and incredibility just does not work. It just shifts the surprise from the spontaneous generation of a complex and highly desired result to the spontaneous existence of an efficient rule which is bound to produce the desired result in time.'[20]

In *Tower of Babel*,[21] Pennock attempts to redeem the situation by claiming that the Dawkins-Sober models were not intended as analogies for natural selection on random variation, but rather for *cumulative* selection. The attempt fails, since the central issue is the process's dependence on a mechanism for comparing an attempt with a target phrase. It is precisely that mechanism's intelligently designed capacity to retain letters in the target phrase once they are obtained and before they have any beneficial effect that makes the selection effect cumulative.[22] There is no cumulative selection without the designed mechanism.

The Dawkins-Sober argument is therefore fatally flawed as an argument giving plausibility to the idea that unguided natural processes can generate information. However, their argument is illuminating in that it could be said to *increase* the plausibility of intelligent design. For it shows that even those attempts to account for the origin of biological information that are based on strong materialistic presuppositions cannot do so without smuggling in intelligently designed mechanisms. Computer scientist Robert Berwick comments that 'all our experience with simulated evolution – from Dawkins' biomorph programmes where he offered prizes to those who could figure out ways to actively select for interesting organism shapes, all the way to the sorry experiences with artificial life that Berlinski notes – demonstrates how hard it is to get anywhere without doing artificial selection or building in the solutions we want'.[23] Phillip Johnson has captured this fundamental problem very neatly: 'It takes more human intelligence to programme the computer to generate 'methinksitislikeaweasel' from a random letter selection programme, than it does just to hit the print key and print the target phrase from the computer's memory where you wrote it in the first place.'

Marcel-Paul Schützenberger, the eminent French mathematician mentioned earlier who participated in the Wistar Conference, gave an interview in 1996 in which he likened mutations to typographical errors. He said: '… evolution could not be an accumulation of such typographical errors'.[24] He went on to analyze Dawkins' model and pointed out that it is out of touch with palpable biological realities since, from a mathematical perspective, it 'lays entirely to the side the triple problems of complexity, functionality and their interactions'.

The origin of information

'In the beginning was the bit.'

Han Christian von Baeyer

'In the beginning was the Word.'

The Christian apostle John

Information and the design argument

The existence of complex specified information, therefore, provides a substantial challenge to the notion that unguided natural processes can account for life and makes scientifically plausible the suggestion that an intelligent source was responsible. Here it is important to realize that such an inference to an intelligent source, based on the nature of DNA, is not simply an argument from analogy. Many classical design arguments were of that kind. In them, an attempt was made to reason back from similar effects to similar causes, so that the validity of the arguments often turned on the degree of similarity between the two situations being compared. This circumstance was famously discussed by David Hume in his criticism of design arguments, as we have seen. But the design inference from DNA is much stronger than its classical predecessors for the following reason given in the words of Stephen Meyer: 'DNA does not imply the need for an intelligent designer because it has some similarities to a software programme or to a human language. It implies the need for an intelligent designer because... it possesses an identical feature (namely, information content) that intelligently designed human texts and computer languages possess.'[1] Meyer is supported by information theorist Hubert Yockey. 'It is important to understand that we are not reasoning by analogy. The sequence hypothesis (that the genetic code works essentially like a book) applies directly to the protein and the genetic text as well as to written language and therefore the treatment is mathematically identical.'[2] We are not, therefore, arguing from analogy, but we are making an inference to the best explanation. And, as any detective knows, causes that we know are capable of producing an observed effect are a better explanation for that effect than causes that we do not know are capable of producing any such effect and, *a fortiori*, causes that we know are not capable of doing so.

Dembski's work *The Design Inference*[3] is devoted to explicating the exact nature of the kind of design inferences that we make from our experience with information-rich systems such as languages, codes, computers, machines, etc. Such design inferences are actually quite widespread in science. A few small marks on a flint are enough to tell an archaeologist that he is dealing with an artefact, and not just a piece of weathered stone. Inferences to intelligent agency are made as a matter of routine in disciplines such as archaeology, cryptography, computer science and forensic medicine.

The Search for Extra-Terrestrial Intelligence and its implications

In recent years even natural science has shown itself prepared to make design inferences, notably in the Search for Extra-Terrestrial Intelligence (SETI). The North American Space Administration, NASA, has spent millions of dollars setting up radio-telescopes monitoring millions of channels, in the hope of detecting a message from intelligent beings somewhere else in the cosmos.[4]

Though some scientists might regard SETI with some scepticism, it clearly raises a fundamental question as to the precise scientific status of the detection of intelligence. How does one *scientifically* recognize a message emanating from an intelligent source, and distinguish it from the random background noise that emanates from the cosmos? Clearly, the only way this can be done is to compare the signals received with patterns specified in advance that are deemed to be clear and reliable indicators of intelligence – like a long sequence of prime numbers – and then to make a design inference. In SETI the recognition of intelligent agency is regarded as lying within the legitimate scope of natural science. The astronomer Carl Sagan thought that a single message from space would be enough to convince us that there were intelligences in the universe other than our own.

But there is a further crucial observation to be made. If we are prepared to look for scientific evidence of intelligent activity beyond our planet, why are we so hesitant about applying exactly the same thinking to what is on our planet? There seems here to be a glaring inconsistency which brings us to the nub of the question we referred to in the introduction: Is the attribution of intelligent design to the universe science? Scientists, we emphasize, seem quite happy to include forensic medicine and SETI in the realm of science. Why, then, the furore when some scientists claim that there is scientific evidence of intelligent causation in physics (small furore) or biology (large furore)? There is surely no difference in principle. Is the scientific method not applicable everywhere?

Once we put it this way, is it not obvious that the next question to ask is: What, then, should we deduce from the overwhelming amount of information that is contained in even the simplest living system? Does it not, for example, give evidence of intelligent origin of a far stronger kind than did the argument from the fine-tuning of the universe – an argument which, as we have seen, convinces many physicists that we humans are meant to be here? Could it not be the real evidence of extra-terrestrial intelligence?

At the public announcement of the completion of the Human Genome Project, its director Francis Collins said: 'It is humbling for me and awe-inspiring to realize that we have caught the first glimpse of our own instruction book, previously known only to God.' Gene Myers, the computer scientist who worked on the genome mapping at the Maryland headquarters of Celera Genomics, said: 'We're deliciously complex at the molecular level... We don't understand ourselves yet, which is cool. There's still a metaphysical, magical element... What really astounds me is the architecture of life... the system is extremely complex. It's like it was designed... There's a huge intelligence there. I don't see that as being unscientific. Others may, but not me.'

Considerations of this kind have been instrumental in altering the thinking of some very prominent thinkers. Observational cosmologist Allan Sandage, whom we mentioned earlier, discussing his conversion to Christianity at the age of 50, said: 'The world is too complicated in all its parts and interconnections to be due to chance alone. I am convinced that the existence of life with all its order in each of its organisms is simply too well put together'.[5] And very recently philosopher Anthony Flew gave as the reason for his conversion to theism after over 50 years of atheism that biologists' investigation of DNA 'has shown, by the almost unbelievable complexity of the arrangements which are needed to produce life, that intelligence must have been involved'.[6]

Information as a fundamental quantity

What we are clearly moving towards considering is the idea that information and intelligence are fundamental to the existence of the universe and life and, far from being the end products of an unguided natural process starting with energy and matter, they were involved from the very beginning. Now such an idea is even being entertained by physicists. A suggestion along these very lines has been made in an editorial in the *New Scientist* in which Paul Davies writes: 'The increasing application of the information concept to nature has prompted a curious conjecture. Normally we think of the world as composed of simple, clod-like, material particles, and information as a derived phenomenon attached to special, organized states of matter. But maybe it is the other way around: perhaps the universe is really a frolic of primal information, and material objects a complex secondary manifestation.'[7] Davies says that this idea was first proposed in 1989 by the well-known physicist John Archibald Wheeler, who said: 'Tomorrow, we will have learned to understand all of physics in the language of information.'

And in the *New Scientist*,[8] under the intriguing title 'In the beginning was the bit', there is an account by Hans Christian von Baeyer of the work of physicist Anton Zeilinger, of the University of Vienna. Zeilinger advances the thesis that, in order to understand quantum mechanics, one has to start by associating information (in terms of bits) with so-called elementary systems in quantum mechanics which, like the spin of an electron, 'carry' one bit of information (there are only two possible outcomes from measuring spin – 'up' or 'down'). Zeilinger argues that his basic principle gains credibility by leading directly to three pillars of quantum theory – quantization itself, uncertainty and quantum entanglement. This proposal, that information be regarded as a fundamental quantity, has profound implications for our understanding of the universe. It adds its weight to the design inference.

But it is no new idea. It has been around for centuries. 'In the beginning was the Word... all things were made by him' wrote the apostle John, author of the fourth Gospel. The Greek for 'Word' is *Logos*, a term that was used by Stoic philosophers for the rational principle behind the universe and subsequently invested with additional meaning by Christians, who used it to describe the second person of the Trinity. The term 'Word' itself conveys to us notions of command, meaning, code, communication – thus information; as well as the creative power needed to realize what was specified by that information. The Word, therefore, is more fundamental than mass-energy. Mass-energy belongs to the category of the created. The Word does not.

It is surely very striking indeed that at the heart of the biblical analysis of the creative acts, so cavalierly dismissed by many, we find the very concept that science in recent times has also shown to be of paramount importance – the concept of information.

This key notion, that the Creator is God the Word, is reflected in the repeated phrase 'And God *said* [Let there be light...]' of the Hebrew creation narrative and it is emphasized in almost all of the statements made in the Bible relative to creation. Of particular interest for our discussion is the statement, 'By faith we understand that the universe was formed by God's word, so that what is seen was not made out of what was visible.'[9] This quotation from ancient biblical literature is remarkable in that it draws attention to a basic characteristic of information, namely, that *information is invisible*. The carriers of information may well be visible – like paper and writing, smoke-signals, television screens or DNA – but the information itself is invisible.

Yet information is not only invisible: it is immaterial, is it not? You are reading this book; photons bounce off the book and are received by your eye, converted into electrical impulses and transmitted to your brain. Suppose you pass on some information from this book to a friend by word of mouth. The sound waves carry the information from your mouth to your friend's ear, from where they are converted into electrical impulses and transmitted into his brain. Your friend now has the information that originated in your mind, but nothing material has passed from you to your friend. The *carriers* of the information have been material, *but the information itself is not material*.

In 1961 Rolf Landauer wrote a famous paper entitled 'Information is physical'.[10] The title seems at first sight to say the exact opposite of what we have just been arguing. However, what he appears to mean is that, since information usually encodes on something physical, then the carriers of information are subject to the laws of physics and so, in that sense, information is itself subject to the laws of physics via its carriers. It can therefore be treated as if it were physical. This does not, however, alter the fact that, strictly speaking, information itself is not a physical entity.

What then of the dream of materialistic explanations for everything? How could purely material causes account satisfactorily for the immaterial?

Divine action and the God of the gaps

I realize that some readers will be impatient by this time because they feel that the kind of arguments being discussed here are open to the charge that they are arguments from ignorance and, possibly, intellectual laziness in that they postulate design (and therefore, by implication, a designer) to cover a gap in the present state of our scientific knowledge, rather than getting on with the hard scientific work of finding out. In other words, they are typical 'God of the gaps' explanations. When science has advanced sufficiently to fill the gap, God is squeezed out. Such a 'god' deserves to fade away. We have already addressed the charge of intellectual laziness in our discussion of the question of the origin of information above, but we need to stress once more that the main arguments for the existence of God are those based not on ignorance but on knowledge – the ordered nature of the universe, its mathematical intelligibility and fine-tuning etc. Bearing that fully in mind, a further point needs to be made here about the nature of 'gaps' themselves.

The reason for that is that there would appear to be two kinds of gap: those that are closed by science and those that are revealed by science – perhaps we could call them 'bad gaps' and 'good gaps', respectively. As an example of a bad gap, we might think of Newton's suggestion that God occasionally had to tweak some of the orbits of the planets to bring them into line. That kind of gap we would expect to be closed by science because it falls within the explanatory power of science to settle. Good gaps will be revealed by science as not being within its explanatory power. They will be those (few) places where science as such points beyond itself to explanations that are not within its purview.

For example, the supporters of the SETI programme would not find convincing the idea that postulating an alien intelligence as the source of an information-rich message which had been received, was tantamount to postulating an 'alien of the gaps'. And if the mathematical and information theoretical analysis is similar, would it not be consistent to postulate an intelligent source for the information-rich messages contained in DNA? Also, as we saw earlier, we find no difficulty in inferring an intelligent author as the source of writing, since we know the futility of attempting to give a reductionist explanation in terms of the physics and chemistry of paper and ink. Putting it another way, when it comes to fully explaining writing on paper, there is a gap in the explanatory power of physics and chemistry. This is not a gap of ignorance, but a gap in principle; a good gap that is revealed by our knowledge, and not by our ignorance, of science. Writing on paper (or paint on a Rembrandt canvas) exhibits what philosopher Del Ratzsch calls counterflow – phenomena that nature, unaided by agent activity, could not produce. Because we know that, even in principle, physics and chemistry cannot give an explanation of the counterflow exhibited by the writing, we reject a naturalistic explanation, and we postulate an author.

Similarly, it is knowledge of the nature of biological information, on the one hand, and knowledge that intelligent sources are the only known sources of information, on the other, taken together with the fact that chance and necessity cannot generate the kind of complex specified information which occurs in biology,[11] that point to design as the best explanation for the existence of information-rich DNA. There is more than a whiff of suspicion that reluctance on the part of some scientists to make a design inference from the existence of information-rich biomolecules has less to do with science than it has to do with the implications of the design-inference as to the possible identity of the designer. It is, therefore, a worldview issue, and not simply a scientific one. After all, scientists seem to be perfectly happy to make (scientific) design inferences to human or even alien agency; so the difficulty certainly does not lie in our incapacity to make design inferences as such.

Now it needs to be very strongly stressed that if there are such good gaps that point towards a Creator, this is far from suggesting that such gaps are the only evidence for his existence. They will at best provide evidence *additional* to the main body of evidence that is provided by the wonder of creation as a whole. After all, serious Christian theology holds that God not only created the universe originally, but he is also constantly active in upholding it and all of its processes – without him it would cease to exist. The bits of it we do understand show us his glory quite independently from whatever we make of the bits we do not understand.

The materialist will of course by definition reject *a priori* the possibility of the existence of good gaps that point to the activity of a Creator.[12] For those who believe in God the situation is different. They will believe, at the very least, that God causes the universe to exist and is therefore responsible for its natural processes. There then arises the question of whether or not these processes are all simply to be regarded as indirectly or ultimately caused by God in that they occur in a universe for which he is ultimately responsible, or whether some of the processes or events that happen in the universe may involve some kind of direct causation. Some theologians take the former view and hold that nature has a sort of 'functional integrity' which means that the world is created but that it 'has no functional deficiencies, no gaps in its economy of the sort that would require God to act immediately'.[13]

However, as Alvin Plantinga has pointed out, it is a matter of logic that if there is a God who does anything in the world indirectly he must ultimately act directly or create something directly. And once we admit that God has acted directly at least once in the past for the original creation of the world, what is there to prevent him acting more than once, whether in the past or in the future? After all, the laws of the universe are not independent of God; they are (our) codifications of the regularities that he has built into the universe. Therefore, it would be absurd to think that they constrained God so that he could never do anything special. Plantinga sums up: 'Could we not sensibly conclude, for example, that God created life, or human life, or something else specially? (I do not say we *should* conclude that: I only suggest that we *could*, and should if that is what the evidence most strongly suggests).'[14] And that is the crux of the matter: Are we prepared to follow where the evidence leads – even if it points away from the naturalistic interpretation of the universe? If there is an active Creator God then it should not surprise us if our attempts to understand the universe on naturalistic presuppositions are for the most part very successful[15] but that we find that there are a relatively few areas (particularly associated with origins) that do not yield, and indeed become increasingly opaque, to any naturalistic methodology.[16]

John Polkinghorne, who, like Plantinga emphatically rejects a God of the (bad) gaps theology, nevertheless insists that we must not 'rest content with a discussion in such soft-focus that it never begins to engage our intuitions about God's action with our knowledge of physical process'. His view is that 'if the physical world is really open, and top-down intentional causality operates within it, there must be intrinsic "gaps" ("an envelope of possibility") in the bottom-up account of nature to make room for intentional causality... We are unashamedly "people of the gaps" in this intrinsic sense and there is nothing unfitting in a "God of the gaps" in this sense either'. As to the nature of God's interaction, it is 'not energetic but informational'.[17]

However, whereas, as Polkinghorne goes on to say, it is important to avoid regarding God simply as a cause among other causes, as a deistic god or as a demiurge in the Platonic sense, nevertheless, if God has done some things directly he is responsible for some energetic action or interaction. After all, the law of conservation of energy tells us that energy is conserved. It does not tell us where that energy came from in the first place – something easily and often overlooked. Furthermore, the central pillar of orthodox Christianity – to which Polkinghorne publicly subscribes – is the resurrection of Christ, an event within history that, according to the New Testament, involved a direct input of immensely powerful divine energy.[18]

The complexity of God: a fatal objection?

But, it will be objected, is not bringing God into the equation in the end a self-defeating move because it amounts to 'explaining' the existence of organized complexity by postulating the existence of a being who is by definition even more complex than that which you are attempting to explain? Richard Dawkins puts it this way: 'To explain the origin of the DNA/protein machine by invoking a supernatural Designer is to explain precisely nothing, for it leaves unexplained the origin of the Designer. You have to say something like "God was always there" and if you allow yourself that kind of lazy way out, you might as well just say "DNA was always there", or "Life was always there", and be done with it.'[19]

However, this analysis is highly confused and inadequate. Firstly, we know that DNA was not always there, nor was life. This is one of the main reasons why we ask for an explanation of their existence. Moreover, 'postulating the existence of a being who is by definition even more complex than that which you are attempting to explain' is something we constantly do. For instance, an archaeologist, on observing for the first time some scratch marks on the walls of a cave, may well excitedly exclaim: 'Human intelligence!' It would be absurd to say to her, 'Don't be ridiculous. Those scratch marks are very simple. What sort of an explanation is it to postulate the existence of something as complex as a human brain to account for such simple scratch marks on a cave wall!' It would be equally absurd to say that explaining the scratch marks in terms of human activity 'explains precisely nothing'. The semiotics of those scratch marks may well be important clues as to the identity, culture and intelligence of the people that made them.

Incidentally, is it not to be wondered at that our archaeologist immediately infers intelligent origin when faced with a few simple scratches whereas some scientists, when faced with the 3.5 billion letter sequence of the human genome, inform us that it is to be explained solely in terms of chance and necessity?

We make such inferences to complex intelligent sources when we find certain structures or patterns that, although they may be 'simple' in themselves, exhibit characteristics that we associate only with intelligent activity. Of course it may be objected that we make such inferences because we are familiar with human beings and their propensity for designing things. But is that really a solid reason for attributing something that arguably exhibits a structure consistent with intelligent activity to a non-intelligent source with which the existence of that structure is totally inconsistent? Remember what we would in all likelihood deduce on visiting a remote planet if we found a succession of piles of perfect cubes of titanium with a prime number of cubes in each pile in ascending order 2,3,5,7,11, etc. We would be very likely to conclude at once that this was an artefact produced by an intelligent agent, even though we had not the slightest idea of what kind of intelligent agent it could possibly be. The piles of cubes are in themselves much 'simpler' than the intelligence that made them, but that fact does not prevent our deduction of intelligent origin as a reasonable inference to the best explanation. The legitimization of the SETI project, as we have seen, uses precisely the same argument: if we were to receive (as featured in Carl Sagan's novel *Contact*) a signal consisting of a sequence of prime numbers we would assume that it is coming from an intelligent source. What is more, such an event, were it to happen, would dominate the world's press overnight and no scientist would ever dream of objecting that postulating intelligent origin for the sequence was not an explanation since it would be tantamount to explaining the sequence in terms of something more complex than the sequence itself. To be sure it would raise many more questions – that of the nature of the intelligence, for instance – but at least we would have settled that there was an extra-terrestrial intelligence. Even Dawkins might regard that as a step of knowledge.

We referred above to his desire to explain everything in terms of the 'simple things that physicists understand'. Now on the one hand, things like atoms are simpler than living creatures since living creatures are composed of complex structures made up of atoms. On the other hand, atoms are far from simple, which is one of the reasons elementary particle physics continues to attract some of the most powerful intellects on earth. The deeper down you probe into the ultimate nature of the structure of the universe, the more complex it becomes.

Think of relativity, quantum mechanics or, better still, quantum electrodynamics. They are so far from being simple that only the most intelligent human minds can grasp them and even then there are many mysteries still unresolved. To start with, no one knows exactly why quantum mechanics works and, as Richard Feynman was also wont to point out, no one even knows what energy is. Now here is the curious thing. If Richard Dawkins objects to the complexity of God as an ultimate explanation, he ought also to object to the complexity of the structure of the universe of particle physics and be totally dissatisfied with ultimate explanations in terms of concepts like 'energy' since we do not really understand them.

Dawkins therefore seems to be wrong here on two counts. Firstly, the things he takes to be simple are not, and secondly, the reason that such complex physical theories are accepted by scientists is not because of their simplicity; it is because of their explanatory power. And explanatory power is just as important, if not a more important criterion for the validity of a scientific theory, than simplicity. Sometimes simpler theories have been discarded because they did not have sufficient explanatory power. It was, after all, Einstein who said: 'Explanations should be as simple as possible, but no simpler.'[20]

Who made God?

Some, who find it hard to accept the notion of God as the ultimate reality, may well continue to ask the question: 'Who made God?' Now any question of the type 'Who made X?' presupposes that X belongs to the category of the made. So the next logical question is: Does the category of the made exhaust all of reality? Is there nothing that is eternal? Of course we can, if we like, make the *a priori* assumption that there is nothing eternal. But we must realize in doing so that that presumption is neither justified by science nor by philosophy. And what is more, there have been times (and are they all past?) when one of the fundamental tenets of materialism was that matter/energy/the universe was eternal, and therefore when adherents of this view asked 'Who made God?', they of all people could not take refuge in the belief that the category of the eternal was empty since they themselves believed very much in the eternity of matter.

It is logically clear that chains of cause and effect either go back eternally in an infinite regression (a notion philosophically problematic in itself), or else there is a point where we stop at an ultimate reality. Explanation in science, if it is to avoid an infinite regress, always leads to certain things that are regarded as ultimate. Austin Farrer reminds us of our childhood explorations of this kind of thing: 'An endless quest for explanation has been praised as a divine discontent. In fact it is a propensity most characteristic of rudimentary minds. "Why does that man wear that hat?" "Because he is a policeman." "Why is he a policeman?" "Because he wanted to be when he grew up." "Why did he want to be?" "Because he wanted to earn his living." "Why did he want to earn his living?" "So as to be able to live – everyone does." "Why does everyone want to live?" "Stop saying 'Why?' darling, and go to sleep." Yes. Some time we must stop saying "Why?" because you have reached the fact that is senseless to question; for example it is useless to ask why living beings want to live. The issue between the atheist and the believer is not whether it makes sense to question ultimate fact, it is rather the question: What fact is ultimate? The atheist's ultimate fact is the universe; the theist's ultimate fact is God.'[21] That is the burning question: In which direction does science point – matter before mind, or mind before matter? The answer to that question will surely have to be determined, as always, by following Socrates advice, examining the evidence and seeing where it leads, however threatening this may turn out to be to our preconceived notions.

James Shapiro asks the question: 'What significance does an emerging interface between biology and information science hold for thinking about evolution? It opens up the possibility of addressing scientifically rather than ideologically the central issue so hotly contested by fundamentalists on both sides of the Creationist–Darwinist debate. Is there any guiding intelligence at work in the origin of species displaying exquisite adaptations that range from lambda prophage repression and the Krebs cycle through the mitotic apparatus and the eye to the immune system, mimicry and social organization?'[22] Biophysicist Dean Kenyon, co-author of a definitive textbook on the origin of life,[23] says the more that has been learned in recent years about the chemical details of life, from molecular biology and origin-of-life studies, the less likely does a strictly naturalistic explanation of origins become. Kenyon's studies have led him to the conclusion that biological information has been designed: 'If science is based on experience, then science tells us that the message encoded in DNA must have originated from an intelligent cause. What kind of intelligent agent was it? On its own, science cannot answer this question; it must leave it to religion and philosophy. But that should not prevent science from acknowledging evidences for an intelligent cause origin wherever they may exist.'[24]

In light of all the foregoing I, for one, find it surprising to read, from the pen of someone as eminent as E.O. Wilson, the following denial of the existence of such evidence: 'Any researcher who can prove the existence of intelligent design within the accepted framework of science will make history and achieve eternal fame. He will prove at last that *science and religious dogma are compatible!* Even a combined Nobel Prize and Templeton Prize (the latter designed to encourage search for just such harmony) would fall short of proper recognition. Every scientist would like to accomplish such an epoch-making advance. But no one has even come close, because unfortunately there is no evidence, no theory and no criteria for proof that even marginally might pass for science. There is only the residue of hoped-for default, which steadily shrinks as the science of biology expands.'[25] I say I find it surprising to read these lines for, even if one were to discount our preceding chapters on biology because they challenge certain prevailing views on origins, how can one ignore the evidence from physics and cosmology that, far from questioning accepted science, flows out of it? Compare Wilson's attitude with that of Allan Sandage, who is regarded as the greatest living cosmologist: 'The world is too complicated in all its parts and interconnections to be due to chance alone. I am convinced that the existence of life with all its order in each of its organisms is simply too well put together.'[26]

We recall that it was the evidence of scientific research on questions of the origin of life that led the eminent philosopher and life-long atheist Anthony Flew to believe that the nature of the complexity of DNA can only be accounted for by an intelligent Creator.[27] Wilson says there is no evidence, Sandage and Flew claim that there is. Both views cannot be right.

Epilogue

'I am very astonished that the scientific picture of the real world around me is very deficient. It gives us a lot of factual information, puts all of our experience in a magnificently consistent order, but it is ghastly silent about all and sundry that is really near to our heart that really matters to us. It cannot tell us a word about red and blue, bitter and sweet, physical pain and physical delight; it knows nothing of beautiful and ugly, good or bad, God and eternity. Science sometimes pretends to answer questions in these domains but the answers are very often so silly that we are not inclined to take them seriously.'

Erwin Schrödinger[1]

So far I have argued that, although science with all of its power cannot address some of the fundamental questions that we ask, nevertheless the universe contains certain clues as to our relationship to it, clues that are scientifically accessible. The rational intelligibility of the universe, for instance, points to the existence of a Mind that was responsible both for the universe and for our minds. It is for this reason that we are able to do science and to discover the beautiful mathematical structures that underlie the phenomena we can observe. Not only that, but our increasing insight into the fine-tuning of the universe in general, and of planet earth in particular, is consistent with the widespread awareness that we are meant to be here. This earth is our home.

But if there is a Mind behind the universe, and if that Mind intends us to be here, the really big question is: Why are we here? What is the purpose of our existence? It is this question above all that exercises the human heart. Scientific analysis of the universe cannot give us the answer, any more than scientific analysis of Aunt Matilda's cake could tell us why she had made it. Scientific probing of the cake may tell us that it is good for humans; even that it was highly likely to have been designed specifically with humans in mind, since it is fine-tuned to their nutritional requirements. In other words, science may be able to point towards the conclusion that there is a purpose behind the cake; but precisely what that purpose is, science cannot tell us. It would be absurd to look for it within the cake. Only Aunt Matilda can reveal it to us. True science is not embarrassed by its inability at this point – it simply recognizes that it is not equipped to answer such questions. Therefore, it would be a serious logical error in methodology only to look within the ingredients of the universe – its material, structures and processes – to find out what its purpose is and what we are here for. The ultimate answer, if there is one, will have to come from outside the universe, from something or someone who stands in a similar relationship to the universe as Aunt Matilda does to her cake.

But how shall we find out? We have argued that there is evidence that there is a Mind behind the universe, a Mind that intended us to be here. And we have minds. It is, therefore, not illogical that one of the major reasons why we have been given minds is not only that we should be able to explore our fascinating universe home, but also that we should be able to understand the Mind that has given us the home.

Furthermore, we humans are capable of giving expression to the thoughts of our minds and communicating them to others. It would therefore be very surprising if the Mind from which we are derived should be any less capable of self-expression and communication than we are. This leads us at once to the question: Is there any serious and credible evidence that that Mind has ever spoken into our world?

Many ancient cosmologies populated the universe with gods of every kind. These deities were usually thought to emerge from the primeval material chaos of the universe, so that they were ultimately part of the basic stuff of the universe itself. They cannot be the answer to our question since we are, by definition, looking for a Mind that exists independently of the universe.

The Greek philosopher Aristotle formulated the concept of an 'Unmoved Mover' which, though changeless itself, imparted change to other things. Regarding as absurd the idea that the principle of change should be inside it, he believed that this Unmoved Mover was in some sense outside the universe. However, Aristotle's Unmoved Mover was much too remote and abstract to have been interested in speaking into the world.

Long before Aristotle, the book of Genesis was penned. It starts with the words: 'In the beginning God created the heavens and the earth.'[2] This statement stands in complete contrast with the other mythical cosmogonies of the time – like the Babylonian, in which the gods were part of the stuff of the universe, and where the world was made out of a god.

Genesis claims that there is a Creator God who exists independently of the universe, a claim that is foundational to Judaism, Christianity and Islam. The Christian apostle, John, puts it this way: 'In the beginning was the Word, and the Word was with God, and the Word was God. He was with God in the beginning. Through Him all things were made; without Him nothing was made that has been made. In Him was life and that life was the light of men.'[3]

This analysis bears close attention. We have already considered its implications for the priority of the concept of information over matter. And there are further implications. In Greek the word translated 'Word' is *Logos*, which was often used by Greek philosophers for the rational principle that governs the universe. Here we have the theological explanation for the rational intelligibility of the universe. It is the product of a Mind, that of the divine *Logos*. For what lies behind the universe is much more than a rational principle. It is God, the Creator Himself. It is no abstraction, or even impersonal force, that lies behind the universe. God, the Creator, is a person. And just as Aunt Matilda is not part of her cake, neither is God part of the stuff of his universe.

Now, if the ultimate reality behind the universe is a personal God, this has very far-reaching implications for the human search for truth, since it opens up new possibilities for knowing ultimate reality other than the (scientific) study of things. For persons communicate in a way that things do not. Being persons ourselves, we can get to know other persons. Therefore, the next logical question to ask is: If the Creator is personal, has he spoken directly, as distinct from what we can learn of him indirectly through the structures of the universe? For if there is a God, and he has spoken, then what he has said will be of utmost importance in our search for truth.

At this point we once again encounter the statement of the Bible, that God has spoken in the most profound and direct way possible. He, the Word who is a person, has become human, to demonstrate fully that the ultimate truth behind the universe is personal. 'The Word became flesh and made his dwelling among us. We have seen his glory of the one and only, who came from the Father, full of grace and truth.'[4]

Now, as Schrödinger points out in the opening quotation, these are things that the natural sciences cannot tell us, and do not claim to. However, as with so many other things beyond the competence of science, this does not mean that there is no evidence for them. Indeed, presenting that evidence would take us far beyond the scope of this present book into matters both of history, literature and experience. I must therefore content myself with quoting Arthur Schawlow who won the Nobel Prize for his work on laser spectroscopy. He said: 'We are fortunate to have the Bible and especially the New Testament, which tells us so much about God in widely accessible human terms."[5]

In conclusion, I submit that, far from science having buried God, not only do the results of science point towards his existence, but the scientific enterprise itself is validated by his existence.

Inevitably, of course, not only those of us who do science, but all of us, have to choose the presupposition with which we start. There are not many options – essentially just two. Either human intelligence ultimately owes its origin to mindless matter; or there is a Creator. It is strange that some people claim that it is their intelligence that leads them to prefer the first to the second.

References

Preface

1. 'The Limitless Power of Science' in *Nature's Imagination – The Frontiers of Scientific Vision*, Ed. John Cornwell, Oxford, Oxford University Press, 1995 p. 125
2. *Dialogues Concerning the Two Chief Systems of the World*, Translated by S. Drake, Berkeley, 1953
3. Radio 4 *News*, 10 December, 2004.

Chapter 1

1. 'Will science ever fail?' *New Scientist*, 8 Aug 1992, pp. 32–35.
2. 'Is science a religion?' *The Humanist*, Jan/Feb 1997, pp. 26–39.
3. London, Bantam Press, 2006.
4. *Daily Telegraph* Science Extra, Sept 11, 1989.
5. John 20:31
6. Romans 1:20
7. *The Language of God*, New York, Free Press, 2006 p. 164.
8. *Dawkins' God*, Oxford, Blackwell, 2004.
9. *A Devil's Chaplain*, London, Weidenfeld and Nicholson, 2003, p. 248
10. 3 April 1997, 386:435–6.
11. Larry Witham, *Where Darwin Meets the Bible*, Oxford, Oxford University Press, 2002 p. 272.
12. *Scientific American*, September 1999, pp. 88–93.
13. *Nature's Imagination – The Frontiers of Scientific Vision*, Ed. John Cornwell, Oxford Oxford University Press, 1995 p. 132.
14. *The Search for God – Can Science Help?*, Oxford, Lion, 1995 p.59.
15. *God and the Scientists*, compiled by Mike Poole, CPO 1997.
16. *Chemical Evolution*, Oxford, Clarendon Press, 1969, p. 258
17. *Science and the Modern World*, London, Macmillan, 1925, p. 19.
18. Cited in Morris Kline, *Mathematics: The Loss of Certainty*, (Oxford University Press, New York, 1980, p. 31.
19. 'Science and Society in East and West', *The Great Titration*, London, Allen and Unwin, 1969.
20. *Theological Science*, Edinburgh, T & T Clark, 1996 p. 57.
21. *op. cit.* p. 58.
22. John Brooke, *Science & Religion: Some Historical Perspectives*, Cambridge, Cambridge University Press, 1991, p. 19.
23. *The Bible, Protestantism and the Rise of Science*, Cambridge, Cambridge University Press, 1998.
24. London, Fourth Estate, 1999.
25. The reader interested in more detail should consult the excellent chapter on Galileo in *Reconstructing Nature*, John Brooke and Geoffrey Cantor, Edinburgh, T&T Clark, 1998.
26. Galileo made reference to this in his famous letter to the Grand Duchess Christina of Tuscany (1615) when he upbraided those who failed to realize that 'under the surface meaning this [biblical] passage may contain a different sense'.
27. It is noteworthy that in 1559 Pope Paul IV had set up the first official Roman Index of Prohibited Books, banning, among many other books, translations of the Bible into modern languages – in light of which one might well ask on what side the church was on!
28. See, for example, *The Wilberforce–Huxley Debate: Why Did It Happen?* by J.H. Brooke, Science and Christian Belief, 2001, 13, 127–41.
29. See 'Wilberforce and Huxley, A Legendary Encounter', Lucas J. R., *The Historical Journal*, 22 (2), 1979, 313–30.
30. *Science and Religion – Some Historical Perspectives*, Cambridge, Cambridge University Press, 1991 p. 71.

31. See David M Knight and Matthew D. Eddy, *Science and Beliefs: from Natural Philosophy to Natural Science 1700–1900*, London, Ashgate, 2005.
32. 'The Conflict Metaphor and its Social Origins', *Science and Christian Belief*, 1, 3–26, 1989.
33. *Beliefs and Values in Science Education*, Buckingham, Open University Press, 1995, p. 125
34. Ed. Honderich, Oxford, Oxford University Press, 1995, p. 530
35. *Oxford Companion to Philosophy*, p. 604
36. 'Intelligent Evolution', *Harvard Magazine*, November 2005
37. Power Lamprecht Sterling, The Metaphysics of Naturalism, New York, Appleton-Century-Crofts, 1960, p. 160.
38. Genesis 1:1
39. 'The Big Bang, Stephen Hawking, and God', in *Science: Christian Perspectives for the New Millenium*, Addison Texas and Norcross, Georgia, CLM and RZIM Publishers, 2003.

Chapter 2

1. *Darwinism Defended*, Reading, Addison-Wesley, 1982 p 322.
2. *The Physicist's Conception of Nature*, London, Hutchinson, 1958 p.15.
3. Their suggestions have resulted in the so-called 'Science Wars'.
4. It is nevertheless important, especially in those areas of science in which the influence of worldview is most likely, for scientists to make a regular health check on the extent to which they are, in the words of Steve Woolgar, 'not engaged in the passive description of pre-existing facts in the world, but are actively engaged in formulating or constructing the character of that world' (*Science: The very idea*, New York, Routledge, 1988. Republished 1993).
5. In *Darwinism, Design and Public Education*, John Angus Campbell and Stephen C. Meyer, East Lansing, Michigan State University Press, 2003 p. 195.
6. *Life Evolving*, New York, Oxford University Press, 2002, p. 284.
7. *Philosophical Essays in Pragmatic Naturalism*, Buffalo, New York, Prometheus Books, 1990 p.12.
8. *The Atheist in the Holy City*, Cambridge, MA, MIT Press, 1990, p. 203.
9. One cannot help applaud Lewontin's openness here: he is neither unaware of his worldview commitment nor does he seek to hide it.
10. Review of Carl Sagan's book *The Demon Haunted World: Science as a Candle in the Dark*, New York Review of Books, January 9, 1997.
11. Which is, presumably, why questions about religious convictions are not normally asked by interviewing committees for scientific positions – though it is not completely unknown.
12. 'Plantinga's Defence of Special Creation', *Christian Scholar's Review*, 1991 p. 57.
13. *The Structure of Scientific Revolutions*, 2nd Ed. University of Chicago Press, 1970.
14. A paradigm need not be as all-encompassing as a worldview, but it is often the case that they are closely related, if not identical.
15. *Mortal Questions*, Cambridge, Cambridge University Press, 1979 p. xi.
16. Associated Press, December 9, 2004.
17. For a nuanced contemporary discussion of the relationships between science and religion see Mikael Stenmark, *How to Relate Science and Religion*, Grand Rapids, Eerdmans 2004.
18. *Nature's Imagination: the Frontiers of Scientific Vision*, ed. John Cornwell, Oxford, Oxford University Press, 1995, p. 125.
19. *Religion and Science*, Oxford, Oxford University Press, 1970, p. 243.
20. 'Why' questions connected with function as distinct from purpose are usually regarded as within the provenance of science.
21. *Advice to a Young Scientist*, London, Harper and Row, 1979, p. 31; see also his book *The Limits of Science*, Oxford, Oxford University Press 1984, p. 66.
22. *The Language of God*, New York, The Free Press, 2006.
23. *History of Western Philosophy*, London, Routledge, 2000, p.13.
24. *A Science of God?* London, Geoffrey Bles, 1966, p. 29.
25. *Creation Revisited*, Harmondsworth, Penguin, 1994, p. 1.
26. *op. cit.* 127–28.
27. *Science and Religion*, Carlisle, Paternoster Periodicals, 1996.
28. *A Science of God*, London, Geoffrey Bles, 1966 pp. 29, 30.

Chapter 3

1. Oxford, Oxford University Press, 1996 p. 68.
2. *The Epicurus Reader*, trans. Brad Inwood and L.P. Gerson, Indianapolis, Hacket, 1994, 10.104.
3. This emptying of the natural world of gods, demons and spirits is often called the de-deification of the universe.
4. Deuteronomy 17.3
5. Jeremiah 8.2
6. See, for example, Edward G. Newing, 'Religions of pre-literary societies', in *The World's Religions*, ed. Sir Norman Anderson, London, IVP, 4th edition, 1975, p. 38.
7. *The Theology of the Early Greek Philosophers*, Oxford, Oxford University Press, 1967 paperback, pp. 16–17.
8. Cited in Anthony Kenny, *A Brief History of Western Philosophy*, Oxford, Blackwell, 1998.
9. Psalm 111.2
10. 'The Scientist as Rebel', in *Nature's Imagination – The Frontiers of Scientific Vision*, ed. John Cornwell, Oxford, Oxford University Press, 1995 p. 8.
11. *Of Molecules and Man*, Washington, University of Washington Press, 1966, p.10.
12. *The Blind Watchmaker*, Longman, London, 1986, p. 15.
13. 'Scientific Reduction and the Essential Incompleteness of All Science', in *Studies in the Philosophy of Biology, Reduction and Related Problems*, ed. F.J. Ayala and T. Dobzhansky, London, Macmillan 1974.
14. *The Tacit Dimension*, New York, Doubleday, 1966.
15. Some may think that I am cheating here. For instance, they might argue that, although the semiotics of the letters cannot be given an explanation in terms of physics and chemistry *directly*, nevertheless my argument fails since in the end the human authors of the writing can ultimately be explained in terms of physics and chemistry. However this simply begs the question that lies at the heart of our consideration: Does such a reductionist explanation for human beings actually exist?
16. *The Experiment of Life*, Toronto, University of Toronto Press, 1983, p. 54.
17. *BBC Christmas Lectures Study Guide*, London, BBC 1991.
18. *The Astonishing Hypothesis – The Scientific Search for the Soul*, London, Simon and Schuster 1994, p. 3.
19. *You're Nothing but a Pack of Neurones*, J. of Consciousness Studies, 1, No. 2, 1994, pp. 275–79.
20. *op. cit.* p. 93.
21. Charles Darwin, *Letter to William Graham*, 3 July, 1881.
22. *One World*, London, SPCK 1986 p. 92.
23. We shall return to this matter later in connection with the attempt to account for biogenesis.

Chapter 4

1. *The Meaning of Evolution*, Yale, 1949, p. 344.
2. 'Energy in the Universe', *Scientific American*, 224, 1971, p. 50.
3. *The Mind of God*, London, Simon and Schuster, 1992, p. 232.
4. 'Das Unverstaendliche am Universum ist im Grunde, dass wir es verstehen'
5. *God, Chance and Necessity*, Oxford, One World Publications, 1996 p. 1.
6. *Letters to Solovine*, New York, Philosophical Library, 1987 p. 131.
7. *The Mind of God*, London, Simon and Schuster, 1992, p. 150.
8. For example the use made in the study of electromagnetic waves (and hence in electronics) of the abstract pure mathematical construction of a number system, in which the number minus one has a square root.
9. E.P. Wigner, 'The unreasonable effectiveness of mathematics', *Communications in Pure and Applied Mathematics*, 13 (1960), pp. 1–14.
10. *The Emperor's New Mind*, Vintage, 1991 p. 430.
11. *Reason and Reality*, London, SPCK, 1991, p. 76.
12. *The Mind of God*, op. cit. p. 81.
13. *God, Chance and Necessity*, Oxford, One World Publications, 1996.
14. ABC Television 20/20, 1989.
15. *Atheism and Theism*, Oxford, Blackwell, 1996 p. 92.

16. 'Is the Universe a Vacuum Fluctuation?' *Nature* 246, 1973, p. 396.
17. *op. cit.* p. 23.
18. *Creation Revisited*, Harmondsworth, Penguin, 1994, p. 143.
19. *op. cit.* p. 49.
20. *op. cit.* p. 174.
21. Reported by Clive Cookson, 'Scientists who glimpsed God', *Financial Times*, April 29, 1995, p. 20.
22. Of whom we shall have more to say in Chapter 5.
23. William Paley, *Natural Theology*, 1802 *op. cit.* p. 7.
24. *New York Times*, 12 March, 1991, p. B9.
25. see *The Timaeus*.
26. Friedrich Engels, *Ludwig Feuerbach*, New York, International Publishers, 1974, p. 21.
27. *A Brief History of Time. From the Big Bang to Black Holes*, London, Bantam Press, 1988, p. 46.
28. 'The End of the World: From the Standpoint of Mathematical Physics', *Nature* 127 (1931), p. 450.
29. *Nature*, 259, 1976.
30. *Nature*, 340, 1989, p. 425.
31. The expression 'quantum vacuum' can be misleading for someone not familiar with the terminology of physics. For the word 'vacuum' tends to convey the idea that nothing is there at all. A quantum vacuum is a term physicists use for a quantum field in its ground or lowest energy state. It is certainly not 'nothing'.
32. That is, they use complex numbers in order to cope with the fact that in their model the geometry of space–time involves two "time" dimensions treated in the same way as the spatial dimensions.
33. *op. cit.* p. 139.
34. Neil Turok of Cambridge is currently challenging the standard model by suggesting that the Big Bang at the start of our universe is only one of many. His view implies a return to the eternity of space–time. The debate is not over yet!
35. *Making Waves*, American Physical Society, 1995.
36. *Annual Reviews of Astronomy and Astrophysics*, 20, 1982, p. 16.
37. *God and the New Physics*, London, J. M. Dent and Sons, 1983.
38. *The Creator and the Cosmos*, Colorado Springs, Navpress 1995 p. 117.
39. See A.H. Guth, 'Inflationary Universe', *Physical Review* D, 23, 1981, p. 348.
40. *The Emperor's New Mind*, Oxford, Oxford University Press, 1989 p. 344.
41. *The Cosmic Blueprint*, New York, Simon and Schuster, 1988, p. 203.
42. *op. cit.* pp. 138–39.
43. Washington DC, Regnery, 2004.
44. *op. cit.* p. xiii.
45. *op. cit.* p. 335.
46. *Cosmos, Bios and Theos*, Margenau and Varghese eds., La Salle, IL., Open Court, 1992, p. 83.
47. For example Barrow and Tipler, *The Anthropic Cosmological Principle*, Oxford, University Press, 1988, p. 566.
48. *Universes*, London, Routledge, 1989, p. 14.
49. See also the discussion in A. McGrath, *The Foundations of Dialogue in Science and Religion*, Blackwell, Oxford, 1998, p. 114 ff.
50. London, Penguin, 1997.
51. London, Weidenfeld and Nicholson, 1999.
52. *One World*, London, SPCK, 1986 p. 80.
53. *Is There a God?* Oxford, Oxford University Press, 1995 p. 68.
54. E. Harrison, *Masks of the Universe*, New York, Macmillan, 1985 pp. 252, 263.
55. In Denis Brian, *Genius Talk*, New York, Plenum, 1995.
56. de Duve, *Life Evolving*, op. cit. p. 299.
57. In Malcolm Browne, *New York Times*, 'Clues to the Universe's Origin Expected', 12 March, 1978 p. 1.

Chapter 5

1. *The Blind Watchmaker*, Longmans, London, 1986, p. 1.
2. 'Lessons from Biology', *Natural History*, vol. 97, 1988, p. 36.
3. Note however, that this is correctly described by Dennett as an *idea*, not a *scientific discovery*.

4. *op. cit.* p. 14.
5. *The Nature of the Gods*, translated by H.C.P. McGregor, Penguin, London, 1972, p. 163.
6. *Natural Theology; or Evidences of the Existence and Attributes of the Deity*, 18th ed. rev., Edinburgh, Lackington, Allen and Co., and James Sawers, 1818, pp. 12–14.
7. *op. cit.* p. 473.
8. *The Structure of Evolutionary Theory*, Cambridge, MA, Harvard University Press, 2002, p. 230.
9. Nora Barlow ed. *The autobiography of Charles Darwin, 1809–1882: with original omissions restored*. New York, W.W. Norton, 1969, p. 87.
10. Paley, *op. cit.* p. 270–71.
11. Gould, *op. cit.* p. 264.
12. Gould, *op. cit.* p 266.
13. Paley, *op. cit.* p. 5.
14. *The Idea of a University*, London, Longman's Green, 1907, p. 454.
15. We note that this is precisely what is claimed by the Christian apostle Paul in his letter to the Romans 1:19–20.
16. *op. cit.* 542–43.
17. Paley's *Evidences of Christianity* remained a required text for entrance to Cambridge University until the twentieth century, which shows, according to Stephen Jay Gould that Paley 'cannot be dismissed as an intellectual slouch' (Gould, *op. cit.* p. 265). Nor should it be forgotten that Paley was no mean mathematician. He had studied mathematics at Cambridge (occupying the very same rooms in Christ's College that Darwin would later have) and it was he who first noticed the important fact that Newton's law of gravitation was particularly stable because of its inverse square form.
18. Russell also notes the limitations of the design argument in demonstrating the full range of God's attributes.
19. *History of Western Philosophy, op. cit.* p. 570.
20. That Paley was well aware of what Hume had written, we have already seen.
21. David Hume, *An Enquiry Concerning Human Understanding*, 1748: ed. J.C. Gaskin, Oxford, Oxford University Press 1998.
22. *op. cit.* p. 46.
23. E. Sober, *Philosophy of Biology*, Boulder, Colorado, Westview Press, 1993, p. 34.
24. *Debating Design*, eds. William Dembski and Michael Ruse, Cambridge, Cambridge University Press, 2004, p. 107.
25. Perhaps this was in part responsible for Newman's reaction?
26. There are scientists who hold the reductionist view that living organisms are nothing but machines. They, one might suppose, should therefore have no objection to the original mechanistic version of the design argument.
27. *Science and Christian Belief*, 2006.
28. *Darwin's Legacy*, ed. Charles L. Hamrum, New York, Harper & Row Publishers, 1983, p. 6–7.
29. *Orthodoxy*, 1880.
30. *Evolution after Darwin*, Sol Tax. ed., Chicago, University of Chicago Press, 1960.
31. *Evolution*, 2nd ed., Sudbury, Jones and Bartlett, 1996 p. 62.
32. *Evolutionary Biology*, 2nd ed. Sunderland MA, Sinauer 1986. p. 3.
33. *The Times*, London, December 1997.
34. *Evolution and the Foundation of Ethics*, MBL Science, Marine Biological Laboratory, Woods Hole, MS, (3) 1, 25–29.
35. *Darwin's Dangerous Idea*, London, Penguin, 1996, p. 18.
36. *The Selfish Gene*, Oxford, Oxford University Press, 1976, p. 1.
37. See, for example, *Intelligent Design Creationism and its Critics*, ed. Pennock, MIT Press, ETC.
38. *The Search for God – Can Science help?* Oxford, Lion Publishing Plc, 1995, p. 54.
39. See David N. Livingstone, *Darwin's Forgotten Defenders*, Edinburgh, Scottish Academic Press, 1987.
40. *The Existence of God*, Oxford, Oxford University Press, 1991, p. 135–36.
41. *The Academy* 1, 1869, 13–14.
42. We shall not elaborate on the fact that the Latin origin equivalent of 'agnostic' is 'ignoramus'.
43. 'Impeaching a Self-appointed Judge', *Scientific American*, 267, no.1, 1992, 118–21.
44. *Dawkins' God*, Oxford, Blackwell, 2005 p. 81.
45. *Rebuilding the Matrix*, Oxford, Lion Publishing, 2001, p. 291.

46. 'Impeaching a self-appointed judge', *op. cit.*.
47. *op. cit.* p. 67.
48. *op. cit.* p. 76.
49. *Darwin's Dangerous Idea*, London, Penguin, 1996, p. 203.
50. 'Put Your Money on Evolution', *The New York Times Review of Books*, April 9, 1989, p. 34–35.
51. Lynn Margulis and Dorian Sagan, *Acquiring Genomes: A Theory of the Origins of Species*, New York, Basic Books, 2002.
52. We would emphasize here that the question of the motivation behind a theory is not the same as the question of the truth or falsity of that theory – a point that will be made subsequently. We are not trying here to prejudice the answer to the latter question by considering the former. What we are trying to do is to tease out a complex relationship.
53. *Evolution*, 2nd Ed., London, Natural History Museum, 1999, p. 120.
54. *Objections Sustained*, Downers Grove, Illinois, Inter-Varsity Press, 1998, p. 73.
55. *The Clockwork Image*, London, Inter Varsity Press, 1974, p. 52.
56. *Christian Reflections*, London, Geoffrey Bles, 1967, pp. 82–93.
57. *Moral Darwinism*, Downers Grove, IVP, 2002.
58. Furthermore, the logic of the relationship is often reversed by sleight of hand, so that the inference from naturalism to evolution becomes 'science (evolution) proves the naturalistic worldview' – a further deception.
59. Cited by Futuyma in *Science on Trial*, Sunderland MA, Sinauer, 1995, p. 161.

Chapter 6

1. *The Beak of the Finch*, London, Cape, 1994.
2. This means, of course, that Richard Dawkins' dichotomy of 'God or evolution, but not both' is far too simplistic. Microevolutionary processes are agreed to occur by all sides and so, from a theistic perspective, the world God created is a world in which natural selection processes have a role.
3. A detailed analysis of the significance of the finch beak story for the theory of evolution and the way in which it is handled in textbooks, can be found in biologist Jonathan Wells' book (*Icons of Evolution*, Regnery, Washington, 2000, chapter 8).
4. *Melanism – Evolution in Action*, Oxford, Oxford University Press, 1998, p. 171.
5. November 27, 2000.
6. London, Anchor, 2000, p. 93.
7. 'Not black and white', *Nature* 396 (1998), pp. 35–36.
8. A detailed analysis of the peppered moth story can again be found in Wells (*op. cit.*), and a fascinating account of the dramatic history of the personalities involved in the story of Kettlewell's original work on the peppered moth is to be found in Judith Hooper's eminently readable book *Of moths and men: intrigue, tragedy and the peppered moth*, London, Fourth Estate, 2002.
9. *The Origins of Prebiological Systems and of Their Molecular Matrices*, S.W. Fox (ed.), New York, Academic Press, 1965, p. 310.
10. For example, the major university text on *Evolution* by Peter Skelton (ed.), Addison Wesley, Harlow, England, 1993 p. 854.
11. 'Intelligent Evolution', *Harvard Magazine*, November 2005.
12. Wilson does not say what these systems are.
13. *Evolution*, 2nd Ed., London, Natural History Museum, 1995, p. 118.
14. In the preface to his book Patterson says that, although he believes in evolution in the sense of common ancestry, he is no longer certain that natural selection is the complete explanation. Nor, indeed was Darwin. In the first edition of *The Origin of Species* he says: 'I am convinced that natural selection has been the main but not the exclusive means of modification.'
15. *op. cit.* p. vii.
16. In fact, Popper himself went as far as calling the theory of evolution 'a metaphysical research programme'.
17. Müller, G.B. 'Homology: The Evolution of Morphological Organization' in Müller G.B. and Newman S.A. (eds.), *Origination of Organismal Form. Beyond the Gene in Developmental and Evolutionary Biology*, Harvard, MIT Press, Vienna Series in Theoretical Biology, 2003, p. 51.
18. *Climbing Mount Improbable*, New York, Norton, 1996, p. 67.
19. R.E.D. Clark, *Darwin Before and After*, Chicago, Moody Press, 1967, p. 88–89.

20. Letter 3831, CUL DAR 101:77–78, 61–62.
21. Letter 3834, CUL DAR 115:172
22. See e.g. *Evolution*, Ed. Peter Skelton, Harlow, Addison Wesley, 1993.
18. *Beyond Natural Selection*, Cambridge, MIT Press, 1991 p. 206.
23. A.P. Hendry and M.T. Kinnison, An introduction to microevolution: rate, pattern, process, Genetica 112–113, 2001, 1–8.
24. *Resynthesizing Evolutionary and Developmental Biology*, Developmental Biology, 173, 1996, p. 361.
25. *The Material Basis of Evolution*, Yale University Press 1940, p. 8.
26. 'The Major Evolutionary Transitions', *Nature* 374, 1995, p. 227–32.
27. *Evolution – Ein kritisches Lehrbuch*, Giessen, Weyel Biologie, Weyel Lehrmittelverlag, 1998 p. 34.
28. *op. cit.* p. 46, translation mine.
29. *Zufall*, Stuttgart, Kohlhammer, 1988, p.217, translation mine.
30. E. J. Ambrose, *The Nature and Origin of the Biological World*, New York, Halsted Press, 1982.
31. Paris, Albin Michel, 1973, p. 130.
32. 'Darwinian or "Oriented Evolution"?', *Evolution*, 29 June 1975, 376–78.
33. D. Papadopoulos et al., *Proceedings of the National Academy of Sciences of the USA*, 1999 (96), 3807.
34. *Mathematical Challenges to the Neo-Darwinian Interpretation of Evolution*, eds. P.S. Moorhead and M.M. Kaplan, Philadelphia, Wistar Institute Press, 1967 pp. 29, 30, 35. *The Mathematics of Evolution*, Weston Publications, Cardiff, University College Cardiff Press, 1987 p. 7
36. *op. cit.* p.9.
37. *World's Classics Edition*, Oxford, Oxford University Press, 1996, p. 227.
38. *The Problems of Evolution*, Oxford, Oxford University Press, 1985, p. 11.
39. *Conflicts Between Darwin and Palaeontology*, Field Museum of Natural History Bulletin, January 1979, p. 25.
40. Evolution's Erratic Pace, *Natural History* 86, 1977.
41. *Time Frames: The Evolution of Punctuated Equilibria*, Princeton, Princeton University Press, 1985, pp. 144–45.
42. *op. cit.*
43. See *The Episodic Nature of Evolutionary Change* in *The Panda's Thumb*, New York, W.W. Norton, 1985.
44. New York, Norton, 1989.
45. *The Crucible of Creation*, Oxford, Oxford University Press, 1998, p. 4.
46. *Reinventing Darwin*, New York, Phoenix, 1996, p. 3.
47. Cited by Pervical Davis and Dean H. Kenyon in *Of Pandas and People*, Dallas, Haughton Publishing Co., 1989, p. 106.
48. Chicago, University of Chicago Press 2004, p. 35.
49. Paul Chien, J.Y. Chen, C.W. Li and Frederick Leung, 'SEM Observation of Precambrian Sponge Embryos from Southern China Revealing Ultrastructures including Yolk Granules, Secretion Granules, Cytoskeleton and Nuclei', Paper presented to North American Paleontological Convention, University of California, Berkeley, June 26–July 1, 2001.
50. *op. cit.* p. 8.
51. *New Scientist*, 90, 1981, pp. 830–32.
52. See e.g. Francis Collins' concept of BioLogos, The Language of God, *op. cit.* p. 205.
53. 'The Methodological Equivalence of Design and Descent', in *The Creation Hypothesis*, J.P. Moreland ed., Downers Grove, Inter-Varsity Press 1994, pp. 67–112.
54. 'On the evolution of cells', *Proceedings of the National Academy of Sciences* 99 (2002), 8742–47.
55. Philip Cohen, 'Renegade Code', *New Scientist* 179 (2003), 34–38.

Chapter 7

1. *Evolution – a Theory in Crisis*, Bethesda Maryland, Adler & Adler, 1986, p. 249–50.
2. *op. cit.* p. 250.
3. *op. cit.* p. 250.
4. *Chance and Necessity*, London, Collins, 1972, p. 134.
5. 'The Cell as a Collection of Protein Machines', *Cell* 92, 1998, p. 291.

6. For a vivid, imaginative account of what it is like inside a cell, see Bill Bryson, *A Short History of Nearly Everything*, London, Black Swan, 2004, ch. 24.

7. *Darwin's Black Box*, New York, Simon and Schuster, 1996.

8. *op. cit.* p. 39.

9. *The Origin of Species*, 6th Edition, 1988, New York, New York University Press, p. 154.

10. *op. cit.* p. 91.

11. It should be noted that some people have claimed that Darwin's theory is unfalsifiable in the sense of Popper: Darwin's concept of irreducible complexity shows otherwise.

12. See, for example, *Intelligent Design Creationism and its Critics*, Robert T. Pennock, ed., Cambridge, MA, MIT Press, 2001.

13. *op. cit.* p. 186.

14. Review of 'The Moment of Complexity: Emerging Network Culture', by Mark C. Taylor in *The London Review of Books*, vol. 24 no. 4, Feb 22, 2002, p. 5.

15. *op. cit.* p. 193.

16. For a full list of the amino acids that can be obtained in such experiments, and a detailed discussion of the whole Origin of Life question, see *The Mystery of Life's Origin*, Charles B. Thaxton, Walter L. Bradley and Roger L. Olsen, Lewis and Stanley, Dallas, 1992, p. 38.

17. see e.g. Thaxton et al. *op. cit.* pp. 73–94.

18. For an account of how the Miller-Urey experiment has been misrepresented in recent literature, see *Icons of Evolution* by Jonathan Wells (Regnery, Washington, 2000).

19. *The Fifth Miracle*, London, Allen Lane, Penguin Press, 1998, p. 60.

20. *op. cit.* p. 61.

21. *The Life Puzzle*, Edinburgh, Oliver and Boyd, 1971, p. 95.

22. It is known that some sites in the amino acid chain of a protein can be occupied by more than one possible amino acid, and so the calculation must be modified to take this into account. Biochemists Reidhaar-Olson and Sauer have done these calculations, and reckoned that the probability may possibly be increased to 1 in 1065 which, in their opinion, is still 'vanishingly small' (*Proteins: Structure, Function and Genetics*, 7, 1990, pp. 306–316). Of course, if we factor in the requirement for L-acids and peptide bonds the probability drops to 1 in 10125.

23. *The Intelligent Universe*, London, Michael Joseph, 1983, p. 19.

24. *De Natura Deorum*, trans. H. Rackham, Cambridge, MA, Harvard University Press, 1933.

25. *Order out of Chaos*, London, Fontana, 1985.

26. Other mixtures produce different colour changes. For example, if the ferroin is replaced by sulphuric acid the change is between yellow and colourless.

27. For a recent account, see Michael Lockwood, *The Labyrinth of Time*, Oxford, Oxford University Press, 2005, p. 261 ff.

28. *The Fifth Miracle*, *op. cit.* p. 122, italics his.

29. *The Return of the God Hypothesis*, Seattle, Discovery Institute Center for the Renewal of Science and Culture, 1998, p. 37.

30. 'The Origin of Life: A Review of Facts and Speculations', *Trends in Biochemical Sciences*, 23 1998, p. 491–500.

31. 'The Origin of life: More Questions than Answers', *Interdisciplinary Science Reviews*, 1988, 13, p. 348.

32. *Life Itself*, New York, Simon and Schuster, 1981, p. 88.

33. *At Home in the Universe*, London, Viking, 1995 p. 31.

34. *The Language of God*, *op. cit.* p. 90.

Chapter 8

1. *The Blind Watchmaker*, *op. cit.* p. 112.

2. Shades of Aristotle! He saw that a living organism could not be explained in terms of material causes alone: the substances of which it was made could not explain its complexity. In Aristotle's view it needed what he called *eidos* or 'form'. And, as the word itself implies, it is in-form-ation that gives to substance its form.

3. It is ironic that the Enlightenment by and large rejected the concept of the universe as machine especially in biological contexts. Now the language of information technology is de rigueur in molecular biology.

4. We speak of *the* human genome as if there were only one. But of course this is incorrect – genetic fingerprinting depends on the fact that human genomes are essentially unique. It is probably true to say that if I compare my DNA with someone else's there will be about 99.9 per cent in common. Differences will consist in part in the accumulation of single nucleotide polymorphisms (SNPs or Snips as they are commonly called), which result from a single nucleotide being miscopied in the process of DNA replication.

5. A report has been issued in *Nature* (447, 891–916, 14 June 2007) of the pilot project of the thorough Encode investigation of a targeted 1 per cent of the human genome that provides 'convincing evidence that the genome is pervasively transcribed' so that there would appear to be very little 'junk' DNA after all.

6. *The Major Transitions in Evolution*, Oxford and New York, Freeman, 1995, p.81; see also *Nature* 374, 227–32, 1995.

7. Cited from Whitfield, 'Born in a watery commune', *Nature*, 427, 674–76.

8. *The Language of the Genes*, Revised Edition, London, Harper Collins, 2000, p. 35.

9. *Harper's Magazine*, February 2002.

10. D.L. Black, 'Splicing in the inner ear: a familiar tune, but what are the instruments?' *Neuron*, 20 (2), 1998, 165–68.

11. 'The Central Dogma of Molecular Biology', *Nature* 227, 1970, 561–63, see p. 563.

12. There is evidence that the repair mechanisms may be even more sophisticated than this. In *Nature* (434, 2005 p. 505) Robert Pruitt reports the astonishing fact that certain genetic mutants of weedy cress (*Arabidopsis thaliana*) produce normal offspring which somehow acquired their genetic information from normal ancestors other than their parents. This should be impossible as it contradicts the received wisdom of Mendelian genetics. Pruitt makes the suggestion that RNA templates inherited from earlier generations may be engaged in repairing the DNA of the mutant genes and bringing it back to its ancestral norm.

13. *A Third Way*, *op. cit.* p. 33.

14. Kenneth R Miller and Joseph Levine, *Biology: The Living Science*, Upper Saddle River NJ, Prentice Hall, 1998 p. 406–407.

15. 'The origin of life – a review of facts and speculations', *Trends in Biochemical Sciences*, 23, 1998, 491–95.

16. *The Road Ahead*, Boulder, Blue Penguin, 1996, p. 228.

17. London, Penguin, 1979, p. 548.

18. *The Touchstone of Life*, London, Penguin Books, 2000 p. 64.

19. 'Life's Irreducible Structure', *Science*, 160, 1968, p. 1309.

20. Cambridge, Cambridge University Press, 1992.

21. H. Yockey, 'A Calculation of the Probability of Spontaneous Biogenesis by Information Theory', J. Theor, *Biology* 67, 1977, 377–98.

22. 'The Selective Chemist', Pre-conference paper for Fitness of the Cosmos for Life: Biochemistry and Fine-Tuning Conference, Harvard University, October 11–12, 2003.

Chapter 9

1. The same applies every time we look up a dictionary to see if our 'Scrabble' word is really a word in the English language.

2. Recent research into the human genome has shown that the situation is even more complicated than this, as indicated in the section 'What is life?' towards the end of the book. This fact only serves to strengthen our argument, which is, however, simpler to state in the present form.

3. There is a delightfully entertaining discussion of this important concept in the book *The Advent of the Algorithm* by David Berlinski (New York, Harcourt Inc. 2000).

4. By contrast with the main thrust of the Shannon theory of information, which is essentially statistical in character.

5. New York, Wiley, 1973.

6. *op cit.*

7. Cambridge, Cambridge University Press, 1998.

8. 20 January 1999.

9. Derek Bickerton, *Language and Species*, Chicago, University of Chicago Press, 1990, pp. 57–58.

10. In this connection, see D.D. Axe, 'Extreme functional sensitivity to conservative amino acid changes on enzyme exteriors', *Journal of Molecular Biology* 301, 585–96.

11. *The Fifth Miracle*, *op. cit.* p. 88.

12. *In Many Worlds*, Ed. Steven Dick, Philadelphia and London, The Templeton Press, 2000, p. 21.
13. *op. cit.* pp. 21–22.
14. *A Different Universe: Reinventing Physics from the Bottom Down*, New York, Basic Books, 2005 p. 168–69.
15. There are many other variants on the theme as a web search will show.
16. *Science and Information Theory*, 2nd Ed. New York, Academic Press, 1962.
17. 'Limits of Science', *op. cit.* p. 79.
18. See Hao Wang's article in *Nature's Imagination – The Frontiers of Scientific Vision*, Ed. John Cornwell, Oxford, Oxford University Press, 1995, p. 173.
19. 'Complexity and Gödel's Incompleteness Theorem', *ACM SIGACT News*, No.9, April 1971, 11–12.
20. 'Der Semantische Aspekt von Information und seine Evolutionsbiologische Bedeutung', *Nova Acta Leopoldina*, NF 72, Nr. 294, 195–219, 1996.
21. 'Intelligent Design as a Theory of Information', *Perspectives on Science and Christian Faith*, 49, 3, 1997, pp. 180–90. See also his, *No Free Lunch*, Lanham, Rowman and Littlefield, 2002.

Chapter 10

1. By Sir James Jeans, *The Mysterious Universe*, New York, Macmillan,1930, p. 4. Jeans gives no reference.
2. Nevertheless what is certain is that Eddington did use such an analogy to indicate the improbability of a gas, once dispersed throughout a vessel, returning spontaneously to occupy just one half of the vessel: 'If I let my fingers wander idly over the keys of a typewriter it might happen that my screed made an intelligible sentence. If an army of monkeys were strumming on typewriters they might write all the books in the British Museum. The chance of their doing so is decidedly more favourable than the chance of the molecules returning to one half of the vessel.' (Arthur S. Eddington, *The Nature of the Physical World*, Gifford Lectures, 1927. New York, Macmillan, 1929, p. 72).
3. *Interchange* 50, 1993, pp. 25–31.
4. *op. cit.* p. 9.
5. The simulator can be found at http://user.tninet.se/~ecf599g/aardasnails/java/Monkey/webpages/index.html.
6. *op. cit.* p. 45.
7. *Climbing Mount Improbable*, New York, Norton, 1996, p. 67.
8. *Evolution From Space*, Simon and Schuster, New York, 1984, p. 176.
9. See also the last chapter of their book, *Cosmic Life Force*, Dent, London, 1988.
10. *op. cit.* p. 68.
11. 'Letter to the Editor', *The Independent*, London, January 12, 1997.
12. Remember that we are talking about the origin of life, so the word selection needs to be treated with care – it does not assume that there exist mutating replicators.
13. It is rather ironic that Dawkins, who decries the use of analogies on the part of those making design inferences, is quite happy to employ them to reject the design inference.
14. Dawkins' original version has only one monkey but this slight variant may make it easier to imagine.
15. Ingo Rechenberg, *Evolutionsstrategie '94*, Stuttgart, Frommann Holzboog, 1994.
16. 'The Deniable Darwin', *Commentary*, June, 1996, pp. 19–29.
17. *op. cit.* p. 221.
18. Behe, *op. cit.* p. 221.
19. *The Genetical Theory of Natural Selection*, Second Revised Ed., New York, Dover, 1958.
20. *God, Chance and Necessity*, Oxford, One World Publications, 1996, p 108.
21. Cambridge MA, MIT Press, 1999, p. 259ff.
22. Here we take 'beneficial' to mean being part of a meaningful entire sequence; in biology a mutation would not be beneficial if it occurred simultaneously with a large number of other mutations that produced a complex (or information rich) new object.
23. Robert Berwick, 'Respond', *The Boston Review*, Feb/March 1995, p. 37.
24. 'The Miracle of Darwinism', *Origins and Design*, Vol. 17 No. 2 Spring 1996, p. 10–15.

Chapter 11

1. *op. cit.* p. 23.
2. 'Self-Organization, Origin of Life Scenarios and Information Theory', *Journal of Theor. Biol.* 91, 1981, p. 13–31.
3. Cambridge, Cambridge University Press, 1998.
4. One cannot help quoting the non-attributed humorous remark to the effect that one of the main evidences that there is intelligent life out there is that it has not tried to contact us!
5. 'A Scientist Reflects on Religious Belief', *Truth* 1, 1985, p. 54.
6. Associated Press Report, December 9, 2004.
7. 30 January, 1999, p. 3.
8. 17 February, 2001.
9. Hebrews 11:3.
10. *Physics Today*, May 1961 p. 23.
11. see Chapter 8.
12. Just as they may also reject arguments, like the fine-tuning arguments, or elegance arguments from mainstream science.
13. See, for example, H.J. van Till, 'When Faith and Reason Co-operate', *Christian Scholar's Review*, 21, 1991, p. 42.
14. 'Should Methodological Naturalism Constrain Science' in *Christian Perspectives for the New Millenium*, Scott B Luley, Paul Copan and Stan W. Wallace, eds., Addison Texas, CLM/RZIM Publ., 2003.
15. As we have said earlier, when we are investigating the laws and mechanisms of the universe for the most part makes little difference whether we suppose that there is real design or assume only apparent design.
16. It is to be observed that even the Genesis account limits the number of such special events. Furthermore, the creation sequence ends with the Sabbath on which God ceases from the direct activities involved in the process of creation (see Genesis 1).
17. 'The Laws of Nature and the Laws of Physics' in *Quantum Cosmology and the Laws of Nature: Scientific Perspectives on Divine Action*, Robert John Russell, Nancey Murphy and C.J. Isham, Eds., Second Ed., Vatican City and Berkeley, The Vatican Observatory and The Center for Theology and Natural Sciences, 1999 p. 438.
18. Paul, Ephesians 1:19–20.
19. *The Blind Watchmaker*, *op. cit.* p. 141.
20. Another important criterion is consistency – both logical consistency and consistency with evidence.
21. Farrer, *A Science of God*, *op. cit.* p.33–34.
22. 'A Third Way', *Boston Review*, Feb/March 1997, p. 33.
23. *Biochemical Predestination*, D.H. Kenyon and G. Steinman, New York, McGraw-Hill, 1969.
24. *Of Pandas and People: The Central Question of Biological Origins*, P. Davis and D.H Kenyon, Dallas, Texas, Haughton Publishing Co., 1989, p. 7.
25. 'Intelligent Evolution', *Harvard Magazine*, November 2005.
26. 'A Scientist Reflects on Christian Belief', *Truth* 1, 1985, p. 54.
27. BBC Radio 4 Interview, 10 December, 2004.

Epilogue

1. *Nature and the Greeks*, Cambridge, Cambridge University Press, 1954.
2. Genesis 1:1
3. John 1:1–4
4. John 1:14
5. Cited by Margenau, Henry, and Roy Varghese, *Cosmos, Bios, Theos*, La Salle, IL, Open Court Publishing, 1992, p. 107.

Index